D0850252

Informal Justice?

Sage Contemporary Criminology

Series editors

John Lea ● Roger Matthews ● Geoffrey Pearson ● Jock Young
Centre for Criminology, Middlesex Polytechnic

Sage Contemporary Criminology draws on the best of current work in criminology and socio-legal studies, both in Britain and internationally, to provide lecturers, students and policy-makers with the latest research on the functioning of the criminal justice and legal systems. Individual titles will cover a wide span of issues such as new developments in informal justice; changing forms of policing and crime prevention; the impact of crime in the inner city; and the role of the legal system in relation to social divisions by gender and race. Throughout, the series will relate theoretical problems in the social analysis of deviancy and social control to the practical and policy-related issues in criminology and law.

Already published

Jeanne Gregory, *Sex, Race and the Law: Legislating for Equality*
John Pitts, *The Politics of Juvenile Crime*
Nigel South, *Policing for Profit: The Private Security Sector*

Library
I.U.P.
Indiana, Pa

306.2 In 3f

Informal Justice?

edited by

Roger Matthews

⑤ SAGE Publications

London ● Newbury Park ● Beverly Hills ● New Delhi

Chapter 1 © Roger Matthews 1988
Chapters 2 and 7 © Tony F. Marshall 1988
Chapter 4 © Anne Bottomley and Jeremy Roche 1988
Chapter 5 © David Nelken 1988
Chapter 6 © David Smith, Harry Blagg and Nick Derricourt
1988
Chapter 8 © Peter Fitzpatrick 1988
Chapter 3 is reprinted by kind permission of Kluwer Academic
Publishers from *Contemporary Crises*, Vol. 9 (1985): 'Beyond
Informal Justice', by Maureen Cain, pp. 335–73. Copyright ©
1985 by Martinus Nijhoff Publishers.

First published 1988

All rights reserved. No part of this publication may be
reproduced, stored in a retrieval system, transmitted or
utilized in any form or by any means, electronic, mechanical,
photocopying, recording or otherwise, without permission in
writing from the Publishers.

SAGE Publications Ltd
28 Banner Street
London EC1Y 8QE

SAGE Publications Inc
2111 West Hillcrest Street
Newbury Park, California 91320

SAGE Publications Inc
275 South Beverly Drive
Beverly Hills, California 90212

SAGE Publications India Pvt Ltd
32, M-Block Market
Greater Kailash — I
New Delhi 110 048

British Library Cataloguing in Publication data

Informal justice? — (Sage contemporary
  criminology; v. 3).
  1. Criminal law. Justice. Administration —
  Sociological perspectives
  I. Matthews, Roger
  306′.2

  ISBN 0-8039-8148-1
  ISBN 0-8039-8149-X Pbk

Library of Congress catalog card number 88-061850

Typeset by Fakenham Photosetting Ltd, Fakenham, Norfolk
Printed in Great Britain by J.W. Arrowsmith Ltd, Bristol

A000005105205

Contents

For john Auld,
who never stopped searching
for better alternatives

1 Reassessing Informal Justice

Roger Matthews

In the beginning there was optimism. The introduction of more informal forms of dispute processing would, it was claimed, provide a greater level of participation and access to justice while overcoming some of the major deficiencies of the formal legal process. Informal justice offered the possibility of more flexible and accountable agencies which would be of benefit not only to the offender and the victim but also to the wider community.

After a period of experimentation with these 'alternative' agencies much of the initial enthusiasm subsided and many observers became sceptical about the possibility of informal justice realizing its promises. Less than a decade after the emergence of the first wave of optimism it was overshadowed by an equally forceful wave of pessimism. Practitioners and academics came increasingly to see the development of informal justice in negative terms. These new forms of adjudication, rather than reducing and transforming the exercise of legality had only succeeded, it was suggested, in expanding and relegitimizing the formal legal system. The more informal neighbourhood tribunals had only effected a shift in the parameters of legal control and created new bodies of paraprofessionals.

The verdict was that informalism was a distraction, an error, an experiment which had failed. But despite these powerful critiques support for informal justice has continued on both sides of the Atlantic and it would seem that we are now entering a new phase in the debate which involves moving beyond the poles of optimism and pessimism and which instead attempts to evaluate the movement towards informal justice in different theoretical and practical terms.

Such a rethink of this process involves a re-examination of the workings of these 'alternative' forms of dispute resolution as well as a more detailed analytic differentiation of the various processes which have become grouped under the general heading 'informal justice'. This in turn invites a reconsideration of the nature of 'social control' in society and by implication the nature of power and the state. That is, a serious reappraisal of these developments pushes us in two oppositional directions. On one hand we are forced to re-examine the specific details of the operation of the various forms of informal dispute processing; while we are simultaneously drawn towards a reconsideration of the wider political and social frameworks within which they operate on the other. In this way we might avoid the twin pitfalls of the idealism and impossibilism which has informed much of the debate so far.

In order to understand exactly how we have arrived at the present position — and how we might move beyond it — it is necessary to begin by briefly retracing our steps.

The era of optimism

The expansion of what has variously been referred to as 'informal justice', 'community justice', 'alternative forms of dispute resolution' and 'neighbourhood justice', involving various forms of mediation, arbitration, conciliation and reparation, occurred in America and to a lesser extent in Britain throughout the 1970s. The term 'informal justice' was widely employed as shorthand for a variety of practices, both public and private, for dispute processing. At the most general level it encompassed all the forms of dispute processing which were seen as departing from the image of the formal legal process based on adversarial procedures.

Like a number of recent developments within the field of law and criminal justice the introduction of more informal modes of dispute processing was not the result of a well-formulated and carefully implemented policy. Instead it appeared as a practice in search of a theory. For many of its supporters the benefits of moving away from the strictures of formal legality were almost too self-evident to need articulation. Informal justice it seemed was an idea whose time had come.

As far as justifications or explanations of informal justice were forthcoming they took two general forms: one positive and one negative. The positive justifications came from a range of anthropological and comparative literature which aimed to show the widespread adoption of informal practices in different cultures. The negative justifications arose, explicitly or implicitly, through an identification of the deepening 'crisis' of the existing judicial apparatus and the dominant legal forms (Marshall, 1985).

Legal anthropologies
Legal anthropologists during the 1970s made a number of (re)discoveries. First, they came to realize that the existing modes of legality are not transcultural but rather historically and socially specific.

Secondly, that the informal processes, particularly those of mediation and arbitration, have been widely employed across cultures and throughout history. Thirdly, that the realization of justice was not dependent on formal systems of legality and that arguably contemporary systems of 'bourgeois legality' might act as impediments to the realization of 'justice'. Fourthly, they made the important discovery that law in all societies operates on a number of levels and encompasses different, and even conflicting, procedures (Auerbach, 1983; Spence, 1982).

From examples of tribal moots, comrades' courts, community courts and the like, anthropologists were able to demonstrate both the 'naturalness' and the 'universality' of these various forms of informal dispute proceedings. From Africa to Russia, from Japan and across to South America examples were produced which illustrated the advantages of informalism.

The apparent naturalness and universality of these different forms of informal dispute processing served important theoretical and political functions. Theoretically they drew attention to the pluralistic nature of the law in society and also reinforced claims about the effectiveness of informal procedures in encouraging compliance and conformity. Politically the anthropological and comparative literature served to broaden the base of support by producing interpretations which appealed to both conservative and radical instincts. The conservatives clearly saw in the literature a reaffirmation of the superiority of traditional values and their potential for establishing order within the community. For the radicals, on the other hand, the reports of post-revolutionary Comrades' Courts and People's Courts conjured up visions of more collective, democratic and egalitarian modes of dispute resolution and the possibility of developing 'prefigurative' reforms within advanced capitalism.

Thus the anthropological and comparative literature performed a dual function. On one hand it suggested that informalism was essentially a transhistorical phenomenon whose relevance had mysteriously been lost, while on the other hand it appeared as a relatively recent development based on the destruction of traditional ideologies and interests. Thus for some it acted as a backward-looking reassuring experience, while for others it provided a futuristic and potentially progressive option. Thus the wealth of anthropological and comparative literature combined communality and individuality, stability with change and experimentation with tradition; it provided a rich resource for the advocates of informalism which engaged readily with widespread critiques of the existing legal process.

The crisis of legality

The term 'crisis' was becoming increasingly employed in the 1970s in relation to law and took a number of forms. It was variously described as a managerial crisis, a crisis of legitimation and a crisis of effectiveness. The deepening crisis of legality, leading social theorists had argued, was the function of the over-use of law as a steering mechanism for the wider socioeconomic crisis (Habermas, 1975; Teubner, 1983). This crisis of management was expressed through the overextension of law and through the overloading of the courts. If the number of cases coming before the courts could be reduced it might improve the quality of justice and avoid delays. The problem of overload was also seen as fuelling the crises of legitimation and effectiveness.

The question of the legitimacy of formal legal procedures was also raised. It increasingly came to be seen — particularly by their radical critics — as class-based agencies serving the rich and oppressing the poor. The lack of equality before the law, the restricted access to legal forums and representation, and the predominance of an adversarial system of adjudication producing either 'winners' or 'losers' appeared unreasonable and inappropriate (McBarnet, 1983).

For some commentators, however, the most serious problem facing the courts was the effectiveness of sentencing. The continued growth of crime, the inconsistency of sentencing patterns, the alienation of the offender and the victim, were all repeatedly identified as indications of the growing inadequacy of the legal process.

The combined effect of these two central strands of explanation/ rationalization was to produce a reservoir of 'evidence' which could be readily mobilized in support of non-judicial modes of dispute processing. Between them they generated a number of central propositions concerning the possible and desirable future direction of the legal process. These included an emphasis on (a) increased participation, (b) more access to law, (c) deprofessionalization, decentralization and delegalization and (d) the minimization of stigmatization and coercion.

(a) Increased participation   One notable difference between the current legal process and those examples drawn from the anthropological and comparative literature was the low level of participation by the two principal actors in the drama — the offender and the victim. Within the current adjudication process the offender will invariably spend much of the time in court, offstage and silent. The victim, on the other hand, is normally reduced to a passive onlooker. As Nils Christie argues: 'The victim in a criminal case is a sort of double loser in our society. First vis-a-vis the state. He is excluded from any

participation in his own conflict. His conflict is stolen by the state, a theft which in particular is carried out by professionals' (Christie, 1982: 73).

Christie argues that the conflict ought to be placed back in the hands of the principal actors who should be allowed to resolve their own disputes. For Christie, the process of participation is more important than the outcome. He is less concerned with 'solutions' and with the determination of guilt. The quest for solutions, he informs us, is 'a puritan ethnocentric conception' (1982: 92).

The courts are also seen as being too remote from the interests of the general public. The repeated claims concerning the 'independence of the judiciary' really mean an independence from public concerns and community accountability. Moreover the employment of 'lay' magistrates is seen as a largely cosmetic and self-legitimizing gesture as magistrates, like professional judges, are invariably drawn from the middle classes and are no more representative of general community interests. This situation has led to arguments for more localized forums involving a genuine level of public participation (Bankowski and Mungham, 1981; Carlen, 1983; Pearson, 1980).

(b) Access to justice One of the major reform movements in the legal field in the 1960s and 1970s was centred around increasing access to justice. This was a two-pronged movement which on one side aimed at opening up the courts and administrative agencies to disadvantaged groups and individuals who were effectively barred as a result of the prohibitive costs of bringing cases to court. The second aim of the movement was to effect changes in the 'quality' of justice and to work for the implementation of 'social justice' (Cappelletti, 1981).

Following the limited achievements of the law centres and legal aid in Britain during the 1970s the attention of the access to justice movement moved in the direction of informal justice which would, it was believed, provide a more accessible and egalitarian framework for processing disputes (Grace and Lefevre, 1985; Stephens, 1980). Moreover by resolving disputes at an early stage informal agencies could reduce the overall level of social antagonism and many potential conflicts could be avoided.

(c) Deprofessionalization, decentralization and delegalization The three Ds of deprofessionalization, decentralization and delegalization were recurring themes which arose in various combinations during the 1960s and 1970s. In order to reduce the social and bureaucratic impediments to more participatory forms of adjudication it was thought that it would be advantageous to operate local

forums which would be less reliant on trained professionals and which could dispense with legal rituals and paraphernalia.

Decentralization also implied the adoption of more 'inclusive' (that is, non-segregative) forms of regulation, and the possibility of exercising sanctions while maintaining the majority of deviants within the boundaries of conventional institutions — the family, the school or the workplace (Cohen, 1987). Through the process of decentralization a change in the locus of power and decision making would occur which would weaken, bypass, or even abolish the conventional structures of legality.

The pressure towards delegalization is far from new and its particular manifestation in the 1970s was only one of the most recent examples of the growing disenchantment with law which has been increasingly evident since the turn of the century (Ewing, 1987). Formal legality appears slow and cumbersome, built on antiquated and incomprehensible procedures, in which the application of law appears inconsistent and unable to provide substantive justice (Abel, 1980; Galanter, 1980).

(d) Minimum level of stigmatization and coercion   Formal criminal courts are often seen to overreact to many cases involving relatively minor infractions. Through the inevitable process of stigmatization these minor offenders are always liable to be transformed into hardened and committed offenders. Dealing with these people in more informal and 'inclusive' ways it is maintained will reduce the level of stigmatization and prevent minor offenders from being drawn into the mainstream of the criminal justice process.

As a corollary formal courts are seen as being unnecessarily coercive and indulging a punitive obsession. The advocates of informal justice argued that the overriding concern with the establishment of guilt and the dissemination of 'just deserts' was an unnecessarily narrow vision of the role of adjudication, and that it should more properly be concerned with repairing social relations, dissolving conflicts and with encouraging compliance rather than relying on coercion. In this way a more effective and less costly (both in economic and social terms) system could be developed. Moreover, the predominant forms of summary and adversarial procedures were viewed as inappropriate in a significant range of cases — particularly those involving matrimonial disputes and juvenile infractions. Such cases, which are rarely contested, are seen to require more sensitive and flexible forms of management offering conciliatory and negotiated settlements (Kilbrandon, 1964; Morris et al., 1980).

These central propositions provide the basic framework on which the expansion of the informal styles of dispute processing was justified. It encouraged the uneven and patchy developments of a range of new agencies including Neighborhood Justice Centers, Children's Panels, a modified Family Court, Small Claims Courts and the like which were all seen to be more appropriate ways of dealing with conflict than the existing formal legal apparatus. Together these diverse agencies would, it was assumed, produce greater community involvement in the process of settling disputes which in turn would strengthen social bonds, repair social relations and ultimately help to re-establish social cohesion.

Within this optimistic, and at times avowedly utopian, discourse, there seemed to be a broad level of agreement about the direction in which reform ought to go. The only major debate was whether or not these new styles of dispute processing would serve to complement the existing system or whether it would provide an alternative which would eventually replace it. Robert Danzig (1973), for example, a leading advocate of informal justice in America, argued that it should operate a complementary system. Although he recognized that transformations of this kind within the field of criminal justice must necessarily involve engagement with the police and other 'corrective' agencies if they are to be fully effective, he believed that the existing legal apparatus does do some things well and it should be allowed to continue to perform some of its more useful functions.

Others, however, like Eric Fisher (1975) wanted a more thorough-going transformation and argued that if community courts are more constructive and more progressive than the formal legal courts then they should be employed across the board. If the aim of community courts is to maximize participation and effectiveness they must be seen as credible agencies capable of performing all the functions currently carried out by the formal legal apparatus. Community courts should therefore be empowered with a full range of sanctions and not simply be limited to providing conciliation, mediation, reparation and arbitration services. Only in this way would community courts avoid becoming dumping sites for discarded and 'rubbish' cases. Some advocates wanted to extend the process of public participation well beyond the process of adjudication itself and saw the community courts (as they were often referred to in this period) as a springboard for a more comprehensive movement which would create a system of 'popular justice' by transferring the overall control of the judicial system to the people. For Longmire:

> The key to the proposed popular justice system is community participation in the distribution of justice. The population will provide a formulation enabling a needs based concept of justice to exist. The allocation of 'rewards' and 'punishments' will be handled by the citizenry thus encouraging a collective, communal sense of needs to flourish. The popular

justice system operating under the basis of needs will actively involve the community not only in the decision making process (e.g. 'Who needs treatment'?) but also in the 'treatment' (e.g. 'How can we help the offender'?). (Longmire, 1981: 25)

This offender-orientated version of popular justice might be difficult to reconcile with Christie's emphasis on process rather than outcomes. But both these supporters of informal justice advocated the abolition of the existing legal apparatus and the removal of disputes from the existing institutions into more accessible forums.

This debate remained unresolved. Towards the end of the 1970s it was overshadowed by a growing disillusionment, not only with the operation of the various forms of informal justice but with a number of destructuring reforms which had been initiated in the 1960s and 1970s and which were seen to be failing (Cohen, 1984). The evaluations of Neighborhood Justice Centers in America, Juvenile Panels in Scotland, Family Courts and a variety of mediation and reparation schemes became increasingly critical. Reports of the operation of the programmes focused on the gap between their original aspirations and their actual operation. As a consequence much of the original optimism began to subside and it was replaced by an equally strong wave of pessimism.

The wave of pessimism

At first the justifications which had been offered on behalf of informal justice were questioned. If informal justice was, as its supporters claimed, the result of a crisis of legality then why had informalism not emerged in this way during previous crises? And even if there was a deepening crisis of legality then why should the response take the particular form of informalism? (Nelken, 1982). The causal relation between the 'crisis' and the expansion of informalism was uncertain because:

> The preference for informalism and the push for 'alternatives' to litigation did not emerge after a careful study of existing litigation practices or the thoughtful weighing up of any evidence of catastrophe. The diagnosis and the cure emerged at the same time. Indeed one could argue that the purported litigation crisis was invented to justify the solution of informalism, rather than the other way round. (Trubek, 1984: 826)

A growing number of critics began to suggest that if informalism was the answer maybe we had been asking the wrong question. In an increasingly fragmented and anomic society, in which disputants may have little more in common with each other than the dispute itself, then what would seem to be required was a more formal and structured process of dispute resolution which could compensate for the increasing uncertainty of social existence (Galanter, 1985a).

The relevance of much of the anthropological material to urban industrial capitalism was also disputed (Merry, 1982a). As Santos (1982) pointed out, once social processes have been absorbed and rationalized by the state they do not re-emerge in their original form. Thus the notion that informalism simply involves a return to traditional values is an illusion.

The central message of the critics of informalism was 'Beware the Rulers Bearing Justice' (Cohen, 1984). This was most forcibly relayed in Richard Abel's two-volume collection entitled *The Politics of Informal Justice* (1982a). This collection aimed to provide a radical critique of the 'liberal' supporters of informalism and served to focus and orchestrate the growing pessimism which had become associated with informal justice.

The experience of a number of projects and agencies which emerged during the 1970s together with the introduction of new comparative and historical material provided timely support for those who doubted the claims of informalism. To some extent, of course, the pessimism which arose was a function of the exaggerated claims which some advocates had made for informalism. But there was also, by the tail-end of the 1970s, a growing number of anomalies which had grown up around informalism and for which it was largely held responsible. For example, in opposition to the claims that informal justice would reduce the burden and size of the legal apparatus, the latter had continuously expanded throughout the decade with the number of lawyers in America more than doubling between 1950 and 1980 (Abel, 1986). There were now more professionals and a new stratum of paraprofessionals, increased formalism and a wider network of legal regulation which, rather than demystifying the operation of the law, increased its opacity and complexity. Also there seemed to be little clarity over what were the most appropriate referral agencies for informal courts, or what level of sanctions they should administer, or why informalism was seen as relevant for some cases and not others, or what kind of training (if any) was required by those who administered proceedings, or what constituted appropriate evidence and critically what kind of 'justice' should be handed out (Marshall in this volume, Chapter 2).

The proliferation of local agencies penetrating deep into the heart of society and personal life, ultimately responsible to an ever-unaccountable state bureaucracy, fuelled popular fears and anxieties about the totally administered society and the advent of '1984'. Behind the engaging rhetoric of informalism the critics saw sinister motives. Informalism, some critics began to suggest, was nothing more than a vehicle for widening the net of social control.

Attention was also focused on the ideological role played by the central notion of 'community' which was identified as one of the most overused and underdefined concepts within the vocabulary of sociology. Paradoxically, it was argued, the notion of 'community' was being mobilized precisely at a time when traditional working-class communities were fragmenting and disappearing. Even where 'communities' could be identified they were not the consensual and harmonious entities which the advocates of informalism had indicated. Instead, they were often conflict-ridden areas in which 'community courts' might just as readily serve to exacerbate as to reduce conflict (Nelken, 1985; Rosenbaum, 1986; Scull, 1982). Apart from the general concerns about 'community control' the critiques of informal justice centred around a number of themes including (a) double tracking, (b) ineffectiveness, (c) relegitimation of law and (d) the expansion of social control.

(a) Double tracking
Rather than transform or subvert the existing legal apparatus the development of 'alternatives' left the core legal institutions virtually untouched. For the formal agencies it was 'business as usual'. Although some of the more minor disputes may have been diverted into more informal settings this only encouraged the formal agencies to concentrate on the more 'serious' and invariably more lucrative cases.

What appears to have occurred was the creation of a dual-track system involving a recognizable differentiation between cases, clientele and the range of sanctions employed. Rather than reduce the ambit of legal intervention the creation of 'community alternatives' resulted in the simultaneous expansion of both the formal and informal processes. In sum, it would seem that what occurred was a combined process of bifurcation, rationalization and expansion (Galanter, 1985b).

One effect of this triangulated process was that it brought a new clientele into a quasi-legal arena, many of whom would have previously been left to resolve their differences informally — either through discussion, avoidance, or simply 'lumping it'. Indeed the central paradox of the movement towards informal justice was that it succeeded in formalizing the informal. A further paradox of this bifurcated system, it was pointed out, was that participants in the informal courts might easily give evidence or provide admissions in this relatively non-evaluative context which could prove incriminating if and when the case was eventually referred to a formal court.

Because sanctions and enforcement in neighbourhood courts tend to be relatively weak participants might drop out of proceedings and as a consequence push the case up into a 'higher', more formal, court. This strategy, if widely pursued, could mean that cases might increasingly come to be processed twice and the system of adjudication becomes even more of a lottery.

Critics also claimed that 'informal' justice provides only second-class justice. If cases are deemed to be serious they are invariably processed in formal courts with clear legal procedures and safeguards. Informal courts, on the other hand, serve as a repository for the less serious 'junk' cases. They are predominantly concerned, it transpires, with interpersonal conflicts, consumer complaints, and public order offences. The majority of cases handled by the Neighborhood Justice Centers were intra-class with 78 percent being domestic disputes between friends and neighbours (Harrington, 1985: III). Also: 'In Atlanta and Kansas City, complainants were disproportionately black and female and in Brooklyn the majority were young, black and Hispanic, poor (56 percent unemployment) uneducated (52 percent without a high school diploma) and female (63 percent)' (Merry, 1982b: 186).

Even in more affluent areas the majority of complainants were female, while 62 percent of the caseloads consisted of disputes between neighbours. But what was significant about these cases was that they served largely as points of exit — normally referred from the formal court — from the justice system, not points of entry into it. Also they functioned, it was suggested, to sever rather than re-establish relationships (Tomasic, 1982).

(b) Ineffectiveness

The doubts and anxieties which some observers had expressed concerning the supposed benefits of the newly initiated forums were fuelled by what was seen as the limited effectiveness of the new initiatives. Preliminary evaluations which were carried out after the first fifteen months of the operation of Neighborhood Justice Centers, for example, found that they were only able to resolve about half of their referrals (Cook et al., 1980). This was largely due to the refusal of the respondents to co-operate or to turn up to hearings. The level of attendance appeared to be a function of the level of effective constraints which the court could exercise, and the coercive powers of the referring agency.

When participants came to court there were further problems in reaching agreements. Where resolutions of cases involved the transfer of goods they were relatively successful but they were much less successful where the resolution involved a change of behaviour.

Interpersonal disputes — which were seen by many advocates as particularly appropriate for mediation — turned out to be less likely to produce long-term resolution than property disputes (Merry, 1982b).

Much to the disappointment of the original supporters of the informal programmes was the realization that a significant number of people — both offenders and victims — were not eager to participate in these informal tribunals. Either they were reluctant to subject themselves to this form of examination, or they saw such forms as ineffectual or inappropriate. Some only participated in proceedings under pressure or out of a belief that participation might reduce the level of the sanctions which they might eventually receive (Smith, Blagg and Derricourt in this volume).

The various surveys did, however, show a surprisingly high level of satisfaction (75–95 percent) with the experience of neighbourhood courts by those who actually participated. This may be due to the fact that, regardless of the shortcomings of the process and the pressures involved, the participants were encouraged to participate actively in the process and the outcome (Felstiner and Williams, 1982; Garafolo and Connelly, 1980).

Satisfaction with the proceedings of the hearing, however, was not universal. Participants in divorce cases who were surveyed, for example, expressed a much lower level of satisfaction (28 percent). In cases of divorce and domestic disputes, it would seem that procedures can become *too* informal. In an emotionally charged situation defendants want procedural safeguards and formal frameworks in which to negotiate agreements. Too much informalism may hinder the rational regulation of terms (Erlanger et al., 1987). Successful outcomes are more likely to be reached, it is argued, through bargaining which is carried out 'in the shadow of the law' and that the introduction of more informal procedures disrupts this effective practice (Mnookin and Kornhauser, 1979). Moreover, there is a real danger that moving domestic disputes out of the 'public' legal system impedes the movement towards formal equality between 'partners' (Lefcourt, 1984). In many cases the final agreements reached in these types of cases is not so much a product of mutual agreement, but rather reflects the relative stamina and vulnerability of participants (Bottomley and Roche in this volume).

In the shift towards informalism the social, personal and economic advantages may remain. In this way informal courts can, behind a mask of neutrality, serve to enforce the existing inequalities and produce 'compromises' which will invariably favour the more powerful. The experience of divorce cases suggests that:

Some informal settlements may be no less imposed than judgements at trial, cooperative negotiating of the dispute to a mutually satisfactory outcome, based on offer and compromise, is the exception rather than the rule. As a result, the positive consequences of informal settlements must be considered variable rather than certain. (Erlanger et al., 1987: 596)

Other disadvantages arising from informalism are reported by Lazerson (1982) in his account of landlord and tenant disputes and the operation of the New York City Housing Court. He points out that the slow, cumbersome and expensive formal courts deterred landlords from taking the tenants to court. However, the creation of a more informal and less costly forum has worked to the disadvantage of the tenants by making it more likely that landlords will employ the courts and thereby further weaken the tenants' already limited negotiating power. In a similar vein some critics have suggested that the creation of the small claims court has created an efficient debt collecting agency for commercial and business interests (McEwan and Maiman, 1984; Vidmar, 1984; Yngvesson and Hennessey, 1975).

(c) Relegitimation

Whether or not it is accurate to refer to the period prior to the expansion of informal justice as one of 'crisis' is uncertain. But what is clear is that the critiques of the formal system were widespread and that the legal process, rather than being seen as solid and reliable, was more often depicted as fragile and uncertain.

The growth of informal courts has served however — rather than to expose these shaky foundations — to relegitimate the ailing legal system. It has performed this function in a number of ways. First, through the proliferation of 'alternatives', it has distracted attention away from the failures of the legal process and by implication reaffirmed its credibility by indicating that its failures were due to overload. Informalism lent weight to the view that the problems of legality stemmed from its being swamped with 'junk' cases.

Secondly, it relegitimated the judicial and state apparatus by reinforcing the claim that the authorities really were concerned with the grievances — no matter how apparently trivial — of their subjects. Some forms of informalism unwittingly serve to reinforce the illusion that commercial and business interests actually care about consumers and that even if these forums do not produce the anticipated results, they still affirm that the state is still taking its citizens' rights and interests seriously.

Thirdly, informalism can also perform a legitimizing function by reaffirming the fundamental individualized and professionalized principles of the formal system. Rather than undermine the existing legal structure, the informal mechanisms replicate the depoliticized and particularized principles of adjudication which are found in the formal system (see Cain in this volume). Thus informal justice, critics argue, tends to be conservative rather than liberating. According to Richard Abel, liberating conflict 'organises the disorganised, allowing them to see the communality of their individual grievances and the power that can be gained by aggregating weakness' (Abel, 1981: 251). On the other hand informal or popular justice can also replicate the operation of the formal system by focusing on the same problem populations and exploring the divisions between the 'respectable' and 'non-respectable' working class (Foucault, 1980).

Finally, informalism performs a relegitimation function, by encouraging individuals on one hand to take more responsibilities for problems which are generated by the wider processes of exploitation and domination and thereby to relieve, in part at least, the state from performing its central functions of providing security of movement and expression for all its citizens (Berki, 1986). In this way, informalism fosters illusions of greater self-determination and competence among even the most impoverished sections of the population. The shift towards informalism serves to conceal the reality that law offers no solution to many of the most immediate problems of daily life (Trubek, 1984: 832).

One of the major and for some the most disturbing aspects of this process of relegitimation was the unanticipated expansion of state control into uncharted areas of personal life.

The extension of state control

As Stephen Spitzer has argued, there appears to be no formal contradiction between decentralization and the expansion of state control (Spitzer, 1982). For Richard Abel the primary goal of informal institutions was to expand the range of intervention and increase the degree of penetration of social control. For him:

> Informalism is a mechanism by which the state extends its control so as to manage capital accumulation and defuse resistance that it engenders. Its objects are not randomly distributed but rather are concentrated within the dominated categories of contemporary capitalism; workers, the poor, ethnic minorities and women. (Abel, 1982b: 9)

The state's purpose in encouraging informalism is to appease the poor and the disaffected and to diffuse the possibility of co-ordinated resistance through a mixture of offensives which combine subtle manipulation with more intensive forms of control. The adoption of these less visibly coercive strategies Abel argues allows the state to control more behaviour. Through these 'top down' strategies the capitalist state actively seeks to undermine and co-opt other forms of social control (Abel, 1982c: 274). These forms of activity which were previously outside the parameters of formal control are now rendered accessible and open to direct manipulation. Within a forum in which participants are encouraged to suspend their formal rights and legal safeguards conflict is effectively depoliticized. Thus Christine Harrington concludes that the new body of disputes expands the state's capacity to deal with interpersonal and minor infractions while 'the ideology of informalism constitutes an administrative-technocratic rationale for judicial intervention to maintain public order' (Harrington, 1985: 170).

In terms of the extension of social control the Neighborhood Justice Centers found themselves in a contradictory position, which involved a heavy reliance on referrals and authority from the official criminal justice system on the one side and yet they claimed to derive their main support and credibility from the 'community' on the other. Although support for 'alternatives' continued, these combined critiques acted to depress the level of enthusiasm and created some uncertainty about which direction, if any, reform should take. Some of these responses to informalism, however, although generally valuable, have come to be seen as overly pessimistic and negative. The theoretical and empirical foundations of this pessimism are beginning to look shaky as a more realistic appraisal is emerging which appears to be moving towards a cautious reaffirmation of informalism.

Some encouragement was given to those who maintained support for informalism in Richard Abel's summing up of the operation of informal justice in America. After mounting a blistering critique which seemed to suggest that the whole informalist project was fundamentally flawed he surprisingly concluded with the recognition that:

> It is advocated by reformers and embraced by disputants precisely because it expresses values that deservedly elicit broad allegiance; the preference for harmony over conflict, for mechanisms that offer equal access to the many rather than unequal privilege to the few, that operate quickly and cheaply, that permit all citizens to participate in decision making rather than limiting authority to 'professionals', that are familiar rather than esoteric, and that strive for and achieve substantive justice rather than frustrating it in the name of form. (Abel, 1982a: 310)

Reassessing informal justice

Part of the reason that the critiques veered so much towards pessimism was a function of seeing these diverse processes as essentially 'top down' strategies which were a by-product of class struggle or a response to the (unspecified) 'needs' of capitalism (Hofrichter, 1982). This implicit functionalism and economism precluded the need for a detailed investigation of the political dynamics which were implicated in the expansion of informal justice. The result was that informal justice remained peculiarly depoliticized. This allowed a number of authors to offer an (overly) conspiratorial view of these processes on the assumption that the development of informal justice was the outcome of a cunning and manipulative strategy designed to shore up a decaying legal system and simultaneously extend the parameters of control. A more detailed political analysis might have revealed a more complex set of forces lying behind the movement towards informalism including a significant demand from 'below'.

There is also an assumption among critics that the law has an essentially integrative function and that its expansion simply extends control (Hunt, 1986). Although there is a recognition of the formally contradictory nature of law and that delegalization and decentraliz-ation have been accompanied by oppositional movements — particu-larly in the form of the 'back to justice' lobby — the double-edged nature of law and the legal process is overlooked and is consequently presented in functional terms (Paternoster and Bynum, 1982).

A prominent feature among both the optimists and pessimists is the tendency to address the problem in terms of exclusive oppositions between formal/informal; conservative/liberating; legalization/ delegalization, etc. Framing arguments in all-or-nothing terms makes for good polemics but bad politics. These exclusive oppo-sitions conceal the complexity and variation between different forms of legality and obscure the pluralistic and uneven character of law. Boaventura de Sousa Santos expresses the problem in the following terms:

> The difficulty lies in that socio-legal life is constituted by different legal spaces operating simultaneously on different scales and from different interpretive standpoints. So much is this so that in phenomenological terms and as a result of interaction and intersection among legal spaces one cannot properly speak of law and legality but rather interlaw and interlegality. More important than the identification of the different legal orders is the tracing of the complex and changing relations among them. (Santos, 1987: 288)

A detailed analysis of law therefore requires the mapping out of both vertical and horizontal relations. In this 'post-modern' conception of law Santos emphasizes that different forms of legality vary in their scale and their range as well as their regulatory procedures. Appre-ciating these complex interrelations involves not only rejecting the crude dichotomy of formal/informal but also demands an analysis of the overlapping and connected elements between these two spheres.

The emphasis on 'interlaw' also prompts a break with legal centralism and indeed with the very notion of a legal 'system'. It also sensitizes us to the notions of justice held by the general public and to the more indigenous forms of rule making as expressed in sport, play, drama and various organizations and to their evaluation not simply in terms of their approximation to formal legality and corresponding conceptions of 'justice' but in terms of their own requirements and their particular scales of operation (Macauley, 1987). In the same vein, we need to differentiate between the variety of forms and procedures and between 'disputes', 'conflict' and 'crimes' rather than treating all these diverse activities as if they are of the same order (McEwen and Maiman, 1984).

There is a certain point at which the scepticism and pessimism slips over into impossibilism. Impossibilism — the belief that 'nothing works' — which was prevalent in the early 1980s seems ultimately to render critique impotent and to suppress the search for progressive alternatives (Matthews, 1987). Critics express both a distaste for the formal legal apparatus and a distrust of all forms of informalism. As Trubek puts it: 'The critics tell us not to believe in the chimera of justice without law. But they also tell us that they do not believe in justice through law. We seem to be left with no way out' (Trubek, 1984: 834).

The implicit legal centralism among the critics is also fostered by a conception of 'social control' which radiates from a central core. Social control is seen as being ubiquitous, expressing an essentially negative and repressive authority. It is also manipulative and sinister. The vision which underpins much of this literature is the Orwellian nightmare of the society totally controlled from a centralized bureaucratic base. It is the language of 'penetration' and 'domination' in which power is 'held' by an elite who 'exercise' it in relation to a subordinate mass. Foucault's vision of the Panopticon and of total surveillance coupled with a more intrusive and disciplining 'carceral' system is also mobilized (Foucault, 1977a).

But Foucault's influential work can also be read as a break with this totalizing centrist vision of control which employs what he refers to as a juridical concept of power which he suggests is outmoded and has been superseded by new forms of 'disciplinary power' (Rajchman, 1983/4). Coming to terms with the problem of power is clearly crucial if we are to overcome the tendency to write off all reforms on the basis that they constitute an expansion of social control. Foucault, as Peter Fitzpatrick (in this volume) points out, has an extremely suggestive but ambiguous theorization of power. An important feature of Foucault's approach is his emphasis on the relational nature of power and that it is always in a sense 'in play'. If we are to change the direction of analysis and try to develop a more adequate understanding of the various transformations which are encompassed by the term 'informal justice' we need a more elaborate analysis of power and social control.

Power and social control

Inasmuch as the critics of informalism operate with a theory of power they tend to adopt a Gramscian notion of 'hegemony' which is used to identify the relationship between the leading group or social class and subordinate groups or classes; a relationship structured in terms of consent rather than coercion. More recent developments, influenced by the work of Michel Foucault, however, have tried to overcome what are seen as the limitations of the concept of 'hegemony' and at the same time to offer some degrees of refinement (Smart, 1986).

Foucault's approach to the question of power has three central components. He emphasizes that the distinguishing feature of power in modern society is that it is productive rather than repressive; that it is not reducible to the interests of one particular group or class and that it is not monolithic but fragmented. Thus he does not deny the reality of domination or subordination but attempts to develop an approach to power which sees it as a series of conflicting methods, techniques and practices which is not unidimensional or certain in its effects and which is not entirely dependent on coercion or consent for its operation.

An important element in this analysis is the notion of 'the social' — a hybrid sphere which links the 'state' and 'civil society' and which Donzelot (1980) claims constitutes a new matrix of relations which involves a new process of 'governmentalization'. This sphere, which includes a variety of educational, health and welfare policies and which although ultimately regulated by the state, does not derive solely from the state. It is in this sphere that informal justice might be located.

There are other dynamics at play within this arena, which are not reducible to the interests of the ruling class and which involve the processes on which the modern human subject is constructed. Through a process of subjectifying practices through which people become classified, examined and trained, new sets of power relations come to play; principally what Foucault calls 'pastoral power' (derived from Christianity) and which is 'salvation orientated (as opposed to political power). It is also oblative (as opposed to the principle of sovereignty); it is individualising (as opposed to legal power), it is coextensive and continuous with life; it is linked to the production of truth — the truth of the individual himself' (Foucault,

1982: 214). The strong appeal of informalism to various religious organizations might be explicable in terms of the influence of 'pastoral power'.

At the same time, however, these diverse and oppositional power relations take institutional forms, which in turn have their own specific effects. They are in a sense both a crystallization of competing powers and a site for the exercise of new power relations. Very briefly, what implications might Foucault's 'analytics' of power have for assessing informal justice? I think there are three general points.

1. Informalism represents a movement towards a more normative, inclusive and decentralized mode of regulation which is not a form of 'deregulation' as such but represents a form of 'governmentality' involving a change in the distribution and organization of power.
2. That this new form of power is located neither properly in the 'state' nor 'civil society' but constitutes part of the 'social' and represents a site for the expression of the individuality of the subject and provides a basis for a more thorough individualizing process.
3. That it is a site of struggle. It is simultaneously a point of resistance not so much against a certain class or group but against forms of power which deny the individuality of the subject. It is a site of struggle over competencies, knowledges and privileges.

These conceptions of power and their possible implications may help to move beyond an uncritical acceptance of these informal processes or a simple dismissal. The potential value of Foucault's analysis to the understanding of changing forms of social control also raises questions about some of the other central concepts within the literature — particularly the notion of 'net-widening'. Although the concept of net-widening has been quite useful in some contexts it can be a limiting and misleading metaphor. To visualize the operation of social control principally as a trawling operation is to present a picture of a unified, co-ordinated and structured offensive aimed at a random population. But it is precisely the population which is predictable whereas the strategies are variable. Also the analogy is deficient in that within the criminal justice system, at least, it is not the 'big fish' who are 'hauled in'. Further, this analogy neglects these multi-layered networks of competing strategies, their varying effectiveness and their differential focus. Most importantly, it does not reflect the invisible but powerful knowledges and disciplines through which social control is exercised. Thus the notion of net-widening cannot adequately grasp the complex overt and covert mechanisms through which 'social control' is normally exercised and in consequence fails to adequately illuminate the significance of informalism.

One of the other leading concepts within social control 'talk' however which does seem to have some direct relevance to the debate is the notion of 'blurring the boundaries'. As the 'boundaries' are rarely clearly identified it is not always easy to recognize when 'blurring' occurs but one of the major reforms in the area is the meshing of 'welfare' and 'law' in the form of expansion of contracts. This development appears to transcend the legalization / delegalization dichotomy and as David Nelken suggests (in this volume) may be 'one of those developments which force us to revise the categories we use for understanding social life'.

The shift towards 'informalism' also involves the 'blurring of the boundaries' between 'public' and 'private' realms. One of the effects of neighbourhood courts is to transform 'private' disputes into 'public' legal issues, as opposed to civil courts which turn disputes, which often have a significant 'public' interest, into private cases.

But in contrast to the twin 'liberal' conceptions which see the referral of 'intimate' relations to a public legal body as signalling a breakdown of social relations on one hand or as the erosion of individual privacy on the other, the transformation of 'private' disputes into 'public' issues can indicate the social recognition of the importance of interpersonal and market inequalities. Thus:

> The general duty substitutes closer bonds of social solidarity than those recognised by the ideal of private autonomy and the special duty emphasises trustworthiness at the expense of authority and discretion. This transition in legal thought implicitly contains a rejection of the traditional liberal view that privacy is essential for human flourishing. (Collins, 1987: 102)

The analysis of social control has recently become more reflexive and more aware of how the language of social control itself structures our thinking and how it can itself act as a constraint. The adoption of statist and centrist views in which informal mechanisms are seen as being 'peripheral' or 'decentralized' involves a type of conceptual mapping and provides a framework in which we have come to locate and evaluate these changes. As Stanley Cohen points out, these master metaphors embody often unexamined conceptions of the nature of power.

> Take the notion of decentralisation itself. This derives from a master metaphor which sees political power in terms of centre and periphery. We are asked to imagine such things as deviants being drawn away from the centre. But the metaphor rests on a largely unexamined view of state power, which at times leads towards the most extreme form of elitist centralism, at other times towards the most amorphous form of pluralism. (Cohen, 1987: 377)

By providing a more reflexive approach to the analysis of changing forms of control we might provide a closer approximation of the significance of informalism and develop a more sensitive and realistic political response. Some of the recent literature has been moving in this direction.

A politics of informal justice?

Many of the critics of informalism were no doubt correct to identify some of the original advocates as too utopian and idealistic. However, most of the critics themselves are not free from the charge of idealism. Just like the 'left idealists' in mainstream criminology the critics of informalism carry a clear suggestion that the conflicts and disputes which are handled by these new informal mechanisms are inherently progressive or liberating (Young, 1986). A significant percentage of the disputes, conflicts and criminal activity processed by these agencies, however, is not an attack upon the dominant sets of individualistic and acquisitive values characteristic of capitalist social relations. Rather, they tend to replicate these values.

As we have seen the participants in informal dispute processing are drawn predominantly from the poor, ethnic minorities and women. The vast majority of cases brought before the Neighborhood Justice Centers were intra-class, not inter-class; while roughly three-quarters of cases involved domestic disputes or conflicts between friends and neighbours.

Just as the creation of crime is overwhelmingly a public initiated act so the majority of cases which come before these informal courts are not instigated by state agencies but arise because one of the respondents is clearly concerned or desperate enough to take action. The state and the criminal justice system is on a day-to-day basis largely reactive to demands from the public (Galanter, 1985b).

However we know little about the conditions under which people refer disputes to court rather than dealing with them themselves. What we do know is that, even in the wake of the so-called 'litigation explosion', most people are very reluctant to engage third parties to resolve their conflicts, and that resorting to 'outside' agencies is widely seen as an indication of personal failure (Engel, 1984; Galanter, 1986). But there do appear to be marked differences in the capacity or willingness of members of different social classes to absorb conflicts. Merry and Silbey, for example, found that the reluctance to take personal disputes to court 'is an important ingredient of respectability for working class and middle class, but not for some segments of the poor' (Merry and Silbey, 1984). It would seem that different social classes not only experience different levels of conflict but are also able to exercise different degrees of tolerance.

Crucially the widespread strategy of 'avoidance' is very much dependent on the range of available resources.

The specific composition of the groups engaging in these new
forms of dispute resolution, and the particular range of issues which
they address, may therefore tell us a great deal about the contemporary social relations among different groups and classes (Touraine,
1985).

Given the focus and the clientele of these informal courts it would
appear that the comparisons which are made between formal and
informal courts in relation to costs, effectiveness and speed are
mostly inappropriate. Clearly, the majority of cases which were
processed by the Neighborhood Justice Centers would not have
received a hearing in the formal courts. Comparisons of this type,
therefore, need to be made between the neighbourhood forums and
leaving participants to deal with the issues themselves.

The 'idealist' critics of informalism tend to suggest that if it were
not for the informal courts that genuine and spontaneous negotiations would occur between the disputants or alternatively that one
party would simply 'lump it'. However, it is precisely because the
mechanisms for dealing with problematic situations are not readily
available that the more impoverished and vulnerable sections of the
population are persuaded to bring in a third party (Lea, 1988). The
alternative to settlement is not limited to the relatively benign options which the critics suggest but may often involve a recourse to
interpersonal violence and intimidation, or alternatively might lead
to prolonged suffering or despair. Either way, these various 'minor'
or 'trivial' disputes can have profound effects on the well-being and
the quality of life of those whose existence is already marred by
deprivation and uncertainty.

It is indicative that whereas the critics evaluate the formal courts
largely in terms of the number of cases which are dealt with by
bargaining which occurs 'in the shadow of the law' (that is, informally) and celebrates the large number of cases which are 'resolved'
without going the full distance, it identifies the inability of informal
tribunals to resolve more than 50 percent of cases as a serious limitation. There is little consideration in these critiques of informal
justice of how its operation might affect the wider networks of social
relations — particularly within urban communities. Informal justice,
however, casts its own shadows. For even when it operates to sever
specific relations it can serve in the process to sustain and enhance
many others.

The critics have played down the important social consequences of
taking these apparently 'trivial' interpersonal conflicts seriously.
They have failed to appreciate the ways in which the operation of

informal justice can serve to facilitate the negotiation of interpersonal and social relations and to strengthen fragile bonds.

The traditional forums with their concentration on specific acts and biographies have been ill-equipped to deal with and shape ongoing social relations. This is not a position of neutrality. For public decisions can significantly affect the balance of power within relationships and influence social norms and expectations. In cases involving domestic disputes, in particular, the concern very often is not with determining innocence or guilt or of finding a 'resolution' as such. For:

> There is no evidence that complainants in these domestic abuse cases use the legal system in order to terminate a relationship. They lack the support networks available in more densely connected social fields and turn to the court as a strategy for limiting violence whilst maintaining an ongoing tie. For these women, the existence of the court as a sanction and not the nature of the court (criminal or civil) is important. (Yngvesson, 1985: 642)

The repeated use of these forums may make difficult domestic relationships more manageable. The very act of bringing such cases before the court may profoundly influence domestic relations in general. In other cases, as Sally Merry points out, 'courts function as a potential sanction by intimidating one's opponents, and as an alternative to street violence' (Merry, 1979: 919).

The cases which actually appear in court, whether formal or informal, are only the tip of the iceberg of conflicts in society. The principal contribution to dispute resolution which the courts provide is to construct a background of norms and expectancies against which social interaction can more constructively take place. The significance of informal courts, then, lies not only in the cases they actually resolve but also derives from their ability to prevent them, to mobilize them, displace them and transform them.

In opposition to the idealist, a realistic politics must ask what forms of adjudication most effectively mediate the problems experienced among different groups and classes and what procedures and practices can be mobilized which will increase the quality of life and improve personal security. This involves a change of emphasis away from the more spectacular and prestigious cases towards the more mundane, regular and everyday disputes and of developing more appropriate forums for dealing with them.

The operation of these informal agencies will invariably have effects on the operation of traditional courts and procedures, just as legal principles, including non-intervention, continue to shape the most basic relations of daily life. Therefore, it is not only a question of more or less law but of what law and for what purpose.

An awareness of the interdependence of formal and informal processes does not mean, however, that we should expect that these different spheres of regulation will create a harmonious and mutually reinforcing system, since all these agencies and institutions are the expression of conflicting interests. Rather than dovetailing into a single unified 'system' they will continue to produce an uneven and unstable mixture of procedures and norms. Thus tracing the connections between these various spheres and evaluating their diverse operations raises crucial political and strategic questions which require detailed exploration.

2 Out of Court : More or Less Justice?

Tony F. Marshall

There is currently a substantial trend in criminal justice circles, across the greater part of the world, towards thinking of alternatives to the traditional legal justice process. The 'community justice movement' arises from a combination of this 'push' away from formal legal mechanisms with a simultaneous 'pull' in the direction of a 'return to community'. There is a superficial appearance of alignment of these separate forces, but this is deceptive. There may be two very different reasons for devolving matters from the law which exist in opposition rather than in parallel. Where economy is the force behind reduction of the role of the law, the community is likely to be viewed as a cheap resource for carrying on what the law is already trying to do but cannot afford to do much longer. The result is likely to be control *by* or *in* the community rather than *for* the community (Nelken, 1985). Where ineffectiveness of law is the spur to alternative action, this is more compatible with the desires of the community empowerment lobby, although the one does not necessarily imply the other. Effectiveness may be achieved in other ways, perhaps, than through community involvement; nor does community dispute settlement have to involve diversion of cases from the law — it may be concerned entirely with conflicts that would never have come to a judicial forum at all.

The oppositions have been seized on by many critics of the community justice movement, as an example of an unholy alliance between right- and left-wing ideologies (Abel, 1981; Harrington, 1985). While the community alternative proponents are seen to be championing liberation, the other camp is accused of exploiting community resources and reducing formal law while holding on to its original law and order aims. A picture has been created of a dichotomy between those who would reduce 'social control' and those who would extend it. There is a substantial literature on the conversion of ostensible exercises in diversion into means of 'net-widening' or increasing control. Although this argument is on solid ground where 'hard' indicators of control such as custody are used (Lerman, 1975), it can become more tenuous when extended to the concept of, say, social work (Scull, 1977). Social control is a difficult concept to measure, or indeed to define, and few texts treat it as other than an 'obvious' feature which needs no further critical analysis. Even in his *Visions of Social Control*, Cohen (1985) avoids defining the term, commenting that

> In sociology textbooks, it appears as a neutral term to cover all social processes to induce conformity ranging from infant socialization through to public execution. In radical theory and rhetoric, it has become a negative term to cover not just the obviously coercive apparatus of the state, but also the putative hidden element in all state-sponsored social policy, whether called health, education or welfare.

This negative tone has been unhelpful, for it leads to the condemnation of anything that could restrict individual freedom and ultimately to the absurd rejection of society itself.

The negative attitude to social control has derived from its identification with state control, and from the assumption that the state apparatus exists to serve only the interests of those groups in power. Although state institutions can, indeed, be used to help maintain an unfair power structure, they only survive in the long term to the extent that they can also maintain legitimacy in the eyes of the ordinary citizens, and thus command their support. The real opposition, then, is not between more or less control, or between control and no control. It is not a quantitative distinction at all, but a qualitative one, between that control which operates in favour of minority groups in power and against more general interests (which we might call 'repressive' social control) and that which serves the interests of society as a whole ('liberating' social control).

This distinction can be applied not only to state-operated mechanisms, but also to all types of 'informal' social control, such as that exercised within the family or by small communities. Thus parental control may be exercised in favour of parents' interests ('seen and not heard') or, for instance, to instil self-discipline that will help the child to perform more successfully in social life later on. While the first can be repressive and inhibiting to character development (or in extreme instances inducive to neurosis or other mental illness), the second is liberating from the unsocialized individual's mess of disorganized hedonistic desires. The outward form of the control in each case may be exactly the same; it is only in the interests served that the two types can be differentiated. Essentially the same distinction is made by Abel (1981) in his analysis of the handling of conflict, which may be

'conservative' (preserving the social structure) or 'liberating' (transforming society).

The interaction between the 'community' and 'diversion' movements can result in either type of social control. It does not depend on
ideologies, but on the real intentions of those who are able to control
the new schemes (who may not be the directors or leaders, but may
be the funders or the agencies on which they depend for assistance or
referrals). The desire for economy, although it does not bear any
necessary relationship to community-based activity (which could in
fact be more expensive), may be 'liberating' by freeing resources tied
up in criminal justice for other services (such as health and education)
or for personal expenditure, or 'repressive' by reducing the overall
level of control and submitting citizens to a higher risk of victimization by crime. The latter tendency may be overcome to the extent
that community alternatives are genuinely cheaper and equally effective in maintaining social order. Similarly, the desire for more effective justice by means of alternatives to formal law may be liberating if
the resulting justice better serves the general interest, but may be
repressive if used as a means of extending control on behalf of a
particular group over the rest of the society (see Cain in this volume).

The critique of neighbourhood justice

Devolution of justice and community alternatives contain all these
possibilities and it is only in a study of their actual operation that the
distinction can be made. Thus Abel (1981) observes that although
formal law tends to be 'conservative' as a method of handling conflict, so do many of the informal alternatives. The blanket classification of law, however, is insensitive to the fact that the law can be
employed by different people for different purposes. Whereas the
expense of law may bias its users towards the more wealthy, ad hoc
organization of the disadvantaged can pool resources to generate
more control in their favour — such as feminist demands for the
police and courts to treat domestic violence more seriously, ethnic
minority demands for more protection against racial attacks, local
community associations advocating greater control of locally concentrated problems like prostitution or the sale of arms (Platt, 1986), or
more general public outcries about child sexual abuse and so on.

While the law itself cannot wholly be dismissed as conservative or
repressive, neither can informal schemes be as simply classified as
Abel does, restricting 'liberating' conflict processes to those involving organization of complainants, undifferentiated roles, lack of rules
(violence not ruled out), norm dissensus, no exclusive focus on the
past (as the law) or the future (as mediation for problem solving), and

without the restriction of social pressures (whether of formal authority or public opinion). In his restrictive definition the only liberating
conflict would seem to be anarchy, and it is difficult to see that this
empowers anyone other than the physically stronger. This is liberation from social bonds, and is far from the liberation that the mass of
people would welcome. Anarchic processes may well be necessary to
combat some examples of extreme repression, but where the over-
throw of tyranny is not the overwhelming preoccupation of a people,
they are as likely to be concerned with maintaining control as with
maintaining individual freedom, with a functioning balance of the
two being seen as truly liberating.

Abel's dichotomy, in fact, seems rather forced — for instance, the
conflation of law and community mediation as both limited by a
time-focus because the one seeks to allocate blame for the past and
the other seeks solutions for the future. It is difficult to conceive what
'liberating conflict' is that 'engages in a normative evaluation of the
past in order to influence the future (e.g. the Nuremberg trials . . .)'
(1981: 254–5), when this sounds so much like what the courts think
they are doing. Abel would seem to be having it both ways —
criticizing the law for being one thing and alternatives for being the
opposite. It is, as Cohen (1985) says, the typical formula of 'analytical
despair' plus 'adversarial nihilism' that always concludes that nothing
works because that is the nature of society. One is left with revolution
(or anarchy) or nothing. It is the result, Cohen identifies, of over-
generalization, of analysis 'quite insensitive to variations, differences
and exceptions' (1985: 240) and 'the persistent tendency . . . to con-
demn a crime-control policy or programme simply by labelling it
"coercive" or "punitive" and, hence, we are invited to conclude, a
failure, unjust or inhumane' (1985: 242).

The problem with analyses such as Abel's is that it becomes difficult to differentiate those activities that can be rightly classified as
repressive and those that are, to a degree, liberating. Harrington
(1985) is led to a blanket criticism of informal justice on the basis of
an empirical study of one American scheme, the Kansas City Neighborhood Justice Center. It is typical of many schemes in diverting
from the criminal justice process cases involving parties with some
kind of established relationship and, if the parties agree to it, settling
them by direct mediation. It is untypical in that, if mediation fails, the
mediator makes a final decision (or arbitrates). This produces an
element of compulsion that may skew the mediation process itself,
and also makes the whole system less distinguishable in aim from that
of the courts. The scheme takes referrals from any agency or from
parties directly, but its caseload is dominated (67 percent) by criminal
justice referrals, which again reinforces its image as an adjunct of the

court rather than a community service. It is, in any case, difficult to perceive its catchment area as a 'community' in any sense of the word, comprising as it does an administratively defined area (a police division) of over 50,000 population, much of it transient and fragmented, and seen as a 'problem area'. Even then, this is only the 'target area' and most cases come from an even wider region. Local laypeople were recruited as mediators, but are hardly representative of the general run of residents, most being experienced social workers.

Harrington questions the accuracy of the assertion that participation is voluntary by contrasting the proportion of cases that reach mediation when there is an arrest charge overhanging the defendant (86 percent) with that when no charge is pending, that is, there is no threat of prosecution (38 percent) or when the referral came from outside the criminal justice system altogether (17 percent). In other words, mediation only seems to be a popular mechanism when the offender is under threat of criminal action. The contrasts are somewhat over-emphasized, however. Some cases not mediated are in fact settled to the mutual satisfaction of both parties by indirect negotiation, without having to bring the parties together round a table. Taking this into account the percentage of cases settled where there is no arrest charge pending reaches 50 percent or more. Even the difference that remains may look a little different if one considers that both victim and offender must agree to mediation, and the victim is under no threat corresponding to that of the offender. It should also be noted that the proportion of cases reaching a court hearing (among those not referred to the scheme), where there has been an arrest charge, is only 53 percent — due to the large number of complainant dropouts. It seems, then, that once the heat of the moment when the complaint is made has passed, the victim is likely to prefer mediation to a court hearing (86 percent to 53 percent). Harrington fails to point this out.

The criminal justice agencies are selective in their referrals, which tend to be the legally less serious, what they regard as 'garbage', cases. Domestic assault is seen as too serious, and the lower criminal courts keep most of the assault, vandalism and trespass charges. The Neighborhood Justice Center receives mostly disorder, harassment, larceny and civil cases (such as child custody), plus a fair number of minor assaults. Harrington correctly stresses that many of these referrals are not diversions from criminal process, because most of these would never have got a court hearing in any case. Moreover, even if dealt with by the courts, they may be processed quickly and easily, with some judges seeing their own role as 'problem solver rather than a law enforcer' (1985: 148). Nevertheless, she does not question how good they are as problem solvers, or how successful they could be if the cases were processed quickly and fluently. If one takes the point that the mediation alternative does not necessarily involve diversion, and may well indeed imply extra effort, it may still be true that this extra effort produces 'better' results, whether in criminal justice terms as settlements that are less likely to break down, or in terms of the parties' interests as being more satisfactory and meaningful to themselves.

Harrington, however, persists in a negative view:

> The type of disputes that are referred to the Neighborhood Justice Center are order maintenance problems that the criminal justice system deals with routinely. Within the decentralized management model, minor disputes are channeled into appended tribunals that emphasize therapeutic intervention by trained lay citizens. Conflict in this setting is absorbed into a rehabilitative model of minor dispute resolution. The creation of a tribunal to mediate these disputes in an individualized therapeutic style signifies a transformation in order maintenance policy that extends the scope of judicial authority. It expands the state's role in identifying and channeling order maintenance problems. (1985: 130)

She concludes that informal justice expands the capacity of the formal system, legitimates the basic approach of that system, fails to expand community control, fails to advance rights and social justice, and diverts attention from the courts as an important arena for struggle.

There are some elements of Harrington's analysis one can accept — certainly the criminal justice agencies are reluctant to yield control. While referring some cases, they are conservative in their definition of what is relevant, and would possibly be less happy with a forum that was more distant from themselves and closer to the community. She is surely also right when she says that the Center fails to expand community control. Nevertheless, one cannot really claim that diverting cases to a forum under the control of the parties and a volunteer mediator (even if a social worker by training) is extending judicial authority. On the contrary, it is expending more resources on cases that might have been dismissed from the formal process, and it does this not in an authoritative manner but in such a way as to better serve the interests of the parties themselves who — it would appear from the figures — mostly prefer mediation. In terms of the discussion earlier in this paper, the alternative forum (avoiding Harrington's vituperative use of the term 'tribunal') is offering supplementary services that the law fails to offer. The overhanging threat of second-class adjudication in the form of arbitration, in which the Kansas City Center is fairly unusual, is the only element that might support Harrington's view; the fact that this is resorted to extremely rarely limits this point, however. The Center may do little to advance rights and social justice, but neither do the courts, and by serving the interests of parties to some degree the mediation alternative may at least be providing more justice in that sense. (The question of justice will be discussed more fully later.)

Harrington's critique is not unusual and many other commentators have shared her misgivings. Although such analyses, like Harrington's — which at least has a more substantial empirical base than most — are often overzealous in their search for evidence of sinister motives on the part of state agencies, they do indicate real dangers that exist for distortion of the original aims of diversion to community control. One certainly cannot assume that the way a scheme's founders presented its objectives is what guides its progress in practice.

Criticisms of actual practice have been of three major kinds — net-widening, bad justice, and conversion of liberating control to repressive control. The first has always been a concern in the study of any kind of diversion (Pratt, 1986). With regard to mediation schemes, Tomasic (1982) has pointed out that many cases referred from criminal justice agencies would have been dealt with informally anyway, often more briefly and less intrusively than through mediation, so that one may in effect be escalating official action rather than reducing it. (If one is thereby providing a better or more acceptable service, this may not be a bad thing, but it remains true that it is not diversion.) Moreover, some of these referred cases will not be successfully mediated, and such cases, in many schemes, will be returned to court for adjudication. This could bring some matters to a hearing that would otherwise not have got that far, increasing court caseloads, not reducing them. Once parties have agreed to mediation, the success rate (in terms of formulating some kind of settlement) is fortunately very high — typically about 90 percent — but quite a significant proportion are resistant to the idea, and, unless there are organizational safeguards, these cases could be received back into the legal system. Nelken (1985) also mentions the danger of net-widening, although he cautions against the exaggeration of such dangers: 'More cautious critics rightly admit that they would have to examine the conditions under which either type of forum and process offered greater advantages for the groups whose causes they favour' (1985: 249).

Nelken also refers to problems of individual justice that may arise. In the first place, the fear of prosecution may put defendants under substantial pressure to accept anything that may offer an escape, without necessarily being fully aware of what they may be letting themselves in for. 'The presence of official sanctions even as a possibility colours the meaning and alters the significance of community programmes ... the impression that the community measures are voluntary, or outside the criminal justice system proper, allows them to be imposed without the application of the usual safeguards' (1985: 247–8). Tomasic (1982: 227) also refers to 'subtle coercive pressure' and the danger that mediators may also press hard for a settlement even when parties are reluctant to agree. Among some American schemes it is not at all difficult to find instances of offenders accepting burdens in reparation for their offence that go far beyond what courts would have been likely (or even empowered) to impose. In one example (Marshall, 1985: 141) from a juvenile pre-trial diversion scheme, a stone-throwing boy was assigned to repay the cost of replacing broken panes of glass, but also to carry out twenty hours of community work, for an offence which here would probably have been dealt with by means of an official caution. A more recent scheme in Tulsa, Oklahoma, employs mediation between offenders, after conviction, and their arresting police officers in victimless offences such as drug- and alcohol-related crimes. The officer is provided with information about the offender, including prior record and other reports. In one case a mentally-handicapped offender agreed to two years suspended custody, a urine-analysis every two weeks, regular home checks by the Department of Corrections, $150 to be paid into the victim fund, $1500 fine and attendance at educational classes for two years. It is not surprising, perhaps, that a pilot study of participating officers showed that 96 percent were keen to participate again. (Information provided by Oklahoma Department of Corrections.)

Nelken also warns of the danger that such schemes may appear to legitimize more severe penalties for cases that do not get the chance to participate in the diversion scheme, on the basis that they are assumed to be more serious or that the offenders are unrepentant. It is also claimed, for instance by Tomasic, that mediation schemes merely provide second-class justice for the poor, without legally protected due process, reinforcing existing inequalities of opportunity to obtain access to the law: '... rather than providing an appropriate mechanism for obtaining access to the justice system, the Neighborhood Justice Centers actually seem to be exit points from the justice system' (Tomasic, 1982: 219). This is similar to the charge made by Brady (1981) about the Dorchester Urban Court, Boston. No better example of second-class justice (if not third-class) can be found than the American Indian Tribal Courts described by Brakel (1978), which provide neither good law nor any effective or beneficial alternative.

It is difficult to reconcile the two accusations of deprivation of access to the law and net-widening, however. One may try to maintain, presumably, that poor complainants are deprived of access, while poor offenders are drawn in further, but as these are not distinct offences, such a ploy still fails to resolve the contradiction. It seems much easier to accept that the mediation schemes represent neither complete neglect nor complete domination by the state, and that they should be evaluated in terms of what they achieve for the various parties involved in comparison to what is achieved through traditional legal procedures, without making any prejudicial judgement about the inherent worth of either.

Perhaps the most serious type of criticism is that what are intended to be, or are represented as, 'liberating' schemes are converted into systems that are in reality repressive. If the community movement stresses that conflict should be brought into the open, aired not stifled, because it may lead to constructive social change, then the interests of authorities charged with maintaining public order may be contradictory, as the 'heavy hand of the law' may only serve to dampen down emotions and restrict energies that might have gone towards a proper resolution. Schemes controlled, more or less, by criminal justice agencies may well, therefore, be more committed to a superficial settlement for its own sake — immediate peace — and chary of encouraging disputes to escalate, even if this might help resolve deeper underlying issues. The opposition may, however, be less than it at first appears. A superficial settlement may have short–term advantages for public peace, but not in the longer term. Moreover, the settlement of superficial issues, and control of unconstructive emotions or violent tendencies, may be a necessary prelude to the identification of the real issues and to a productive course of conflict resolution. Feminists have been rightly chary of mediation in domestic violence cases because of the need to establish before anything else occurs that physical force is unacceptable and not a matter for compromise (cf. Lefcourt, 1984). There is a case to be made, therefore, on behalf of a process of conflict management that is not so 'liberating' as to be anarchic, but sufficiently empowering to the parties not to be repressive. The degree of control that needs to be exerted over individuals will vary with circumstances, but the role of the state, in the expectation of the vast majority of citizens, will be to hold the line firmly where violence or abuse of power is involved. There is no need to see such state intervention as repressive. If carried out with the right motivation, it is necessary to libertarian control and the empowerment of citizens to solve their own disputes.

What is proper in mediation to facilitate community control is therefore a fine distinction which passes beyond the typically heavy-handed critiques that have sought wholesale condemnation if they could not see their way to wholesale praise. It is important, once again, to see them as helpful warnings about what might go wrong rather than sensible judgements about the overall worth of the basic ideas. Given the intention to empower citizens to take more control over their own lives, and for local communities to do the same, the move away from professional control, for instance, is an important attribute of the schemes we are discussing, but as Cohen (1985: 66) observes, '. . . the potential for volunteers to be absorbed into the official system is high. Often the volunteers are retrained or formalized into para-professional or professional status. . . .' Davis (1983) supports this diagnosis in relation to divorce conciliation.

While it may not always be right to impute sinister motives either to governments or professions, it does remain true that some people will find a vested interest in exploiting the skills they have learnt and protecting themselves from too much 'amateur' competition. Maintaining the truly informal nature of any initiative is difficult unless there is real involvement of local people of a widespread kind. If the character of a scheme remains that of a service provided by a small clique which monopolizes (in fact, even if that was not their intention) the experience of informal dispute settlement, quasi-professionalism and specialization will inevitably grow. Such a tendency is also likely to be supported by other professional agencies with which they interact (community welfare as well as legal) simply because it is far easier for them to communicate with other specialisms with tight organizational structures than it is to relate to inchoate, decentralized community schemes. It is a little worrying that one of the pioneer American experiments in diverting offences involving related parties to a mediation forum — the Columbus, Ohio, Night Prosecutor's Program — has spawned a large organization with multiple departments, a bureaucratic structure and a large staff of employed professionals. One of the latest innovations in America — like the Columbus programme with roots in legal rather than community development thinking — is the Multidoor Courthouse Program, in which a disputant would bring his/her problem to a central court-based agency where, as the founder of the idea, Frank Sander, puts it, 'a sophisticated intake officer would analyze the dispute and refer it to that process, or sequence of processes, most likely to resolve it effectively' (Sander, 1983). With admirable candidness, however, he does go on to admit 'there is also a real danger — as with all administrative innovations — that it will become the genesis of a new bureaucracy that will result in Kafkaesque shunting of individuals from one "door" to another without any genuine effort to address the problems presented.'

Although projects like the San Francisco Community Boards and the Newham Conflict and Change Project in the UK (Miller, 1986) strive continually to involve local residents as far as possible and to maintain their community base, it is easy for many schemes, under pressure of restricted funding and the desire to get on with 'focal' activities like dispute resolution, to neglect the difficult and time-consuming task of building community skills and indigenous powers of self-help. The 'community' then degenerates into something like an excuse or a mere location, as both Tomasic (1982) and Nelken (1985) have pointed out. In Clarke's (1976) terms — referring to the diversion of mental illness patients from hospitals — the community becomes a 'dustbin' into which problems are deposited without any development of that capacity within the neighbourhood that is needed to cope with them: 'The community is a euphemism for the world at large, in which the disadvantaged citizen is dumped and told to make out as best he can and not to return to be a burden on the state' (1976: 235).

These problems can come about simply through 'benign neglect' or muddled policy development, but they may also arise because the interests of the general community were never paramount at the start. Trubek (1984), for instance, sees the move away from law, insofar as the initiatives originate within the justice system, as a defensive one intended to shore up repressive control and prevent the growth of liberating alternatives. He sees the development as

(i) a tactic designed to accomplish a concrete set of political goals; [e.g. to counteract the success of some organized groups that have managed to obtain access to legal justice, as, it is claimed, have tenants' associations in America; one might also read the growing interest in methods of dealing with domestic violence cases without resorting to prosecution as a reaction to the increased influence of the women's movement]

(ii) a defensive move by the legal profession to co-opt and control popular movements which threaten the profession's economic interests [the alacrity with which American lawyers have been moving into the provision of mediation services themselves, especially for divorcing couples, is quite remarkable]

(iii) a response to the need to legitimate the legal system by offering new ideals that hold out new promises of fairness after others have been exposed as shams

(iv) an effort to create an atmosphere in which the role of law in America could be altered [as an example, Trubek refers later to diversion as a reaction to the growing success of 'rights' movements in use of the law in America: mediation instead of litigation is certainly being stressed nowadays in the context of race and sex discrimination issues]

(v) a way to introduce a new form of social control that is more pervasive and powerful than formal law.

This critique is like that of Abel (1981), who characterizes 'informalism' as a means of protecting the formal system from criticism (unsuccessfully, it seems!) and as being modelled on formal mechanisms, not a true alternative; or that of Santos (1985), who sees the transference of control functions to the workplace, the community or the family as a proliferation of 'law-type' relations into those spheres rather than a reduction in law — 'deregulations are reregulations'.

The problem with this type of critique is that it involves speculation about the motives of agencies and governments that are difficult to substantiate. Although moves away from litigation may serve the interests of established groups in various ways, they may also serve the interests of the general population if established on the right foundations. Theoretical discussions at the level of such schemes as a totality can reveal potentialities and pitfalls, but without empirically based discriminations between types of diversion they will ultimately be vacuous as a guide to appropriate action.

Varieties of diversion

The simplest form of discrimination is to contrast, as Shonholtz (1984) does, agency-based mediation programmes (such as the American Neighborhood Justice Centers) and state programmes (such as the Polish Social Conciliatory Commissions, or the takeover of traditional Chinese mediation practices for the purposes of state indoctrination and control) with the 'pure' community scheme, of which he takes the San Francisco Community Boards as representative. This is a distinct improvement in the sophistication of discussion, although one can argue that it is still too simplistic. If one leaves out the programmes associated with totalitarian states as irrelevant, in any case, to the totally different national structures obtaining in western democracies (however limited one may view that 'democracy' as being), then Shonholtz's argument rests on the view (like Harrington's) that insofar as cases are genuinely diverted from the courts they involve at least covert coercion, and that insofar as such cases would not have been processed officially anyway they represent net-widening and a state takeover of what are really community concerns. This fails to recognize that individual citizens have voluntarily referred such cases to formal agencies and sought some form of resolution. It may be that if there were proper facilities or indigenous powers in the community, they would choose not to invoke the law, but while most disputes remain unresolved and their parties unaided within the community, the demand for some official action will remain and should be met. The need to build up community resources is not an argument for ignoring all the problems that arise until community programmes reach universal perfection. If the law, through adjudication, tends to provide unsatisfactory resolutions as far as the individual parties go, then it is right for it to seek better alternatives. These will inevitably have overtones that informal measures outside the law do not have, but often these overtones, such as the authority to control violence by physical means, are necessary for the establishment of fair mediation.

Nor, on the other hand, can one accept Shonholtz's rosy vision of the potential for community mediation entirely uncritically. He encourages the early expression of conflict, but such escalation is not necessarily the best way of proceeding with every dispute. Some suppression and self-control, leading to mature consideration, may well indicate constructive ways forward on individual initiative. Encouragement of early referral to third parties may be just as much a form of net-widening as that of which the agency schemes are accused, the net being that of community control instead of state or legal control. It is stated that people need to resolve their own problems, but there are some acts that call for clear denunciation and hence wider social involvement, even if this often involves prolonging the anguish of the victim, as it does in rape cases.

In Shonholtz's view, the community itself may take over the state's current role of denunciation and the expression of shared, normative values, but the prevalent values in the community are not necessarily the same as the scheme's organizers — they may be less addicted to 'democratic values' and to the tolerance of diversity than is Shonholtz himself. He therefore does not deal adequately with the dangers os scapegoating minority groups or individual deviants, or of vigilantism. As Fielding (1986: 185) says, 'The principal issue is how community programmes handle competing interests and conflict in pluralistic societies'. Shonholtz does recognize that 'civic activity may become monopolized by a particular group if resident representation and participation is not broad, and that can diminish its potential impact and vitality' (1984: 26), but believes such problems can be overcome, without really suggesting practical measures for doing so. Broad representation and participation is unlikely to be adequate. The problem is not simply that cultural differences exist but that these are associated with real differences in social power. He advocates the natural development of community mechanisms without intervention by existing elites, but it is difficult to see in such a case how power differentials will be overcome and discrimination eliminated, nor does it square with the reality of development of even his own Community Boards which are very much the creation of some kind of elite — perhaps not in terms of economic power, but certainly in terms of altruistic attitudes and social skills. It is this very injection of atypical values which enables such schemes to develop in acceptable ways and provides a safeguard against 'natural injustice'. Given existing power differentials, intervention must be biased in favour of the underdog in order to create that thriving democracy of universal equality on which Shonholtz's ideals are founded.

The division between agency-based and pure community schemes is not, therefore, one which survives critical examination. The only pure community control arises internally without intervention and cannot be created. It may well not, moreover, partake of those democratic characteristics that would make it acceptable to its advocates; nor is there any guarantee that such control will be liberating rather than repressive. In some cases an agency base may be the only way in which democratic liberties can be safeguarded, because of the backing either of legal guarantees or professional standards. In the end, one is faced with a dilemma. Either one takes devolution as one's main aim and accepts the consequences (which may not appeal to a liberal, educated intelligentsia); or one takes the attack on prejudice and inequality as one's aim — and accepts that these may well necessitate some external control of a professional kind. Shonholtz, I believe, wants to have it both ways, presumably on the basis of a belief that people will be peaceful, tolerant and egalitarian if only one allows them to control their own lives. This may be a brave assumption — even if one wishes it were true.

These issues need to be examined further in the light of actual developments in mediation processes, but first there are two conceptual notions that have to be explored — those of justice and the nature of conflict. Both are fundamental notions in the ideology of alternative dispute resolution.

The nature of conflict

As Cain and Kulcsar (1982) observe, the concept of dispute is not integral to any sociological theory and its ramifications have not been adequately explored in the academic literature. They point out some of the problems with current discussions — the tendency to lump together many disparate phenomena, to equate conflict with disorder, to abstract disputes from their structural context and to assume that their mode of resolution can also be generalized across different contexts.

Another assumption they particularly attack is that courts, or the law, exist to process disputes. Cain (1983) herself has shown in an empirical study that much of the business of civil courts can hardly be described as disputes. There is usually no real argument over facts or rights. A large category of business, for instance, is simply concerned with the collection of bad debts. Although evidence of rights has to be presented in court, which makes the case look superficially like a contest, it is in reality just one step in the enforcement of obligations.

Rather than a two-sided contest, as implied in the idea of dispute, a court case is much more often (and this applies a fortiori to criminal cases) a one-sided action intended to re-establish parity by a person who feels him/herself wronged.

The ideal concept of dispute can be similarly elusive outside the legal system. A typical neighbour dispute over a fence or a tree, noise or whatever, will often not be seen as a dispute by the parties concerned, but as the result of bad behaviour, bad faith or unco-operativeness on the part of one party, even though there may be cross-accusations. This fits with the findings of one of the few social anthropological studies that has focused on disputing as a social phenomenon, Strathern's (1985) research in a New Guinea community. She found that disputes were not isolated eruptions in a state of normal tranquillity, but part of an ongoing and endless political process. Dispute-settlement was a normal part of the system of interpersonal and intergroup exchange, and thus merely another aspect of social relationships, seen not as in a steady state but as in constant transition, as each side, in shifting combinations, continually seeks advantage. The idea of restoring equilibrium found in our western courts is imposed on disputes, and not necessarily part of their nature. Merry's (1979) study of litigation in an American urban area also supports this idea that 'going to court' is just one step in the process of the struggle for dominance between people and groups.

This intimate connection between 'disputes' (as conceived by outsiders) and the general ongoing social process means that they cannot simply be isolated as distinct and limited problems as the law tries to do, and as some dispute settlement schemes also attempt. As Cain and Kulcsar (1982) argue, disputes must be seen as interrelated in the present and as having histories of other altercations in the past. This complexity makes it unrealistic to talk in terms of 'settlement', although the substitution of the idea of 'outcome' by Cain and Kulcsar, while widening the concept, still has an unhelpful implication of finality. Better still would be to talk in terms of the 'future' of a dispute, in which a 'settlement' at a particular time is but one step in the process, temporarily shifting the balance of power one way rather than another.

If a dispute is but one stage in ongoing relationships, it can nevertheless be isolated, at least in theory, and can possibly be settled in its own terms, although such settlement must be recognized as but one phase of a continuous process in which the battleground shifts from place to place. Seen in this way, a settlement is not the creation of balance or order, but may just as easily be viewed as creating imbalance by defining a new interpersonal or intergroup situation (whether a judicial finding in favour of one party, a negotiated compromise, or a creative solution serving the immediate aims of both sides) which will occasion the need for further inter-party adjustments as time proceeds.

The theory of disputing has thus moved from a static model (disputes as temporary disruptions of a system generally in equilibrium) to a process model (disputes as phases in an ongoing struggle for potency). Whereas the first has its inadequacies, so has the second, for it tends towards a Hobbesian view of society as a war of one against all, tenuously held together by authoritarian forces of law and order. Whereas the static model encourages authoritative intervention in the same way that 'illness' calls forth medical attention, so the process model also encourages authoritative intervention as the only way of holding society together. They are equally crude as sociological paradigms.

Although disputes do have histories and futures, and also lateral ramifications, it is not true that the ongoing process of which they are part is characterized by continuous struggle. The energy, time commitment and emotional drain that disputing entails prevents a single person continuing indefinitely at the same emotional pitch. At times conflict may be welcomed, may actively be sought, but at other times one tires of the continual bickering and desires peace above all. The process of developing relationships that is society is not one of never-ending struggle but of surges of conflict interrupted by surges of pacification. Given that time and energy must also be spent on essential co-operative endeavours, the process is normally marked by longer periods of relative peace than of outright conflict.

This alternative view of conflict (a 'phase' model) has elements of both the more extreme models but uniquely lacks the necessity of social intervention in disputes that these entail. Most disputes will fizzle out anyway, because the parties tire of them, and they are not all therefore threats to social order or future peace. They are, indeed, a necessary, or at least unavoidable, part of social relationships and are not to be discouraged. They are part of that process of social change in which unfairness and inequalities are both created and resolved. Conflict is neither good nor bad, neither positive nor negative in social 'function' (cf. Coser, 1956), but a morally neutral fact of life, given that we are each more conscious of our individuality than ants or bees, but must nevertheless live with, and can only survive through, social bonds. '[I]t is important not to presuppose that conflict ought to be solved' (Christie, 1982). Intervention may, in fact, be deleterious if it interrupts this natural process which, as Christie (1977) says, belongs to the parties — is of their making and requires their involvement if it is to progress meaningfully.

The 'community control' movement has very much adopted

Christie's idea of 'conflicts as property', but it does not prevent members from advocating intervention. This is because intervention does have a rationale, and this occurs when the natural process 'goes wrong' in one of a number of ways. It goes wrong when there is an imbalance of personal power or commitment between the parties, when one party is prevented by social barriers from participating equally, or when the conflict develops beyond the point where either party can disengage despite a desire to do so. These are all reasons internal to a conflict. From a more general standpoint a conflict can also go wrong by passing beyond the bounds of propriety or acceptable behaviour, or by threatening the wider involvement of other parties in social disorder. Disputing, like war, has its rules, its self-imposed order, and does not, unless it gets out of hand, have to upset society itself.

There are thus two reasons for intervening, one as a service to one or both parties, the other in the interests of maintaining social order. The two may be in opposition. For instance, intervention to preserve social order because the parties have resorted to limited violence, such as a punch-up, may interrupt a natural process of dispute settlement according to local community mores that stress the importance of 'standing up for one's rights', 'saving face' and demonstrating 'virility'. In a case referred to the Cumbria Reparation Scheme, a schoolboy refused to apologize and make amends to another because of the loss of face it would have entailed in the eyes of his peers, despite the fact that he freely admitted he was in the wrong and would personally have liked reconciliation. (Personal communication from Harry Blagg.) This case also illustrates clearly the nature of conflict as embedded in wider social processes and relationships.

Intervention as a service to the disputants may also seem to be wasteful of resources from a general point of view, if the dispute seems unlikely to erupt into social disorder, but this is to ignore the fact — which does seem to have gone unrecognized until very recently with the start of community mediation schemes — that parties locked into a dispute may suffer from untold unhappiness, grief and frustration, loss of time and energy, and a total alteration to their preferred way of life, especially where the disputant is unavoidably close, as one in the same household, living next door, a close colleague at work, or a classmate in school. Such suffering has gone undocumented for too long, except when (surprisingly rarely) it has finally escalated into desperate violence, as in domestic murder (in a personal context) or an urban riot (in a social one). Intervention reserved purely for law and order purposes could find itself either too late (parties committed to the conflict and unable to change course rationally) or blackmailed (by parties who precipitate violence in order to invoke help). The provision of dispute settlement services, just like social work or psychiatric services, can therefore be justified in terms of public good as well as compassion for human suffering. Moreover, it may not be just suffering that is saved, but also the resources of citizens released from debilitating and fruitless conflict.

The problem is not, therefore, the justification for intervention, but discrimination between cases that would be genuinely assisted and those where the natural process would be stultified. The difference corresponds once again to the distinction between 'liberating' and 'repressive' control, the one helping parties to use their differences constructively and to collaborate with one another, the other suppressing the conflict and stifling the expression of grievance and aspirations for social change. The problem of discrimination, moreover, is not one simply of types of dispute, but also of timing, for some parties will find a resolution by a certain point when others will find themselves entangled in an escalating spiral of unhelpful antagonism. The distinction has to be made ultimately, assuming there is no immediate threat of socially unacceptable behaviour, in terms of whether the parties have the power of control over their relationship — that is, have a realistic knowledge of what is going on and a rational orientation towards future action, plus the power to act on their better judgement. The distinction is difficult to make from a removed position, unless events have got well out of hand — rather late for effective intervention. Therefore the provision of conflict resolution services on demand by either party is probably the only way of ensuring both the need to intervene and its timely initiation.

This argument concerning whether or not to intervene is separate from that concerning the form of intervention — legal, non-legal professional, or community control. We do, however, need to consider the relationship between dispute and offence, for mediation is predicated on the former and alternatives to law on the latter. At first sight they appear to be quite separate concepts with potential overlap, as when offences arise out of a dispute or a dispute is caused by a prior offence. The majority of 'crimes of violence', so-called, arise from ongoing relationship problems, and it is relatively easy to see how they might be reframed in mediation terms, but what of 'property crimes' that typically occur between strangers?

There are two answers to this question. One is to argue that all offences where there is a personal victim create a situation of potential conflict. The fact that the victim seldom meets, or even comes to know, the offender may prevent the realization of that conflict as an actual dispute, but that does not alleviate the victim's problems; indeed, it exacerbates them, in that it prevents him/her resolving the issue directly. We now know from several empirical studies (Shapland et al., 1985; Maguire and Corbett, 1987) the suffering that victims of crime may endure, including the inability to express their anger, to obtain the reassurance of observing the offender's remorse, or to alleviate fears for their future security by establishing the offender's identity as a fellow citizen with his/her own problems. 'Above all, perhaps, victims need an experience of forgiveness . . . forgiveness is a process of letting go. Victims need to be able to let go of the crime experience so that . . . it will no longer dominate their lives. Without that, closure is difficult and the wound may fester for many years' (Zehr, 1985). Dissatisfaction with the legal process on the part of victims, as Shapland et al. demonstrate, is partly a reflection of the fact that legal processing, for all that it saves of the victim's time and energy, does nothing to compensate for these more emotional features. The more prominent the psychological, rather than the financial or the physical, impact of a crime, the more the victim may find advantage by involvement in the resolution of the offence, including encounter with the offender, despite the loss of time, and possibly other resources, that will be implicated.

Even if one considers that the above argument stretches the concept of 'dispute' to breaking-point, it is still true that the emotional sufferings of victims of crime and of parties to debilitating conflict are often very similar, and in many cases can only be adequately resolved through direct encounter (via mediation). On the other hand, the second method of argument makes an even more direct connection between dispute and offence. Like disputes, offences also arise out of ongoing social processes and relationships. Although victim and offender may not have known each other before, they are related by membership, in many cases of the same neighbourhood, in almost every case of the same society as fellow citizens. The victim, to the offender, may represent the wealthy class whose exploitation has created his/her poverty, or the lucky ones who have found status, comfort and happiness when he/she lacks these. The offender, to the victim, may represent a threat to expected security which may be more or less prevalent in the victim's thoughts — whether to leave the house, walk certain streets at night, etc. Personally strangers, they know one another as types, or rather stereotypes, because most often they are quite wrong in their pictures of each other. But it is not only the past and the present they share, it is the future too. The conflicts mirrored in these stereotypes — class, status, culture, scapegoated minorities — are real conflicts that prevent communities functioning as well as they might. In a small village community everyone knew everybody else; in present-day communities we face the tall order of managing social interactions between people who are personal strangers. This can only be satisfactorily resolved through personal interaction and the breakdown of false stereotypes. Offenders may find it less easy to take a predatory attitude towards strangers (potential victims) if they are forced to recognize their individuality and their similarity of social status. Victims — as average citizens — would need to see their responsibility as citizens (not as victims) to preserve their community against the prejudices, intolerances and exploitative attitudes that create the very crime from which they hide in fear, and to create the positive mechanisms for co-operative informal neighbourhood control that will bring people together, not force them apart as members of stereotyped classes, black and white, victim and offender.

This second argument regards offences not as personal disputes, then, but as aspects of social conflict. A crime, from this perspective, is an incident arising out of underlying social problems that is identified by state agencies of social control and classified as an offence in order to process it through the legal system. This process facilitates essential declaratory and expressive purposes, but other processes and other definitions are possible for other purposes. Seeing such an incident as arising from social inadequacies, as an expression of grievance on one side and helplessness on the other, provides one with a definition in quite different terms from legal ones, and suggests quite different forms of resolution. Although the latter cannot be achieved solely through one encounter between two representatives of the local community, the change in attitude from the alienative judicial process to collaborative mediation may, in the long run, over many cases, make a significant impact on social attitudes and behaviour. The devolution of all responsibility for dealing with crime to the state is a situation that allows people to continue operating with misperceptions of society that prevent them adopting rational solutions.

These arguments depend on analyses of the origins of crime and the nature of social life that are difficult either to prove or disprove. Their present potency (in the alternative dispute resolution movement) lies only in the failure of alternative visions to prevent a growing problem of social disorder and community breakdown. They pass beyond the bounds of any further examination here and must remain merely as hypotheses. However correct they may be, too, it must be remembered that in the short term society must cope with a few individuals whose behaviour is either beyond rational control or is deliberately antisocial, exploitative, predatory and dangerous, to whom the sort of alternatives discussed here will not be relevant — even if their characters have been formed in social inadequacies of the recent past that are ultimately a communal responsibility. The distastefulness of our legal process is the price one pays for neglecting that prior responsibility.

The nature of justice

The other issue that demands some theoretical exploration is that of 'justice'. Justice may take a number of forms. The legal system operates around a particular conception of justice in terms of desert, where punishment is measured in terms of the severity of the offence, although other considerations also enter in — the attitude and previous behaviour of the offender (an expanded concept of desert), his/her social background (closer, perhaps, to justice in terms of need than in terms of desert — cf. Honore (1962), Miller (1976) — seen particularly in the Scottish Children's Hearings). In British courts, the effect of the offence upon the victim (which may, for instance, be greater for the elderly or the nervous in disposition) is more rarely a consideration in sentencing and no arrangements for reporting this to the court exist. The 'victims' movement' in the United States has been instrumental in establishing 'victim impact statements' as a court input (Bureau of Justice Statistics, 1984), but the British victims' support movement has resisted such measures as an 'unfair' influence on sentencing. The scope of the courts in sentencing is quite wide, however, and it is likely that in Britain a crime deliberately committed against an elderly or disabled person, for instance, as an easy target, would be dealt with more severely. In other words, the practice of courts tends towards a 'natural' or pragmatic concept of justice which contains elements of different kinds. Surveys of public opinion have shown close agreement in Britain between the judgements of appropriate sentences by laypeople and actual sentences given in court (Hough and Mayhew, 1985).

The justice system may well congratulate itself on maintaining public confidence to the extent that it can still act as the prime model of justice, but cracks in that confidence are apparent, as perhaps they have always been. Crime is a growing problem, not a decreasing one. High rates of custody are criticized by many, whether on humanitarian, utilitarian or financial grounds. Despite agreement in general, sentences are criticized by some groups for excessive punitiveness, by others for excessive leniency. What all these criticisms amount to is a growing perception that legal justice founded on abstract rules, while it may be more or less fair, is not effective. 'The more equity is sacrificed to the logic of rules, the greater the distance between official law and the lay sentiment of right. As a result, the law loses its intelligibility as well as its legitimacy in the eyes of the layman . . .' (Unger, 1976). The movements away from the traditional legal system are movements towards not only alternative methods but also alternative justice.

The single most important feature of the legal-judicial approach, which distinguishes it most clearly from more informal systems studied by social anthropologists (Marshall, 1985: 45–9), is its alienative character. It is predicated on separating an 'offender' from the rest of society; opposing him/her to the 'good' victim or the state (represented through legal functionaries, and by the symbolic appearance of Her Majesty as one of the parties, as in R. [Regina] v. Smith); and, in sentencing, to place the whole blame for what has happened upon the offender, who may then be further separated from 'good' society by being placed in custody or under regular supervision, quite apart from the labelling as criminal which occurs through the public nature of the courtroom and the permanence of a criminal record. This is the legal-judicial method and it works well as a means of clarifying right and wrong in abstract moral terms. It does not work at all well in reforming individual offenders; in fact, it may make them all the more difficult to reform. Imprisonment is particularly severe in this respect, by breaking ties with the legitimate community not only for the period of custody but thereafter (because of lost employment, broken marriages and psychological impairment). Even short of custody, however, the whole legal process alienates the offender from the community (self-concept as 'bad', resentment at the overreaction of the formal process) and the community from the offender (rejection of 'criminals', lack of desire for reconciliation).

The 'community control' movement has formulated an alternative to legal process that would not be alienative. Though still pronouncing right and wrong, this judgement would refer to specific acts and not be generalized to an individual's total character. The greater part of the effort in an alternative forum would be devoted not to cutting off the offender but to establishing more effective ties between him/her and the general community. Unger (1976:204) foresaw such a trend away from formal law towards justice based on equity ('intuitive sense of justice in the particular case') and solidarity ('procedures concerned primarily with reconciling the parties . . . and . . . developing moral ideals'). Unlike traditional social work attitudes (which have until recently been seen as the main alternative to the legal punitive approach), the new alternatives would still assign responsibility to individuals; unlike the formal courts, however, they would seek to operationalize that responsibility not symbolically through an imposed act of retribution, but by involvement of the offender in a real act of reparation to the victim and the community. The burden assumed by the offender would not simply be a passively received punishment, but a contribution — in association with others, possibly including the victim — to his/her reintegration into normal social relationships. The burden, objectively, may be greater or less than in the judicial process, but what is distinctive is its meaning to the offender and to others. The meaning of retributive justice is 'Go and stand outside until you learn to behave properly'; the meaning of integrative or reparative justice 'Join us in putting things right again'. In Zehr's clear exposition:

> Judges often talk about accountability, but what they usually mean is that when you do something wrong, you must take your punishment. I want to suggest that real accountability means something quite different. Genuine accountability means, first of all, that when you offend, you need to understand and take responsibility for what you did. Offenders need to be encouraged to understand the real human consequences of their actions. But accountability has a second component as well: offenders need to be encouraged to take responsibility for making things right, for righting the wrong ... Unfortunately, though, our legal process does not encourage such accountability on the part of offenders. Nowhere in the process are offenders given the opportunity to understand the implications of what they have done. Nowhere are they encouraged to question the stereotypes and rationalizations ('It's no big deal; they deserved it; insurance will cover it') that made it possible for them to commit their offenses. In fact, by focusing on purely legal issues, the criminal process will tend to sidetrack their attention, causing them to focus on legal, technical definitions of guilt, on the possibilities for avoiding punishment, on the injustices they perceive themselves to undergo. (Zehr, 1985)

The 'new justice' takes a number of different forms according to the procedures advocated. We have already seen how Shonholtz emphasizes democratic principles and direct community involvement. The San Francisco Community Boards that he inspired are panels of five or six local volunteers, usually acting in a public forum, who encourage the parties to tell their own stories and to participate in the process of establishing the facts and their relationship to social norms of good behaviour, and who work towards a resolution that is the product of parties' own ideas in collaboration. From a general community standpoint, the process is more important than the details of the resolution (unlike a judicial forum where the high points are the conviction and the sentence), for it is the process which would achieve the longer-term aims of community integration and individual rehabilitation. This process would be empowering in terms of negotiation skills (educative) and in terms of keeping control over one's own conflicts.

'Community justice' of this kind, however, is not the only way that has been contemplated of introducing the 'new justice' principles. Others such as Zehr (1985), Christie (1982), and Raynor (1985: ch. 9

on 'participatory justice') have argued for the incorporation of reparative justice in the formal courts, as a substitute for the usual retributive and rehabilitative principles. While retributive justice is state-centred and rehabilitative justice offender-centred, reparative justice would seek to involve the interests of all parties (including the victim and the community). Christie, for instance, proposes a system based on restitution or compensation rather than the infliction of pain, with full participation of the affected parties and opportunity for airing expressive as well as material concerns, such as repentance and forgiveness. Zehr includes these features in a more general paradigm of the 'new justice' that contrasts with the traditional process in various ways: in defining crime as a conflict between people, in its focus on establishing or re-establishing relationships, in its future-oriented, problem-solving nature, in its encouragement of a sense of community, in its concern with behaviour in context, and in its assessment according to the outcome rather than obedience to 'correct' procedure (due process).

These ideas have been operationalized (by Zehr among others) in the development of Victim/Offender Reconciliation Projects (VORPs) in North America, beginning as an initiative of Mennonite communities that reject resort to external law in favour of resolving trouble within the community (religiously as well as geographically defined). In the origins of this movement religious notions of personal responsibility (sin), atonement (setting matters right with God) and the 'church' (as a living community) were important (cf. Umbreit, 1985), although they easily translate into secular concepts that have lent themselves to the extension of the VORP idea beyond Mennonite communities.

The same concepts of reparation and restitution have begun to percolate through to Britain, helped by the growth of the victims' support movement, and have greatly extended the idea, at the time tentative, incomplete and imperfectly understood in terms of its ultimate implications, of 'community service', first introduced experimentally as a court 'penalty' in 1973. 'Of all the modes of community control,' Cohen (1985) is now able to say with the benefit of hindsight, 'only "community service" (restitution, reconciliation, reparation, compensation) evokes most directly the vision of community. These schemes have been heavily criticized as forms of net-widening, cheap labour, new sanctions in the sentencing tariff, and as a version of the same ideology of work and discipline developed in the prison, but they do come close to the original vision of involvement and integration. This is particularly so when punishment takes the form of direct victim compensation — vandals repairing the windows they have broken.'

This idea is an 'alternative' not in terms of the locus of control, as in community justice, but in terms of the principles on which justice is based. It operates either within, or in association with, standard legal procedures and agencies. In terms of the argument in the first part of this chapter, the VORPs supplement or complement the law, they do not replace it. They carry out the tasks that the law itself leaves incomplete. How far they can achieve such a revolution in approach from within remains to be seen. At the same time, how far modern communities can effectively manage their own internal troubles outside the formal system is an equally pressing question.

Despite the obvious differences, the VORPs share many aspirations and concepts with community justice. They are predicated on personal active involvement, particularly in a meeting between victim and offender, mediated by a third party, who may be a law volunteer or a professional (in Britain, for instance, often a probation officer, although this practice has been tried and rejected in America). They rely on mutual agreement between the two parties, not on authoritative judgements. Insofar as victim and offender know one another personally, the mediation may be identical to that involved in a community dispute settlement scheme but, on the basis of the assumption that all fellow citizens are related in a sense, VORPs do not select only related parties but include 'stranger' crimes as well.

Underlying both community justice and the VORPs is a common ideology based on 'co-operative problem solving', the principles of which are developed by Fisher and Ury (1981). The crucial elements of this approach are: (a) direct and active collaboration between the parties involved; (b) a concern with the future and how the relationship between the parties can be managed for mutual benefit; a concern with the past only insofar as it holds lessons for the future; (c) creativity in finding solutions, avoiding adherence to rigid procedures and trying to escape restrictive assumptions and prior definitions that induce false oppositions. It is based on the assumptions that disputing is often unproductive because parties concentrate on their differences rather than their common interests and interdependency; that adversarial methods are not fruitful in the long run, although they may lead to deceptively easy victories in the short term; and that, a fortiori, violence, as an extreme form of adversarial disputing, is socially unacceptable and particularly unproductive (and this would include the use of violence by the law, except when there is no option for proceeding otherwise).

These general principles pass beyond any particular method of practice. Mediation and reparation are grounded in them, but they may also inform a variety of other activities — personal negotiation, management, social planning, peacemaking, and pressure group politics, for instance; and be employed by all kinds of people — as professionals and citizens — in any sphere of social activity. A participatory, problem-solving approach has also been suggested for social and probation work (Raynor, 1985: ch. 5; Bottoms and McWilliams, 1979) and the growing popularity of these ideas explains the origin, in initiatives by members of these two professions, of most of the new schemes in Britain described in Chapter 7.

We are taught to fight or oppose others effectively — debating societies, competitive games and sports, legal and rights education — but are hardly ever taught to co-operate. The idea of 'co-operative problem solving', in the eyes of many of its advocates (Beer, 1986: ch. 9, 'Dreams of Justice, Dreams of Peace'), could, if it attracts widespread adherence, constitute a reform of fundamental proportions in the nature of society.

3 Beyond Informal Justice

Maureen Cain

The debate about informal justice, deregulation and popular justice has run into stalemate. Once again, it seems, high hopes shared by both left and liberal reformers have been dashed.

Academic criticism and negative evaluation have created a growing chorus of despair, a feeling that the devil of formal justice whom we know may, after all, be better than his dangerously unfamiliar informal brother. This chorus is occasionally punctuated by an attenuated left-wing squeak of hope that by some dialectical feat a 'genuinely' human and popular form of justice may emerge in spite of all from this newly identified diabolical situation (Abel, 1982; Cohen, 1984; Hofrichter, 1982; Santos, 1979, 1980; Spitzer, 1982).

This chapter is an attempt to make that squeak a little stronger. I argue that the pessimism arises from a failure to distinguish between types of informal justice in a theoretically adequate way. When all modes of adjudication other than the formal and professional are conceptually conflated, the failures *from a working-class standpoint* are bound to outweigh the successes. Not only does this lead to pessimism and nihilism: it makes it impossible either to learn from the mistakes or to identify a direction for future efforts.

The argument here has the following form: there follows a brief discussion of my choice of standpoint; in the next section the already established criticisms of informal justice institutions are briefly reviewed, and some additional ones put forward; following that, the general requirements for a more adequate theory in this area are specified; the final sections of the chapter deal with three main types of informal justice which can be empirically identified and theoretically established. The dynamic of the relationship between the types is then briefly considered, and the inherent instability of progressive forms explained. In conclusion it is argued that the identification of these types establishes provisional criteria of progress.

It is seen that when collective justice is used as the yardstick against which other types are measured, then the picture that emerges is very different from when the customary yardstick of professionalized justice is used.

It is by now commonplace in sociology to argue that knowledges are not absolute but depend on the structural location of the knower. In recent writings I have argued (1) that this does not preclude but rather necessitates technical excellence and the application of scholarly standards (Cain and Finch, 1981); (2) that standpoints are recognizable in theoretically determinate ways; not all 'groups' or structural locations are or can be standpoints (Cain, 1985; Hartsock, 1983); (3) that for this reason epistemological conflation — to know or to construct knowledge from several standpoints at once — is not possible. However, at the level of politics there can be alliances and, on the basis of these, knowledge produced from one standpoint may sometimes be of value to those whose practice and knowledge is from a different standpoint (Cain, 1985). Thus in this chapter I write usually of knowledge from a working-class standpoint, and this is the site from which I hope I have spoken in elaborating this analysis. I do not know if the analysis would have been different if I had approached it from a feminist standpoint: probably so. I believe that this is a case in which knowledge produced from one standpoint (that of the working class) could be useful to people working from another (feminists). To indicate this I have from time to time strung together in the text the working class–black people– women. But I do not believe such alliances are best forged by pre- suming their existence *at any level*, including the epistemic. Such conflations can only be a way of disguising the need for intellectual and practical work.

The standpoints from which it is possible for any one person to speak are given, although they must also be chosen. Here I have approached the problem of informal justice from the standpoint of the working class primarily for the practical reason that the literature and 'social experiments' on which I base my analysis make this possible. Extrapolation from historically frozen or existing examples is crucial to my method, as will be seen.

Before proceeding, one further qualification is necessary. The discussion is intended to illuminate questions of informalism in ad- vanced capitalist societies. Some of the points made may have a bearing on related problems in post-colonial societies or in socialist societies, but these are not my central point of reference here.

The critique of informalism in advanced capitalist societies

Critics of informal justice argue that it is unnecessary, that it has failed, that it is sinister and that it is impossible. Let us consider these points in turn.

Felstiner (1974) taking issue with Danzig (1973) and also, although not explicitly, with Christie (1977) argues that in complex and technically advanced societies people typically deal with their problems and resolve their disputes by avoidance or by lumping it. Thus elaborate, semi-official agencies of the type proposed by Danzig are neither necessary nor appropriate. On the other side Danzig and Lowy (1975) have argued and Merry (1979) in particular has demonstrated that avoidance is emotionally and financially expensive for working-class people in the United States. The practice of lumping it could be used empirically to found a radical non-interventionist strategy: the cost of lumping it could be used to argue for either more formal or more informal mechanisms: so this discussion was inconclusive.

In the same way, the second critique, the argument that informal justice is a failure in its own terms, points to no clear alternative. This line of argument arose mainly from evaluations of US neighbourhood justice programmes (Felstiner and Williams, 1980; Tomasic, 1980; Tomasic and Feeley, 1982) and consumer protection agencies (Nader, 1980). It had been hoped that neighbourhood justice would be cheap, express community values, be socially integrative, non-coercive, and individually therapeutic. The model was the post-colonial African community moot (Christie, 1977; Danzig, 1973). In the event it was found that informal justice could cost more in time and money than formal adjudication, that its practitioners were middle-class people and expressed professional values, that neither the issues raised nor the clients of the centres were representative, with courts tending to offload family matters and (other) 'trivia', and clients being disproportionately black and/or female. Moreover, the fact that most referrals came from other social control agencies, as well as the class of the mediators, meant that the system tended to be alien at best, and at worst coercive, while any potentially therapeutic results to be derived from a refereed face-to-face encounter were lost because the procedure did not allow for such confrontations.

A number of other studies have discussed the co-optation or capture of agencies of informal justice either by various groups of professionals or by what Thompson (1983) has called a professional laity — a group of experienced lay people of proven reliability from the standpoint of those who established the tribunal or other adjudicative agency. Frost and Howard (1977) and Hetzler (1982) have demonstrated an alliance between chairpeople and professionals in various welfare tribunals in the UK and Sweden, which effectively inhibits participation by other lay members. Blegvad has made a similar point in relation to consumer tribunals in Denmark (Blegvad, 1983; see also Eisenstein, 1979). Dickens (1983) has pointed to the secondary role played by lay members of industrial tribunals in Britain, compared with their legally qualified chairpeople.

Chairpeople are frequently appointed by or with the approval of the agency on whose actions the tribunal will adjudicate, as in the case of Supplementary Benefit Appeal Tribunals in the UK (Frost and Howard, 1977). Those recognized (probably by the agency to be adjudicated) as experts have ideological advantages best described as a legitimacy bonus. Other tribunals, such as British Mental Health Review Tribunals, have legally qualified chairpeople who are presumed to be 'expert in the impartial examination of facts' (Wraith and Hutchesson, 1973: ch. 10). Thus even where lay members are regular participants they are at a structural disadvantage.

Like the neighbourhood justice centres, these agencies too fail to fulfil their own objectives, as at least one official report (Franks, 1957) has pointed out. The voice of the person in the street is not heard, the criteria of adjudication are either professional or class biased, and the 'informality' of the hearing itself exists only in comparison with the ritual of a high court. Private rules of procedure, evidence, and entitlement are inevitably substituted for the public ones which are waived.

Proposed solutions to these problems range from reaction (re-professionalization), through reformist measures (representation by non-lawyers; legal aid to 'litigants'), to despair. This lack of guidance towards an alternative results from the lack of a theory which goes beyond the structure of the specific institution(s) under discussion, a theory with adequate conceptual links with a general theory of social structure. Only such a general theory can give adequate guidance as to how desired changes may be achieved, and only such a general theory will contain within it a political morality and the concepts necessary for realizing its vision. This is the familiar problem of the limitations of middle-range theorizing, and the neighbourhood justice studies in the United States and the lay justice studies in Europe have willy-nilly shared these failings, whatever the practical and political intentions of their authors.

Nonetheless, these studies have considerable value precisely because by and large they are informed by a concern for the clients of these institutions and have been carried out from their standpoint. The negative demonstration that these agencies do not work may not have been sufficient in pointing to an alternative direction, but it has demonstrated the need, both practically and theoretically, for alternative formulations.

The third argument, that informalism is sinister, has various levels of complexity. Mathiesen (1980) and Santos (1980) for example, develop their analyses from complex attempts to reformulate the place of law in the modern capitalist state, whereas Abel (1981, 1982), Garth (1982), Hofrichter (1982), Scull (1982), Wahrhaftig (1982) and Winkler (n.d.), either presume a neo-Marxist theory of the state, or regard states per se as dangerous. The arguments, however, are similar; not only has the state encouraged informal justice in order to solve its own political legitimacy or fiscal crises, but in so doing it has co-opted voluntary groups and deeply penetrated the social structure, taking over and transforming common-sense evaluations and traditional patterns of relationships. Thus the apparent off-loading of state functions is a disguised form of state expansion, as Cohen (1985) has also argued. But with the notable exceptions of Mathiesen and Santos, who in their larger theories create a space for political action, the other contributions to the 'informalism is sinister' school of thought adopt an instrumentalist position in which the question addressed by the analysis is 'how do these institutional arrangements serve the needs of capital/the state?' When the question is posed in this way, positive answers as to what might be achieved are impossible, as is any elaboration of the theory of the state itself, about which it is presumed we know already.

With the same two exceptions these arguments can be characterized as a form of socialist idealism, that is, they present a theoretical discussion of capitalism from which informalization movements are somehow derived, even deduced. No one attempts to use the by now considerable range of materials *about* these movements to construct a theory.

Thus a majority of writers who have seen informalism as sinister have been unable, because of the limitations of their own theoretical positions, to formulate any alternative. A defensive formalism, following Thompson (1975) becomes the only conceivable tactic. As indicated, Mathiesen and Santos are exceptions in that the concepts they use to identify and distinguish informal structures can be integrally related to their theories of the total social structure. Thus for these authors it is only certain types of informalism which are sinister. Their relative success in making these distinctions and elaborations has profoundly influenced my own position.

Fourthly and finally there are those critiques of informalism which argue that it is impossible, that informal justice is, in the context of advanced capitalist societies, a contradiction in terms. Once again, scholars of the 'impossibility' school can be divided into two groups. First there are those who have contributed to the transferability debate set in train by the arguments of Danzig (1973) and Christie (1977) that the western world would benefit from the importation of African models of judicial decision making. Merry effectively concluded this debate in 1982, demonstrating that the argument was based on a romantic idealization of pre-capitalist (but non-feudal) forms. Contrary to this idealized view, mediation in such societies is typically influenced by high status people appointed to the role, it is coercive in that there are strong sanctions against breaches in agreements reached, and it depends on patterns of continuing relationships which do not exist in the capitalist industrialized world.

In Europe informalism has not shared the anthropological premise, although it has shared the objectives. There have been warnings about transferability, albeit from historical (Dawson, 1960) perspectives, or as between advanced capitalist societies (Blanken-berg and Reifner, 1981). Both versions, however, are vulnerable to the theoretical attack which argues that informal law cannot be law. As early as 1926, Pashukanis (1980) argued that the concept of law, like the concept of commodity, should be historically specific in its derivation. The argument has been developed theoretically by Edelman (1979), and by Medcalf (1978) with a brilliant concrete illustration of a North American case revealing how successful struggles for economic and civil rights internally transformed (destroyed) native American cultures. Plainly this discussion has relevance for the debate about the transferability of institutions between different modes of production, for the arguments show that law is fundamentally and inevitably destructive of collectivities. The use of legal means to reinforce community or neighbourhood ties thus involves a contradiction. Informal law is a contradiction in terms so far as the working class is concerned. In so far as informal law is law it is destructive of collectivity, the only source of countervailing power to capital. In so far as informalism does not destroy collectivity, that is in so far as it constitutes its subjects in non-individual ways, then this informal procedure is not law. It must be some other form of justice or of social control.

Towards a theory of collective justice

In elaborating a materialist theory of justice, from a working-class standpoint, a number of important methodological principles must be adhered to. I have elaborated these at considerable length else-where (Cain, 1985; Cain and Finch, 1981). As far as the present attempt is concerned, they boil down to the following interrelated principles.

First, the categories will be elaborated in such a way that they are integrally related to an existing theory; in more precise terms, the categories will be *objective*, existing independently of particular thinkers, and capable of critical scrutiny in their relationship with the rest of the theory. Class categories developed within the Marxist tradition are used, for several reasons. The most important of these is that one-dimensional conceptions of class, based on life chances in a market situation, or distinctions between rich/poor, privileged/underprivileged, do not account for the observed differences between agencies, *all* of which (that is, all of those studied) would claim that their purpose was to help the poor and the underprivileged, who are their prospective clients. Marxism allows for the elaboration of qualitative distinctions between classes: the distinction between an independent shopkeeper and an industrial worker remains even if their incomes are the same; the distinction between a houseworker and a waged worker remains even if their life chances are the same. Secondly, and for the same reason, Marxism makes possible the adoption of a standpoint in the sense used here. Thirdly, a theory emphasizing qualitative rather than purely quantitative distinctions is prima facie — but still only potentially — better able to take account of complexities such as those introduced by racism and sexism.

Next, the theory will be historically specific in that it will depend on 'data', in this case secondary source materials about actual informal justice institutions. Materialist theories cannot be constructed out of ideas alone, but most extrapolate working principles from the various 'practical utopias' which it has been possible to develop at particular historical moments. When Marx attempted, so briefly, to give an indication of how a class-free (or proletarian?) future would look, he analysed the short existence of the Paris Commune (Marx, 1969). All we have to start with, in building such practical experiments, is class-specific knowledge of the forms of exploitation and oppression which are given by our theorized experience. We therefore 'know' that which we oppose, and we proceed not by reversing the institutions of the other, but by experimentation with ways of overcoming those forms of oppression which we know. We construct, that is, prefigurative institutions.[1] The task, therefore, for the theorist from a working-class standpoint is to notice these prefigurative institutions where they emerge, and to identify their salient features.

A direction of advance will be integral to the (standpoint-specific) formulation. Materialist theories, while they cannot capture future history in a blueprint, must be useful for their clients, those from whose standpoint the theory is constructed. The aim here is to extrapolate key characteristics from prefigurative collective justice agencies in order to make the concrete direction of progress that little bit more clear for other groups of people making similar attempts to overcome their experiences of oppression.

These methodological points may seem tedious, but they are not trivial. This approach is essential for the development of helpful distinctions between informal justice agencies; without a method we shall all be overwhelmed and ultimately stultified by the contradictions which left scholars have so ably identified.

This chapter therefore has the aim of *identifying success stories, from a class standpoint*. The characteristics identified are the ones used as the *basis* for identification of three other 'types' of justice. Hitherto, scholars have sought to distinguish informal or popular justice from professionalized justice; thus, unintentionally, giving the professionalized form pride of place, allowing it to set the agenda, and determine which attributes are to be examined. Using this strategy one can come up with only negative characteristics for informal justice, or inversions of the professionalized version: informal justice is cheaper, closer to the needs and aspirations of its clients, faster, and so on. One can never identify an attribute which cannot even be conceived of by the professionalized form. One cannot say anything radically new or transformative. Here, in contrast, instances of working-class justice are captured and constituted as a yardstick, so that what is new will not be lost, and so that people may learn from each other.

In identifying success stories one is catching at so many chimerae. It is in the nature of expressions of working-class justice that they should encounter problems, attract opposition, and be, in the main, short lived. Yet these fleeting histories must be caught and inscribed in our political theory if we are to advance.

Collective justice: some success stories

I have chosen the term 'collective justice' to characterize those working-class instances which I shall describe. This is for the practical purpose of distinguishing this emergent form from the catch-all categories of informal or socialist or so-called 'popular' justice, as well, of course, as from the other types of informal justice distinguished here. It refers to a unique characteristic of the form: the way in which the *subject* of justice is constituted within it.

Our limited knowledge of collective justice is derived from scattered historical and contemporary sources. Typically, this has been a repressed knowledge, as Foucault has argued in both his discussion of repressive justice (1978) and popular justice (1980), as well as in his analysis of intellectuals (1977). This repression, or inhibition of reflexivity by collective justice practitioners, has itself contributed to the instability of the form.

But we do know that there were the 'Knights of Labour' trade union courts in the early twentieth century USA (Garlock, 1982); there were the workers' offices in Weimar Germany (Reifner, 1982); in recent times in the United States we have seen the San Francisco

Consumer Advice Agency (Wilson and Brydolf, 1980) and of course 'the first law commune' (Lefcourt, 1971: 310–26) and the civil rights and later poverty rights lawyers (Carlin, 1970; Cloward and Elman, 1970; Ginger, 1972; Handler et al., 1978; James, 1973; Medcalf, 1978). In Britain, the law centres movement is documenting its own history in the form of its annual reports and beginning to publish the results of its own self-reflections (Grace and Lefevre, 1984, 1985; Stevens, 1980).

In Portugal, popular courts had a brief life after the revolution of 1974 (Santos, 1979). There are historical examples of mass resistance which has taken an adjudicative form, and numerous Third World instances of post-colonial locally based courts.[2] These last examples are not central to this analysis, which concerns itself with what can be done in a non-revolutionary situation in an advanced industrial and capitalist society — a limited aim. Nonetheless, a knowledge of these instances can help clarify some of the issues, particularly in those cases where contradictions are identified and where policy choices must be made, as in Sachs's (1979, 1985) discussions of Mozambique, Spence's (1982) research on Chile, or Thome's (1984) consideration of alternative strategies for legal services.

When relatively stable and institutionalized instances of working-class (collective) justice in advanced industrial societies are considered, it can be seen that they exist in two modes, corresponding to what they seem to regard as their two tasks. These tasks can be identified as the maintenance of internal discipline (the defensive mode) and advancing the position of the collectivity they represent (the attacking or advancing mode). There are few examples in the literature of agencies which move between modes. The 'Knights of Labour' courts described by Garlock were predominantly defensive, concerned primarily with questions of union solidarity and internal petty crime. Similarly, in Latin America the 'barrio' courts discussed by Karst et al. (1973), Santos (1981) and Spence (1982) are concerned with the resolution of internal disputes between residents. More dramatically, Hillyard (1985) and Munck (1985) have described the popular justice of the Provisional IRA in Ulster. Quite clearly, in the case of the 'Knights of Labour' and the Provisional IRA the 'advancing' mode was and is organizationally independent of the 'defensive' structures. In the case of the 'barrios' this distinction is less apparent because the same meetings might serve many purposes.

This raises a question about the British and North American institutions discussed here, for these are mainly legal services agencies with neither official status as, nor unofficial claims to be, courts. Yet it emerges from the analysis that they are indeed sites of judgement, sites at which a decision is taken not just about which party to an action to support but about who is deserving of support, about who is right in a moral and political sense, and in their own legal sense. For these agencies, as will be seen below, the question of who is adjudged to be right in a conventional legal sense is not decisive, and rarely more than an interim objective. Because they are agencies in the 'advance' mode, self-consciously seeking new and better ways of achieving their objectives, because they are not simply reacting to, mirroring, or inverting conventional practices, but functioning experimentally, they are the most promising source of a prefigurative model.

From accounts of these agencies it has been possible to extrapolate ten characteristics which can be empirically observed and which hang together theoretically.[3] These are explored below, and listed in summary form in Table 3.1.

1. The first characteristic of collective justice agencies is that their class identification is open and explicit, and pre-exists specific events affecting clients. This is clearest in the case of the two union-based agencies and in revolutionary courts, as in Portugal (Santos, 1979). The shanty town courts of Brazil and Chile claim a community rather than a class base, but the communities are homogeneous in class terms, and politically aware of their class position. The British Law Centres movement has also seen the local community as its client. However class-based organizations within the community (the local association of trades union delegates or Trades Council, tenants' associations, black people's groups) may form major clients as well as members of the management committee (Grace and Lefevre, 1984, 1985). Some centres have a policy of excluding certain types of client; for example, they will not act for a landlord in a dispute with a tenant.[4] Many have 'closed door' policies, focusing on community rather than casework problems. The limiting case with regard to this criterion is perhaps the San Francisco Consumer Agency, as consumers cannot be theorized as a class. For this agency class identification must be extrapolated from the actual class characteristics of its clients, and from the location of the agency in a working-class area.

2. and 3. Secondly, (2) the client is constituted (or seen) as a *collective subject*. This means that (3) the 'other side' in matters dealt with by the agency in its 'advance' mode must necessarily be seen in class terms also. A collective subject cannot have an individualized, de-classed opponent. Both these characteristics of collective justice agencies derive logically and necessarily from their explicit class standpoint and purpose. As the Schwendingers (1978) have shown, these collective characteristics of subject and object can also be found in feminist sites, such as rape crisis centres.

In the 'defensive' mode the client remains a collective subject —

the community, a class to be protected. The other side, when this community has been threatened, may be individualized, as may be the case when two community members are in conflict. These cases differ from conventional practice in their procedures and solutions (below), but also because the individual is conceived concretely and politically, as taking his or her identity from a discursively negotiable status, rather than abstractly. In formally abstract justice the individual disappears and only the rule and its privileged custodians and spokespeople remain. The individual of collective justice in its 'defensive' mode is a being and human.

4. If the objective is to advance a class then (a) long-term and prophylactic solutions are required. The total situation should be prevented from occurring again: that particular experience of oppression must be eliminated for the class as a whole to be said to have made an advance. (b) The prophylactic function can be performed negatively, by requiring some action on the part of the opposing class, or positively, by education. Thus all the agencies produce newsletters, posters, have public meetings and seek to involve clients in their work — in making decisions and in contributing to the agency's understanding of the options. The German agencies made a point of presenting archetypal case histories in their newsletters so that the class basis of the problems could be more readily understandable than if discussions were either theoretical or based on generalizations. Thus clients are brought to a fuller understanding of their own class position, and so of the political strategies necessary to counter the class oppression they experience.

5. It again follows logically that the kind of evidence required for either negative or positive prevention, and for identifying the class character of the issues and the opponent, are different from the kinds of evidence required for adjudication in a narrower, individualized sense. Thus the workers in Germany found it necessary to conduct surveys of housing conditions, industrial injuries, and so on. In Britain, one London Law Centre, Brent, commissioned studies of shopping intentions and practices for use in a land use struggle. San Francisco CAA made a point of aggregating individual complaints and of testing products, so that particular producers could be identified as creating problems for their clients.

6. All presenting problems are generalized empirically and/or theoretically. Particular instances of problems with the police, with landlords, with employers, with producers or retailers are analysed as well as aggregated to identify their class basis. This is how the correct 'other side' is established.

7. Because ideal solutions will be long-term and prophylactic, as a result of modifying the structure of class relations in the area in

question, the seventh characteristic must be that these agencies do not limit themselves to the use of established 'courts' for possible solutions. This is because courts cannot offer changes in the structure of class relations, on however local a level, as a routine solution, although their decisions may under pressure, or, in particular 'test case' instances, affect the structure of those relations (Lazarson, 1982). Basically, even in aggregated actions courts do not recognize the same two opponents as collective justice agencies, so even apparently favourable decisions may leave the main problem untouched (Moore and Harris, 1976). And even if the solution is relevant, there are enforcement problems requiring continuous monitoring and continuous action on the part of the agency. Collective justice agencies do not see a court decision as the end of a process of problem solving, but as an occasional stage in that process. A good example here is provided by the San Francisco Consumer Agency which found the manipulation of publicity, and in extreme cases the tactic of picketing factories which produced faulty or dangerous products, more effective in many instances than court actions.

Courts are therefore used in pragmatic and tactically useful ways. According to Pashukanis (1980), this was what Lenin advised. However, the classical theorists of the left have in general had rather little to say about the question.

8. The eighth characteristic of these agencies is of crucial importance in guaranteeing their continuing collective character. Workers in these agencies are *accountable to the collectivity* (class) *they work for*. They are not accountable primarily to their individual clients, to the organization which employs them, to each other as an activist group, or to the state. This accountability guarantees that the collective justice agency remains organically linked, in Gramsci's (1971) sense, to the class it serves; that the intellectuals (again in Gramsci's broad sense of those who theorize the way forward for a class) who work there do not begin to follow the inner logic of their own ideas, or their established and habitual practices, and in so doing lose touch with the concrete demands and experiences of those from whose standpoint they claim to speak.

Accountability structures are institutionalized in a range of ways. Trades union electoral patterns and constitutional structures themselves vary, but accountability to the class via the trades union movement was the objective of the 'Knights of Labour' (Garlock, 1982) and the workers' offices (Reifner, 1982). Community-based agencies may elect officials, or accountability may be achieved by means of a management committee which includes as its major constituent delegates from the various clients of the agency (Grace and Lefevre, 1984, 1985). San Francisco CAA tried to realize the objective by involving individual clients directly in decision making relevant to their own problem. Adequate accountability in practice is not always achieved by these agencies, but the objective and the attempt is there. The criterion by which collective justice judges itself is adequate representation of and accountability to the collectivity which it serves.

9. This accountability structure is also the guarantee of the validity of the emergent theory of its practices which a collective justice agency develops. This is the ninth definitional characteristic of these agencies. The rules governing their decisions will be derived from a self-critical (reflexive) moral and political theory which itself is in a continuous process of elaboration. The purpose of the theory is a guide to effective collective action via adequate analysis of problems and past practice. The objective is not to be able to predict a decision, but to achieve adequate theorization of the problem and to devise an adequate strategy and tactics in the light of this. Adequacy is not an absolute criterion, but one which is decided, both from moment to moment by those working on the problem, and in the longer term via the accountability structure, in the light of a particular historical constellation of forces.

10. Finally, collective justice agencies experiment with forms of internal democracy. These include de-specialization of work (so that each person does his or her own typing, for example), randomizing the allocation of cases so that the most pushy, often male, do not claim the most interesting ones, equal pay for all staff members, collective decision making in which all staff (both volunteer and paid) have an equal voice, and client involvement in decision making (Grace and Lefevre, 1985; Lefcourt, 1971; Stevens, 1980; Wilson and Brydolf, 1980).

It is difficult at first sight to see a logical necessity for relationships of this kind. Whereas the first nine characteristics are, on examination, integrally related to the explicit collective (class) identification of the agencies, the tenth characteristic of internal democracy seems to be related rather adventitiously to this fundamental defining characteristic. It seems to be derived from a moral-political theory which identifies democratic practice as a crucial means of overcoming — permanently — forms of repression and oppression which are part of a collective class experience. Thus the democracy of the internal practices of some, but not all, of these agencies is consistent with their more general philosophy, and presumably both internal and external tensions would arise were this not the case.

A closer look, however, suggests that the logic of internal democracy may also be related to the accountability structure. Thus it becomes a necessary rather than a merely useful or correct mode of organization for collective justice agencies. Sociology of organization has over and over again demonstrated the blocking, filtering, gate-keeping (at the least) powers of lower status members of organizations which are hierarchically ordered. Thus a hierarchic structure in which, for example, high status members were accountable *to* the collectivity *for* the practices of low status members, could not guarantee the overall objective, which is that each member of such an organization should herself be an organic intellectual of the client collectivity. Democratic internal organization recognizes in its practices the close relationship between knowledges and powers, and seeks to maximize the accountability of both.

Agency workers are not vulnerable to the contradictions which could arise in a dual accountability structure, to both bureaucratic managers and to the collective client. As Grace and Lefevre (1985) have suggested, internal democracy may well be a practical necessity as well as a good-in-itself (which it surely is). In this sense it is not just an exemplar of the general direction of advance, but a necessary condition of it.

These characteristics, conceptually and practically interrelated as they are, make it possible to distinguish working-class or collective justice from other forms. The argument is that they are a necessary part of both defensive and offensive strategy. Defensively, the distinctions are important because the legitimacy of collective justice practices is often challenged by the simple polemical device of conflating all forms of justice which are not professionalized, and therefore creating the possibility of attributing the very obvious faults or failures of these other forms, here identified as *incorporated* and *populist* justice, to collective justice itself. Moreover, as the final section of this chapter describes, collective justice agencies are always vulnerable, are always under pressure to dissolve themselves into one of the other types which are acceptable within the capitalist world. The distinctions developed here are intended to reveal the dangers inherent in such pressures, which are usually expressed as plausible arguments and tempting offers rather than as coercion.

Offensively, apart from overcoming the depression alluded to in the first section, which results from these false analyses, the distinctions are important because they provide a temporary yardstick by which progress can be measured. If one or more of these characteristics is missing, an agency can ask itself why this is so. This might reveal a problem with the structure, and a direction for the agency's advance; or it might reveal instead some special characteristic of the agency's work or of the concrete historical setting within which it functions, thereby explaining its atypical structure or practices, and perhaps making it possible to elaborate the model. This would assist

Table 3.1 *A typology of justice in capitalist society*

Characteristics	Collective justice	Professionalized justice	Incorporated justice		Populist justice
			State	Capital	
Class base	Explicit/capable of theoretical identification	Class basis concealed by occupational autonomy	Class basis concealed by experts/lay members	Apparent but denied	Class base concealed by economic/political disjunction/ideology of the whole
Subject/client	Client constituted as collective class	Client constituted as individual subject with rights	Client constituted as individual subject	Client constituted as individual subject	Totality manifested in agents
Object/other side	Opposing class(es)	Object constituted as individual opponent	Existence denied	Existence denied	Penal law: outsider/non-person. Otherwise aspect of the totality
Objectives	Class advance (education) and defence (prophylaxis, individual rehabilitation)	Resolution of immediate issue/output of institutional forms for capital	Legitimation	Legitimation	Destruction of opposition/elimination of conflict
Originating incidents	Generalized to identify class base	Narrowly defined/de-classed	Generalized to personal characteristics/de-classed	Narrowly defined/de-classed	Generalized in unpredictable ways
Basis of decisions	Objective rules derived from emergent moral/political theory	Objective rules unrelated to other purposes	No public rules (possibly theoretically grounded)	No public rules	No objective rules
Evidence	Broad/theoretical criteria of relevance	Restricted by internal rules and definition of the incident	Discretionary Broad re. subject Narrow re. object	Discretionary Narrow re. both subject and object	Broad and variable
Sites decision/enforcement	Decision agency based/enforcement anywhere	State authorized institutions	State authorized institutions	'Private' sites	Any setting
Accountability	To class subject (institutionalized mechanisms) specialists accountable	To other practitioners	Hierarchic/'experts' non-accountable	Hierarchic/'experts' non-accountable	To 'totality' Effective accountability nil
Internal organization	Democratic: non-hierarchic/non-gendered	Collegial/segmented (some judiciaries are hierarchic)	Hierarchic/segmented	Hierarchic/segmented	Hierarchy may be by-passed by discretion or spontaneous order

other agencies with similar experiences. Table 3.1 sets out in simplified form the characteristics which typically distinguish these types of
agencies.

Plainly there is a 'more or less' element in the extent to which any
particular concrete instance fits its type, which is an abstraction from
a diverse reality. But this simplification is not so much a weakness as
one of the things the model is for![5]

Professionalized justice

This is the form of justice which has until now monopolized the
language of legitimacy, to the extent that it has become synonymous
with the concept of justice itself. Its characteristics have been ably
described by many commentators, most notably Unger (1975), in his
analysis of contemporary liberalism. For this reason — because this
form is familiar both common-sensically and analytically — its characteristics are simply listed here without elaboration. A fuller discussion can be found in Cain (1984).

1. The bourgeois class basis of professionalized justice is concealed by an undoubtedly considerable professional autonomy.
However, this class base can be demonstrated. Weber (1954: ch. 7)
noted that it is predominantly capitalists who demand creative work
from lawyers. Auerbach (1976) has recorded a correlation between
the expansion of the legal profession and the rise of capitalism in the
United States. I myself have argued (1979) on the basis of ethnog-
raphic evidence that lawyers are the *conceptive ideologists* of the
bourgeois class, thinking creatively new forms of organization for
capital. It also seems to be the case, secondly, that recruitment
processes to law work are such as to secure the predominance of
capitalist common sense within the bar and judiciary in Britain and
the United States in particular (Cain, 1984: 23–4).

2. In systems of professionalized justice the client is constituted as
an individual subject, in whose individuality and intact subjectivity
consists his or her humanity. Professionalized justice depends on
an individualized notion of the subject-as-client (Pashukanis, 1980;
Unger, 1975, 1976).

3. Professionalized justice also depends on, and constitutes, an
individualized conception of the opponent, the individual subject as
the model of what British practitioners call 'the other side'. Both
parties are subjects at law in this conception, hence justice has no
object other than itself.

4. Solutions are usually characterized as one-off and short-term.
However, this is only the character they typically present to the
litigant who is seeking a particular 'application' of the rules, as in

most contract and tort actions. It is also the character they present to working-class litigants, hence the insistence of collective justice agencies on doing community work rather than case work (Carlin, 1970; Grace and Lefevre, 1984, 1985; Lefcourt, 1971; Reifner, 1982). Moreover, the working class(es), as the weaker party in terms of any current analysis, will have to struggle continuously to guarantee effective enforcement of any relatively favourable court decision. And finally, positive prophylaxis by means of education and organization has no place whatever in the world of professionalized justice.

On the other hand, solutions for the clients who generated the legal profession as their organically related intellectual workers are indeed prophylactic — the joint stock company (brought about by statute with the help of lawyers) prevented major losses by small investors in the eighteenth century — and long term. This criterion, therefore, only distinguishes professionalized from collective justice if one adopts the standpoint of the subaltern classes, for whom even positive solutions are rarely prophylactic. In Britain, certainly, class successes are more likely to be achieved legislatively than in an adjudicative site.

5. and 6. Rules of evidence within professionalized justice are strict and circumscribed. They serve to constitute a narrow, declassed definition of the incident. Whereas collective justice searches for an analysis which will indicate the correct way of conceiving the class structure of the incident, its status as an example of a wider category of patterned events, professionalized justice insists on the incident being dealt with in isolation (or at best in aggregated form) as an occasion complete in itself. It is important to realize that the rules of evidence are *active* in this respect. In legal theory the incident is pre-defined, exists in itself independently of these rules which simply state what information 'about' the incident may be used. In the material world, on the contrary, it is the rules of evidence as they are used by lawyers which make the incident what it is, which set it up, which constitute it as an occasion without a relevant past, as unique, and as complete unto itself.[6] The rules of evidence guarantee the ostensibly apolitical and asocial character of professionalized justice. They therefore underpin the reality of its class character.

7. The legitimate solutions in professional justice systems are those which are offered by the courts or those settlements which a court could support. Other means of persuading the other side are not allowed. Innovative solutions are acceptable in only very limited cases, such as conditions of probation orders.

8. Professionalized justice takes its name from this eighth characteristic, namely, the successful achievement of autonomy by an

occupational group. Lawyers have successfully claimed a non-accountable status over large areas of their work. Even in the case of a career judiciary this may be so, with effective control being exercised by senior judges (Di Federico, 1976). Only a lawyer can decide whether another lawyer's conduct has breached the occupationally constructed ethical rules governing membership and practice. Lawyers set and mark their own entrance examinations and control, by informal means, mobility within the occupation so that, for example, at the bar in Britain, the non-deferential may find career advancement difficult (Cain, 1976) while women may be marginalized in gender-specific work roles or segmented into lower status work areas (Boigeol, 1984). In the United States the bar has achieved considerable influence over appointments to the Supreme Court (Grossman, 1965).

As far as the legal occupation goes, the autonomy claims mean that the lawyer cannot be directed as to how his or her 'professional' judgement should be exercised. Within the space of his or her relationship with the client, the lawyer is non-accountable except to the occupation itself. The collegial, non-hierarchic internal structure of the occupation reflects this ideology; assessment by peers is the practice, and in negligence matters even the formal courts rely heavily on the opinion of other workers in the same occupation. Typically, the organization and administration of legal aid schemes reflects these autonomy claims (Zander, 1978; Zemans, 1979).

9. The rules governing the decisions are, it is claimed, derived autonomously. This relates to the first characteristic, the fact that the class character of professionalized justice is concealed. However, the claimed autonomy is also a real structural constraint on lawyers and their clients. It shapes the forms which discursive translations and conceptive ideological work can take, and ensures that the rules do work, that is, do set limits to deviant practices and in so doing establish some parity of form and practice between capitalist enterprises. The rules also work, that is, appear as fixed and autonomous, in relation to those people or legal persons who lack the resources to challenge or re-create them by means of the elaborate processes established precisely in order to maintain these autonomous appearances. Their side-effect is to make the autonomy real! The fact that only a member of the occupational group can address or interpret the rules also secures their internal consistency of logical structure, which is essential to both the reality and the appearance of the autonomy of the rules.

10. Finally, the internal organization of the legal occupation is collegial, as a result of the claim that hierarchic organization and bureaucratic direction is impossible within the protected relationship

with the client. Thus intra-occupational differences are those of status and of work segmentation rather than bureaucratic rank. On the other hand, ancillary workers in legal offices, whether legal executives or secretaries, are outside the collegial structure and can, therefore, be subjected to managerial direction.

Incorporated or 'colonized' justice

Incorporated justice is a form which lacks both the reality and the appearance of autonomy, although parts of the rhetoric of professionalized justice may be retained. The name derives from the key characteristic, which is that this is a form of adjudication which has been taken over by or embodied within either an agency of capital itself or an agency of the state.

How one regards the latter form is a function of the theory of the state which one employs. This problem is simplified here because it is only forms of justice in capitalist society which are being examined, so that one can at least assume a capitalist form of the state.[7]

First, the class basis of this form of justice may be direct as well as overt. A good example is the Better Business Bureau (Eaton, 1980), a consumer organization founded by a group of companies with a view to protecting their image as well as to resolving the 'reasonable' grievances of consumers. More frequently, however, the state mediates the class relations, as in Britain, the FRG and Scandinavia in industrial relations tribunals, and in a range of agencies responsible for adjudicating welfare state law (Blegvad, 1983; Farmer, 1974; Frost and Howard, 1977; Hetzler 1982; cf. also Abel-Smith and Stevens, 1967). In this latter, more typical, situation which also describes a number of semi-autonomous Federal Control agencies in the United States, the class character of the justice delivered is disguised in two important ways, which have come increasingly to displace the rhetoric of professionalized justice. This still emerging and complex situation demands analysis in some detail. If the class bases of incorporated justice cannot be identified then the distinction from the collective form will not hold.

The first complex mediation of the power of capital involves the use of *experts*. Public, or usually state, recognition as an expert in a field accords the entitlement to self-legitimating knowledge. An expert's judgements are valid because he or she has access to a knowledge which renders it impossible to make an *in*valid judgement, although a mistake, a false application of one's self-legitimating knowledge may be possible. The position of the expert is closely related to, but not isomorphic with, the position of scientist. It is easier to have claims to expert status formally acknowledged if it can be argued that they are based on positivistic scientific knowledge, the self-legitimating form of knowledge par excellence in the twentieth century. Non-experts are more sceptical of claims based on experience — a problem faced by teachers, police officers and social workers, among other occupational groups. Such workers may seek a more scientific theory of their jobs to underpin their claims to expert status.[8]

The scepticism is of course well founded, for all occupations generate self-closing knowledges — the very reason why intellectuals must retain organic (institutionalized) relationships with those whom they seek to serve as a means of preventing such knowledge closures. The argument, therefore, is that there should be scepticism about scientific knowledge too, for all expert knowledges are spoken from a site in the social structure which has been created and is maintained by a political process. It is correct to enquire of a scientific expert also *whose* knowledge does he or she speak, and on whose behalf.

In the context of incorporated justice, however, the knowledges of experts are presented as neutral and incontrovertible. Experts are used to present decisions as the outcome of non-negotiable truth. Thus as Blegvad (1983) has shown, the trade experts in consumer affairs are seen as having direct access to a knowledge about whether claims in the dry cleaning industry, for example, are reasonable. And in Swedish pensions councils, the official of the agency concerned is treated as having more 'true' knowledge of the facts (Hetzler, 1982). In these situations the claim to a larger than average share in decision making is based on a closed, allegedly true, knowledge, which is not open to debate. The political bases of knowledges of this kind are hidden and denied. Thus class-based knowledge sneaks in covertly, while incorporated justice is able to present itself as neutral, science-based and value-free.

This argument should not be seen as a denial of the value of expertise, for the democratic use of expert knowledges is possible. In one instance reported in the literature, that of land use planning appeals in Northern Ireland (Thompson, 1983), the expert knowledge was treated not as a knowledge of facts but precisely as a knowledge of policy. This is an acceptable use of experts, consistent with collective justice. It is therefore important to secure the distinction. When an expert presents herself as being most familiar with *policy*, she is basing her claims to a better than average influence on decision making on privileged knowledge of a socially constructed reality, that is, policy, by definition the outcome of a political decision. This is to admit that the knowledge, or the policy from which it derives, could be changed as a result of a political process. The knowledge is not foreclosed, therefore, but is open to scrutiny and debate. From the standpoint of democracy and collective justice, therefore, such ostensibly expert knowledges are acceptable. This is not how expert knowledges are typically regarded in incorporated justice agencies, however.

The second complex mediation of incorporated justice results from the second typical legitimacy claim, namely to represent the average person, the man (sic) in the street, the reasonable lay person's view. It is from this second kind of legitimacy claim that the confusion with collective justice arises.

State-run lay justice tribunals attempt to maintain the appearance of a state-sponsored popular court by means of their powers of selection of personnel. But there is an endemic contradiction whenever a capitalist state presents itself directly as representing, or indirectly as sponsoring, the collective totality, in this case by means of an allegedly representative selection of individuals.

The most fundamental contradiction is that the state must first construct the totality which it claims to represent, and also itself as an abstraction serving the interests of the total society (Engels, 1970; Jessop, 1982). However, once the mystique of the state is penetrated it can be seen as a set of interrelated institutions which collectively and separately are the ever-changing outcome of class struggle. The forms and practices of the agencies which constitute the state are constituted by different constellations of class forces, but, in capitalist society, the state as a whole is dominated by the various, often competing, segments and fractions of capital itself. This changes as, and only as, the balance of economic/political/ideological powers in the society is changed by political practice.

This formulation means that the precise constellation of class forces in any particular agency of incorporated justice will vary. However, some abstractions can be made from the studies so far carried out.

The mediation of the class basis of incorporated justice agencies is effected through the chairperson. There are ample studies which demonstrate an alliance between chairpeople and experts in arriving at decisions (Dahl, 1982; Frost and Howard, 1977; Hetzler, 1982). The chair may be a lawyer or a lay person. Four further points can be made, which have a bearing on lay chairpeople in particular.

First, as already noted, chairpeople are often appointed by a state agency, often too the one whose activities they are supposed to adjudicate.[9] Secondly, they are appointed as lay people in the very specific sense in which the state deploys this term; they are lay in the sense that they are not qualified lawyers nor currently employed as experts in the field to be adjudged. (Retired experts, apparently, can 'pass' as laity, cf. Thompson, 1983). Because they are lay in this sense it becomes possible for the state to claim that they represent the people, the person in the street, etc. At the same time they are in fact chosen from a very limited pool of eligible people who have been tried, tested, and approved by various agents and agencies within either the state or the direct institutions of capital (Thompson, 1983). Similar arguments have been put in relation to the lay magistracy in Britain, although the courts in which they adjudicate are not informal in the usual sense of the term (Bankowski and Mungham, 1976; Bankowski and McManus, 1983). Other members of these agencies are variously appointed, but the chair will usually have a substantial say in the matter, and the other arguments as to lack of representativeness apply.

Thirdly, as discussed above in relation to experts, members of lay tribunals who are neither chairpeople nor have expert status are typically passive. This applies also to trades union representatives, who may come to the conclusion that in order to keep their legitimacy going — and to get reappointed on the grounds that they are reasonable — they should fight only exceptional cases, and express their position in terms of the dominant discourse. Thus ordinary lay members rarely offer a contrary view, but limit their participation to making statements in support of the opinion of the chair or experts or officials (Blegvad, 1983; Dickens, 1983; Hetzler, 1982). Therefore even if a representative panel, in a class cross-sectional sense, were constructed, the opinions expressed would not carry equal weight. Certain knowledges would still be regarded as more authentic and legitimate than others; and the organizational structure (role of chair) and even the seating arrangements (Hetzler, 1982) would effectively, if unofficially, give the state control over possible deviant interpretations and decisions.

Fourthly, there is the historical evidence that these agencies have been created in and through continuously waxing and waning class struggle (Carson, 1981; Marx, 1954: ch. 10, sec. 6; Phillips, 1977; Vogler, 1984). This struggle was and is about, for example, what kinds of form magistrates' courts (as well as other state agencies) will have, not simply about which class would run a pre-existing institution with a fixed form. When the adjudicative agencies of the welfare state were established in Britain it was the intention of the Labour Party (the then government) to create a genuinely popular form of adjudication. That this did not occur may partly have resulted from the fact that the processes whereby popular justice can be subverted were at that time less well understood on the left; but more important than this theoretical failure was the political struggle concerning the structure of the new agencies — the main protagonists being the trades unions, lawyers, various associations of capital and employers, and state officials (Abel-Smith and Stevens, 1967; Colwill, 1984). What was different about this struggle from the eighteenth and nineteenth century struggles for the control of the magistracy was that it took place within and was therefore mediated and ultimately controlled by the state. The incorporation of these bodies as part of the state apparatus should therefore come as no surprise. But although the outcome of these struggles was the structure just described, it was by no means the inevitable outcome and, indeed, the struggles continue in the debates about expanded legal aid, about legal versus informed lay representation, and so on.

The other characteristics of incorporated forms of justice can be dealt with rather more briefly.

1. Clients of the agencies — those seeking justice or, in our language, the subjects of it — are constituted as individuals, sometimes with particular rights and always with particular grievances.

2. The existence of opponents in the cases is frequently denied, for the opponent is usually the agency itself, and to recognize it as an opponent would be to recognize, willy-nilly, the clients of the agency as a single category of people, a collectivity if not a class. Thus incorporated justice typically denies the existence of its object. And in extreme cases, merging on the populist form, this denial makes possible a complete inversion of the subject and object of justice. In such cases the agency itself appears as subject and the client/subject as the victim or accused — effectively the object.

3. This individualization of the client and denial of the opponent means that the incident itself which gives rise to the judgement situation can only be constituted in a limited number of ways. This is discursively necessary because as there could be only one conceivable opponent (if any opponent were admitted) so a decision that someone else was responsible is not possible. Two or three theories of the origin of such incidents are conceivable. One is that there has been a well-intentioned mistake by a junior employee; another is that there has been a malign mistake by such a low level employee, but that he or she is an atypical example of employees in general (the rotten apple theory); another is that the client did not put the initial case well enough, clearly enough, etc (blaming the victim). Such arguments allow these agencies to grant a minority (Frost and Howard, 1977) of claims, without conceding that there is any fundamental problem with the defendant agency (as it should surely be from a collective standpoint) itself.

When claims are being denied it is typical to displace and deny the originating incident altogether, so that the client of the agency is seen as having been unreasonable, as having, that is, made a 'normal' event into an incident.

4. Justice agencies which have been incorporated tend to demand two types of evidence, and again this requirement is related to the other characteristics of incorporated justice. As regards the alleged incident, rather strict rules may well be applied, although (as in the Danish dry cleaning instance, Blegvad, 1983) there are occasions when expert testimony may be invoked. Nonetheless, evidence is customarily admitted only about the single incident under discussion. No broad review of product reliability or officials' practices could be introduced as evidence relevant to the matter in hand.

As regards the characteristics of the client (or claimant), however, different evidential practices are involved. Here it becomes possible for the agency to examine a broad range of background characteristics in order to determine whether or not the claim is likely to be deserved. The record of past contacts with the agency, appearing like all records to represent facts, but in reality compiled by the agencies in terms of their relevancies, and representing their construction of events, is an important factor in this characterological reconstruction. Thus incorporated justice agencies can be said in general to apply strict rules of evidence to the incident but broad, and largely implicit, rules to the client.

5. Incorporated justice agencies see themselves, and are regarded, as complementary to the professionalized form rather than as an alternative. Thus it is quite possible for these agencies to maintain quite formal links with professionalized state courts. These may be at the beginning by referral or at the end by appeal, and in many cases the two systems work in parallel, with incorporated agencies adjudicating matters which fall also within the jurisdiction of professionalized state courts.

The general picture then of relations between incorporated justice agencies and professionalized state courts (PSCs) is one of reciprocal legitimation and lack of competition, with the PSCs being accorded senior place. This relation is the same whether the incorporated justice agency is in fact itself a state agency, or whether it has been incorporated directly by capital.

6. Incorporated justice agencies have no prophylactic concerns but limit themselves to the resolution of the particular case. This is Nader's criticism of a range of consumer protection agencies in the USA (Nader, 1980) and also the criticism that the welfare rights advocates have made of the British tribunal system (cf. Brooke, 1969, 1979). What these critiques have often failed to recognize is the integrity of the discourse constituting these agencies. Prophylactic solutions could not make sense unless the meanings of 'popularity' and 'expertise' deployed were changed, with vast structural repercussions; unless clients were constituted as a collective and the opponent

was recognized rather than denied; unless the incident itself were constituted as an example of a relationship rather than a uniquely caused occurrence; unless a broader range of causal and theoretical evidence relevant to these prophylactic concerns were to be collected. All this would place the agencies in an antagonistic–cum–instrumental relation with professionalized state courts, the legitimacy of whose practices would now be undermined. In other words, effective prevention is not discursively or politically possible for these agencies: it may, however, be rhetorically invoked.

7. Accountability poses few problems for these agencies. Staff are accountable to their employers within the framework of a bureaucratic hierarchy. Processing of cases is thus carried out by employees, often of the agency being investigated, although this is not necessarily the case.

The position of members of the adjudicative panels is more complex. Those representing organized interests such as trades unions may regard themselves as accountable to the sponsoring organization; experts may consider themselves accountable to their occupational groups. But given the method of appointment and the sociology of the hearing process, objective accountability is to the agency which established the incorporated forum. Subjective feelings of accountability may give rise to personal tension, even some maverick decisions, but the trade union, the occupational group, can rarely recall a member whom they did not appoint, and certainly they cannot appoint his or her substitute. Only the agency which incorporates the forum can make accountability bite in these ways.

8. It is not possible to trace a general pattern in relation to the sources of the rules invoked and applied by these agencies. What is clear is that the rules to be applied are rarely public or known in advance, there is little autonomous elaboration of them and they are derived from notions of what is reasonable and to which the personnel of the agencies subscribe, in particular the administrative staff who pre-process, construct, and filter the cases, and the chairpeople. This creates an organizational space for a totally unmediated class discourse. Alternatively, certain categories of experts may claim an authoritative view in relation to what is reasonable, particularly in relation to client behaviour. In these last cases the rules governing the adjudication will be elaborated in quite another setting and in accordance with various (but specific in each case) sets of occupational criteria, each with its own class articulations. The structures are such that they generate very particular and localized rules. This of course makes it extra hard for a client or her adviser to know what arguments can most effectively be used.

9. As noted in the discussion of accountability, the internal structure of incorporated justice forums is hierarchic and bureaucratic as
far as the permanent secretariats are concerned. Work roles are
likely to be segmented by gender, with women doing typing and
initial intake (reception) work. As indicated, the filtering work of the
clerks plays a larger part in the processing of cases in incorporated
agencies. (In professionalized justice pre-trial negotiations are carried out by 'professionals'; in collective justice the aim is not to filter
out cases but to collect all relevant examples). Thus middle-class
women in clerical and secretarial positions may have a considerable
influence. The adjudicators themselves are formally equal with the
exception of the chairperson. This formal equality has already been
seen to bear no relation to practice.

The hierarchic structures of organization and accountability, with
the elaborate blurring of both at the summit, may not be necessary
forms for incorporated agencies, but they do reflect the essential
ambiguity of these agencies which are both owned and free, part of
the state (or of commerce) yet purportedly independent, agencies for
self-criticism and agencies for self-defence, agencies, essentially, for
state-controlled lay justice.

When these characteristics are reviewed simultaneously it can be
clearly seen that *from a working-class standpoint, while collective
justice is the ideal, professionalized justice is greatly to be preferred to
either variant of incorporated justice.* In professionalized forms of
adjudication the rules of evidence and the relatively public character
of the substantive rules provide protections against the unmediated
class justice which may be on offer in incorporated agencies.

Populist justice

The literature on populist forms of justice is sadly limited. Such as it
is, it is of two broad types: there is the literature dealing with fascist
legal theories and legal forms (Brosznat, 1981; Haley, 1982, Kirchheimer, 1940, 1969; Neumann, 1957; Poulantzas, 1974) and the even
more scanty literature on contemporary societies (Ietswaart, 1982).
Observers of increasingly repressive tendencies in the UK (Hall,
1980) have also noted populist tendencies.

Populism can be characterized as a view of society as an organic
whole constituted by separately and independently constituted individuals. At one level, the society alone creates the unity among these
individuals; at another level the unity is constituted arbitrarily (non-
theoretically) by any identifying feature which the populace can be
persuaded to regard as relevant. Skin colour, place of birth, 'race',
legal status (slaves, insane people versus the rest), 'moral' behaviour

and political subjectivity have all been bases for distinguishing between in-laws and out-laws, members and others.

Politically, attempts to resolve the paradox between separateness and organic interrelatedness take the form of referenda, emphasizing the individuation prior to agglomeration/incorporation, or mass demonstrations of those claiming to be or to speak for the totality, emphasizing organicism. As is clear, these forms merely represent and restate the paradox.

The *theory* of society as whole which underpins populist forms of justice (and other civic expressions) is therefore diametrically opposed to the theory on which collective justice is based, although the rhetorics may at times be similar (Ietswaart, 1982). The collective form, it will be recalled, depends on a theory of society as constituted by fundamentally separated groups whose unity in a social formation depends on the nature of their separation. How then are these differences manifested in the theory and practice of justice?

1. In populist forms of justice the class basis of adjudication is denied. Whether the residual professional courts are the forum, the police station, or the streets, the claim is made that the norms are those of the whole society on whose behalf the justice is being administered. Populist justice does not claim to be a neutral adjudicator as does professional justice; rather it claims to be a *true* adjudicator. Truth, in this view, is not seen as standpoint-specific as in collective justice and collective theories of knowledge (Gramsci, 1971: 352, 408, 455) but as unproblematic and total. The truth claims are similar to those of the incorporated justice form. As both Neumann and Kirchheimer pointed out so forcefully, judgements are given in the name of collective morality, to which 'adjudicators' invariably claim a hot line. This claim to legitimacy may remain at the level of common sense, or as in Germany in the 1930s, be embodied in a jurisprudential theory.

The material class base of populist justice appears to be even more complex than in the situations discussed so far. Moreover, the comparative base is more limited. The literature deals with pre-Second World War Germany, Italy and Japan, and pre-election Argentina. What seems to be the case is that the class base is not apparent because there is a real disjunction between monopoly capital, which is the site of power, and its functionaries, drawn from the petit bourgeoisie, who achieve a quite considerable autonomy by monopolizing key positions within the repressive state apparatuses. Poulantzas argues that this dominance also extends to ideological state apparatuses (trade unions, youth groups, etc), but that the specific ideologies of the petit bourgeoisie leave space for monopoly capital to function, in spite of a rhetoric of 'status quo anti-capitalism'

(1974: 241). This class base is disguised not just by the believed-in rhetoric, the imaginary relations of the participants, which constitute their practice, but also politically, by the fact that monopoly capital is no longer represented by a political party, and by a duality of str;c-tures within the state which undermines the apparatuses of the liberal state while remaining hidden. In the judicial field the relevant proces-ses here are the creation of special courts, to deal largely with political offences, and the delegation of either general or specific penal powers to a range of organizations — the military, employers — or administrative agencies. Private law also became more arbi-trary in certain areas; in both Japan and Germany relationships between creditors and small debtors were dealt with administrat-ively, and titles to land in Germany and Italy apparently became less secure. Monopoly capital itself was able to achieve the certainty necessary for its adequate functioning by other, non-legal means. The precise structures which claimed to give voice to the truth in these circumstances are considered below.

An even less tractable problem is offered by the on-street forms of 'summary justice' which Ietswaart (1982) contrasts with 'popular justice' in pre-election Argentina.[10]

What could be the class base of what appears to be a manifestation of an underclass — and popular — morality? We have two clues: one is the evidence of this and the other studies cited that the repressive state apparatuses, in this case the army and the police, are controlled by the petit bourgeoisie, and function largely independently from monopoly capital. The other is Ietswaart's sophisticated notion that on-street justice, even if apparently supported by sections of the populace (although in Argentina this was not the case) represents 'a rather extreme form of *dissociation* between instances of social real-ity and their authoritative verbal descriptions' (1982: 161). As Hall (1980) has indicated, these manifestations are media controlled, frequently in their generation, and almost inevitably in their author-itative representation. The class bases of these forms of justice are therefore disguised by the mass media's typical presentation of itself as universal and authoritative, or in some cases neutral. Struggles over the control of the media themselves are another question and a longer story.

2. The subject or client of populist justice is seen as the totality. The range of institutions claiming to speak for the whole of society or the good of society tends to proliferate in fascist regimes; but populist forms, as all of the other forms analytically distinguished here, can also be found in varying degrees in most contemporary social forma-tions. The subject/client of populist justice presents itself as spokesperson or people for the organic unity.

3. Conversely the 'other side' in populist justice is conceived as an outsider, a non-member, and therefore a threat to the organic unity, and, whether intentionally or not, therefore an enemy of it. As indicated earlier, there is no theorization of the other but rather the random invocation and non-rule-governed application of negative definitions. The genesis of these definitions, and their availability within the discourse, can be examined empirically in each specific case. Whereas in collective justice the other side is a theoretically (objectively) identified enemy, so that the risk of such an identification could be calculated in advance, the risk in the case of populist justice can be calculated empirically only retrospectively; for example, following a spate of attacks on black people. Populist justice is in this sense, therefore, fundamentally non-rational.

4. and 5. The incident giving rise to the judgement, in the populist form of justice, may not necessarily be known at the time, and may be unknowable in advance. In part this is a result of the integral unpredictability referred to above and in part a result of the attempt to police morality, which becomes in the end the policing of imputed subjective states such as, for example, having sympathy with the guerillas or the communists or being a 'nigger lover' or . . . Thus the defendant or object of the justice may be unaware of the originating incident. It is therefore inevitable that what counts as, or is allowable as, evidence varies from case to case. As in every form of justice, rules of evidence and relevance are established by those judging: here the judges are also the subjects of the justice. In this respect also, populist justice is closer to the two forms of incorporated justice analysed here than to either the collective or the professionalized form, for both of which types these rules can be identified theoretically/objectively. In populist justice what counts as evidence depends on situational exigencies and the vagaries of the stereotype in use.

6. Outcomes in populist justice are not institutionally restricted. They may include lynching or death mobs or ostracism or a range of less severe penalties. In private law, as we have seen, outcomes may be more benign than in the professionalized form, for instance, small debts may be absolved by discretion and administrative decision. What populist justice shares with both professionalized and incorporated forms is that outcomes depend on individualized characteristics, whether subjective (moral state/intention) or objective (what can she afford to pay?). In a system of collective justice outcomes depend on the social position of the individual, and the theorized or publicly/politically decided requirements of the class.

7. The above implies that the objective of populist justice in its pure form is to preserve the totality and reintegrate members within it while destroying the other. This is why populist penal forms have

the ferocious quality so frequently observed. Populist justice is not intended to be prophylactic in the individual case. General deterrence of fear may, however, be an objective.

8. Populist justice forms are not accountable. Indeed the nature of the organization/non-organization (see 10 below) renders this inevitable. The totality is constituted as the subject of justice, and provides legitimation for these actions, but it has no institutional expression which could render anyone answerable for his or her judgements. And while accountability exists within the hierarchic organizations of exceptional states, the discretionary space at the top — the leader — also ensures the ultimate non-accountability of judicial decisions to the legitimating populace. Populist justice, being founded on an organicist conception of the totality, is *incapable* of being accountable, either internally or externally, to its organization or to its subject.

9. The lack of rules or of a theory from which rules could systematically be derived has already been noted. Insofar as rules can be extrapolated from relatively consistent patterns of behaviour they are seen to be derived from the arbitrary stereotyping constitutive of organicist ideologies, and the public expressions of this in the media of mass communication. It is, perhaps, worth mentioning here that communication in a populist regime is necessarily 'mass' as opposed to collective, since collectivities other than those which are conceived as sub-parts of the organism cannot be identified. In terms of populism's own theory of itself, communication must be unstructured, expressing the view of the totality (although of course un-structure is not a possible concept within social theory). In contrast, the theory of collective justice recognizes that all communication is necessarily political (Foucault, 1978, 1980), and thinks the politics of it in terms of a theory of structure. Therefore, rules under such a system are both overtly political *and* objective (theoretically grounded).

10. Populist justice has a restricted institutionalization, with few permanent organizational roles. The structures of street justice are essentially fluid. In the closely related fascist forms there are hierarchies within repressive state apparatuses, although the summit of these hierarchies is constituted by a totally discretionary space. Thus the contradictory and dual nature of the class base of populist justice is reflected in the continuing contradictions between order and non-order.

Tactical and strategic notes

I have argued, in listing these characteristics, that the class base of the adjudicative form, with the manner in which this class basis is identified or concealed, establishes the remaining characteristics not as necessary or inevitable, but as consistent. It is this conceptual consistency between the characteristics that makes it possible to claim that one has identified a specific type or form. Bourgeois legal theory reduces the alternatives to professionalized justice to a single oppositional form. Here three have been identified. Intellectual discrimination in terms of the class base of these forms is important because it makes it possible to choose between political strategies. Indeed, Table 3.1 is intended to be capable of being used as a kind of checklist by working-class justice practitioners, so that it can be readily seen how closely any particular agency approximates to the collective justice model. The respects in which would-be collective justice agencies differ from the model will at least provide a basis for reflection, and a self-aware decision as to whether change is necessary. More realistic and refined evaluations of strategy in relation to agencies of other types should also be possible. And most important, collective justice agencies will have the beginnings of an elaborated theory of themselves with which to resist attacks on their legitimacy and direction.

As suggested, empirically these four recognizable abstracted types of justice most frequently coexist in capitalist society. The class struggle which continuously defines and redefines the distinctions between them is a process which produces many forms, or at least elements of them, in any social formation. These complex struggles may be simplified for analytical purposes into conflicts over legitimacy and conflicts over resources.

At present in capitalist societies collective justice is the most unstable and vulnerable form. This is endemic in its prefigurative character. A prefigurative institution exists in advance of the class forces which could sustain its fully developed form, although of course its very existence presupposes a sufficient base of working-class power. Secondly, prefigurative institutions are necessarily experimental structures attempting to express class interests and to formulate visions of how life might be. For this reason prefigurative institutions, or collective justice institutions, lack a fully developed theory of their being. This renders them intellectually vulnerable. This is why an enterprise such as this one, an attempt to construct their concept, is also an attempt to contribute to their viability.

Collective justice forms are at risk of being professionalized, as a response to the legitimacy problem, or incorporated, as a response to the resource problem. Recent British examples illustrate this point.

First, a number of local authority and central government-funded law centres and advice agencies have been urged or required to abandon collective work in favour of dealing with individual cases in a recognized 'legal' way. This ideological attack is possible not only because of the resource dependence, but also because professional-ized justice still has a monopoly of legitimacy in British society. This is exacerbated because there is a theoretical inconsistency in defen-sive claims that the only way to help 'the poor' is by collective action, for the necessity of a collective approach is derived from a theory of discontinuous and qualitatively different classes, which is not or cannot be expressed because of the prevalence of the notion of the givenness of the possibility of consensus, involving unidimensional concepts of social differentiation. Where classes are conceived as qualitatively different, 'consensus' involves political work, the formation of alliances, and the establishment of hegemony.

The theoretical weakness in collective justice agencies' presenta-tion of themselves enhances their ideological vulnerability. This diffi-culty will be exacerbated in any society with (i) a strongly organized profession and (ii) a lack of left resistance to consensus politics. In this situation it is difficult for these prefigurative agencies to present an acceptable account of themselves.

On the resource front, law centres in Britain are vulnerable to closure as the price of nonconformity. But they are also — and this is more sinister — vulnerable to incorporation. The Royal Commission on Legal Services recommended precisely such an incorporation within the central state, effectively in exchange for a financially secure future (Royal Commission on Legal Services, 1979: especially ch. 8).

In addition to these endemic risks, popular justice forms are vulnerable when they directly challenge the existing state, presenting themselves as alternative authorities. Morrison (1975) has described how the rules of property developed by Canadian miners were over-turned by the Mounted Police; the Portuguese forms described by Santos (1979) have been supplanted. On the other hand, if the state is weak or unstable these alternative sites may coexist with it over extended periods, as in Latin America.

An understanding of the reason for the observed short lives of effective collective justice agencies should not only help us to counter arguments that they demonstrably don't work, but also enable us to develop more effective defensive tactics. An elaboration of a concept of these agencies is one such tactic. Some of the relationships be-tween the other forms also have a bearing on these tactics. In particu-lar, it is hoped that the evaluative rank ordering of these forms from a working-class standpoint — collective, professional, incorporated, populist — will clarify a number of real life political questions.

The main contribution of professionalized justice to the dynamic relations between the forms is an imperialist one, purporting to take over not only collective justice (which would be a retrogressive step) but also incorporated justice (which would be progressive). It is partly for this reason — the dependence of one's evaluation of an expansion of professionalized justice on a particular analysis — that it has been necessary to draw the distinctions presented here. When it is argued (Brooke, 1969; Frost and Howard, 1977; Reich, 1964) (i) that clients of state forms of incorporated justice should be constituted as subjects with rights, (ii) that rules governing the decisions should be public and consistent and (iii) (only) capable of being argued by professional representatives, (iv) that other aspects of the discourse — characterization of the originating incident, rules of evidence — be similarly accommodated to the 'professional' legal model, then these changes should be encouraged (although the third is problematic because it supports the unnecessary monopoly position of a particular occupational group). Professionalized justice is closer to the interests of subaltern classes — workers, women, black people — than any incorporated form could be, since incorporated forms create a site for the direct penetration of dominant class norms.

Incorporated forms of justice are vulnerable to encroachment from each of the other three forms, as a result of their lack of a consistent legitimating ideology. On the other hand, the very fact of their incorporation indicates that as long as they continue to fulfil their objective they are not going to encounter resource difficulties.

The legitimacy problem for incorporated forms which can be posed by collective justice results from the dual legitimation of these forms in terms of their 'lay' element and their 'expert' element. First, these two forms of legitimation cannot function simultaneously. Yet both elements — the lay and the expert — are used to justify the departure from professionalized justice, the form, as has been stated, which undoubtedly carries highest legitimacy in contemporary western capitalist societies. The problem of the internal contradiction arises because of the scientific truth claims made by and particularly about experts. Because if there is a person who can directly divine the truth of a claim or a situation, then there is no need for a court of adjudicators at all. Their only function could be to reinforce the truth, which is unnecessary, or to subvert it. On the other hand a decision by an expert alone is plainly not regarded as adequate. Many experts — planners, welfare officials — do not carry wide popular legitimacy. Therefore the present two-tiered legitimacy structure is in practice more effective. The incorporated justice agency claims legitimacy from the outside world by virtue of being 'lay' or popular, while a pattern of acceptable decisions is legitimated internally, to the lay members, by virtue of being expert.

However, this structurally useful device creates a second legitimacy problem, apart from that of internal consistency. Lay members' claims to speak for a populace they in no way represent can very easily be rendered suspect. Thus the class base, the organization, and the procedure of incorporated justice, can be directly challenged by collective justice forms, which are a living demonstration of what 'lay justice' might become. An analysis of the practice of these institutions also reveals and explains the typical subject–object inversion presented above, so that their legitimacy can be challenged on the grounds of blaming the victim. These contradictions could therefore be exploited in progressive directions.

However, incorporated justice is also at risk of lapsing into the worst form of all, from a working-class standpoint, namely populist justice. It is 'protected' from this only by a different mode of constituting the subject, but the inversion of subject and object which may take place renders the form virtually indistinguishable from populist forms except as a matter of degree. There is always the danger that the response to the challenge from collective forms, if these emphasize strengthening the lay element, or from professionalized forms, if these emphasize individuation of the subject, may be a reactive movement towards greater incorporation, and total control. This last is the organizational (rather than the on-street) manifestation of populism at its anti-democratic extreme.

The best historical example of precisely this series of shifts has been offered by Reifner (1982) in his powerful account of how Workers' Offices (collective justice forums) in pre-fascist Germany were first incorporated as government-sponsored law offices, and then finally absorbed into the fascist totality. This is why professionalized justice forms are essential to the working class at defensive moments in their struggle: they are resistant to incorporation without massive organizational and ideological restructuring, as Thompson (1975) so forcefully pointed out.

Finally, what is the relationship between populist and collective forms? This has to be a crucial question for the left since populist extremes are invariably invoked as arguments against progressive measures. This chapter has shown that these two forms are not just diagrammatically but also conceptually and politically poles apart. There seems to be no real risk of collectivism degenerating (from a class standpoint it is possible to use such an evaluative term) into populism. And can populism become collective? It is of course extremely vulnerable to legitimacy challenges from both collective and professionalized forms. If these become sufficient then the structural rift between monopoly capital as financier and the petit bourgeoisie which controls the state might cause a dramatic lurch back towards professionalized forms. But here we are talking of a class struggle and the balance of class forces in particular situations, not of relations between abstracted justice types. And of course, both legitimacy and resource claims and deficits are effective only if political action makes them so. An analysis of this kind can only provide some indicators of the directions for political action. And successful working-class political action would render it obsolete, for like all material analyses, its truth-claims are temporally bounded.

Notes

My thanks go to the EUI for the Jean Monnet Fellowship which gave me time to do this work, and to the many friends who have commented on earlier versions of this text: Rick Abel, Piers Beirne, Peter Fitzpatrick, Clive Grace, Audrey Harvey, Paddy Hillyard, Richard Hofrichter, Tony Jefferson, Sean Loughlin, David Nelken, Ralf Rogowski, Carroll Seron, David Sugarman and Gunther Teubner. I am also indebted to Sim Smiley and Lisa Alisi who typed various versions, always at short notice, with care and skill, and to Stan Cohen for his insightful and patient editing. I am responsible for what remains.

1. This discussion owes much, in general terms, to Foucault's discussion of repressed histories and experiences. See Foucault (1977), pp. 205–17.
2. See Cain (1984) for references to these, which have had to be left out for reasons of space.
3. One practitioner (Clive Grace, personal letter) has expressed scepticism about this, saying: 'This seems to me less a "theory" than drawing out some of the themes of the work of some agencies which have expressly committed themselves to helping working class communities.' Exactly. But it will be easier to evaluate these practices and for more people to try to do them, if they are shown to make theoretical sense. At least I hope so.
4. Source: pilot research conducted in 1979 by the author, and financed by the Nuffield Foundation.
5. Nonetheless, the consistent variation of continental European legal professional organization from the model concerns me (see Cain, 1984). An additional category 'between' professionalized and incorporated justice may be necessary. But I have insufficient data as yet to construct this type.
6. McBarnet (1976, 1981) has revealed how legal rules, and in particular the discretionary spaces which they create, shape the work of police, prosecutors, and criminal courts. The same is true in private law (see Cain, 1979: report to the Nuffield Foundation on pilot study of County Courts, Appendix B).
7. This form is not, of course, unproblematic. Jessop (1982) provides the most useful summary of the debates in this area.
8. There are of course exceptions. As Napier (1979) shows, some labour courts in particular resist incorporation of this kind. Most notably in France all adjudicators of the *conseils de prud'hommes* are elected directly by members of either trades unions or employers' organizations.
9. A good discussion of how this situation came about can be found in Bell (1969). She does not, however, share my scepticism about experts and chairpeople in general,

but rather interprets the question as one of the quality of the particular participants the system is able to recruit.

10. Ietswaart's distinction here provided the seminal thought giving rise to this article — a considerable debt which I gladly acknowledge.

4 Conflict and Consensus: A Critique of the Language of Informal Justice

Anne Bottomley

Jeremy Roche

Introduction: setting the scene — dispensing (with) justice?

In the last decade in Britain a plethora of 'alternatives' to law, or specifically dispute resolution through the court process, have developed to the point where it might be fair to characterize it as fashionable, if not evidence of the establishment of a new orthodoxy. One of the most visible and seemingly popular developments has been that in family law of mediation or conciliation by social welfare professionals and volunteers as an alternative to court decision making. The development of mediation was characterized as a fresh approach, a movement away from both adjudication by the courts and the adversarial model employed by the legal profession. Many of those involved in the political struggle for the recognition and funding of such schemes consciously employed a language of dissatisfaction with law, courts and lawyers — a language which cast the legal process as fundamentally alienating. It was presented as a movement on behalf of the dissatisfied consumer, one which replaced third party decision making and unnecessary conflict with a process of negotiation and decision making by the parties themselves. Such sentiments paralleled Nils Christie's argument for the return of the property of conflicts to the parties themselves; an argument that negotiation geared to settlement based on consensus and agreement was not only possible but preferable to an adversarial process in which a third party decided the 'winner' of the dispute (Christie, 1977). Celebrated was party control and the minimization of third party intervention, gone was the inappropriate and socially destructive language of conflict, of winners and losers.

Of course, on closer examination it was obvious that many of those involved in championing the alternatives were offering their own languages, arising out of their own practice. The probation service and social workers were the main actors (especially those with a background in family therapy). The rhetoric of 'empowering the client', for instance, has a significance for those involved in forms of therapeutic practice in which empowering is a tactic designed to encourage clients/patients to take responsibility for their own lives and decision making. Within this tradition a third party overtly making decisions is a prop for the irresponsible and immature. This tradition perceives the very method of law, as well as its objectives, as wrong. In relation to mediation on divorce what was offered was an alternative focus, one which replaced divorcing adults with parents who were responsible for the previously unrepresented: the children. Thus for many a concern to educate and persuade the divorcing parties on the need to provide a suitable environment for continuing parenting was a fundamental part of the rhetoric and practice of mediation. This was particularly visible in the work of probation officers acting as court welfare officers and in their participation in the development of court-based mediation services. Client decision making became subsumed into a process of preparing the clients for the 'right' decision, and offering a forum in which it was emphasized that they themselves were the initiators and guardians of that decision. What cannot be denied is that in the deployment of the language of participation and empowerment a chord was struck in the popular imagination. Not only did the presented themes seem to make sense but there already existed sufficient client dissatisfaction with lawyers and courts to find a ready audience for alternatives.

Indeed important sections of the legal profession and Parliament welcomed these moves as a recognition of the unsuitability of law and the adversarial process in dealing with family matters, especially child custody disputes. The only voices raised in opposition were from some feminists and some academics influenced by either feminist work or the emerging critique (mainly from the USA) which argued that processes of 'informal dispute' resolution operated to the disadvantage of less powerful individuals or groups within a hierarchical society (see Bottomley and Olley, 1983; Erlanger et al., 1987).

These arguments have been reviewed elsewhere but it is important to recall the basic outlines of the debate. The critics argued two points. First, that the seeming benevolence of the development of alternatives to law actually hid the extension of patterns of control and authority which effectively extended state power[1] through other disciplining agencies, ones which were by their very nature more difficult to expose and challenge than the orthodoxies of formal legal practice. In a sense this paralleled work on 'welfare' models operating in juvenile justice (cf. Morris and McIsaac, 1978). Secondly, that

the development of informal processes of dispute resolution operated as a diversion from the legal system freeing courts and lawyers to
deal with the business of powerful sections of society or those areas of
conflict which state institutions wished to continue to regulate
through law. This had the effect of marginalizing other conflicts and
groups which had begun to learn to use the courts and the rhetoric of
due process and rights in their own struggles.

This is rendering the argument at its most simple level and in doing
so does not do sufficient justice to the complexities of both the
evidence and the models of analysis used. From the start particular
difficulties were encountered in constructing this critique of informal
justice. The thrust of the argument was that whereas models of
informal justice may have a proper place in more 'progressive'
societies they were unsupportable in hierarchical societies operating
a capitalist economy and a political system continuing to utilize the
rhetoric and institutional agencies organized around the rule of law.
Insofar as the rule of law could be used as a countervailing force
against authority, or the power of certain individuals and groups,
then within terms of dispute resolution the formality of law was a
better protector for oppressed groups than the emergent alternatives. While it was recognized that formal law could never fully
deliver that which it was held to offer even more so the images
contained within the offer of informal justice were illusory. The
utilization of languages of consensus, agreement and community
were even more elusive and unreal than those surrounding the
machinery of legality. What was rejected was the possibility that
informal justice, for all its rhetoric of returning disputes to the people
and an emphasis on group and community solidarity, could be part of
a transformative political practice. The particular difficulty with this
critique was that it threw us back into a defence of the rule of law and
formal justice in circumstances where we were only too aware of its
frailties to the individual consumer. In the face of increasing political
support, including that from the legal establishment, the critics constructed a critique of informalism through a defence of formalism.

As Trubek (1984: 835) so succinctly put it in his review of both
Auerbach and Abel:

> The ultimate paradox of the story is that no one really seems to believe in
> law anymore. The elites who champion alternatives question law's effica-
> cy, but so do the critiques. Auerbach sees legalism as the antithesis of
> community and humane values. Abel and his colleagues see formal law as
> at its best a weak reed that the poor can occasionally hold on to and at
> worst as the very heart of oppression. The high priests celebrate an
> informalism they don't believe in, while the critics reluctantly champion a
> formalism they distrust.

On the naming of the parts and the problem of the whole

This then was the most obvious and constraining difficulty. While at one level it was an acceptable strategy to expose the practices and rhetoric of informal justice, and while we had sufficient evidence to give our case credence, we were left with a number of unresolved problems. This dilemma could be summed up by the recognition that our concern was not merely to try and understand changes within the legal process and its penumbra but to understand them for the very purpose of evaluating their potential in terms of progressive political action. The relationship between understanding and intervening was, and is, crucial to our work. The question then was whether a strategy and analysis, essentially defensive and based on not only the use of models of formality and informality but an espousal of formality, could carry us into the future — a future in which we looked for change not stasis, and a future in which we had to recognize that not only were the alternatives becoming well-established but that their appeal to certain sections of society had to be understood. We also had enough evidence to realize that the complex interaction of agencies of disciplining authority and their different discursive practices could not be explored within the crude frames of formal and informal justice. Indeed both historical evidence and contemporary practice alerted us to the very inadequacy of posing these models as alternatives or of identifying law simply with formal justice and in particular court-based adversarial proceedings. It was clear that 'the law' was and is much more complex than this. It was clear also that we had to be much sharper in our analysis of the specific interrelationship between law and other knowledge in such shared sites as family law and criminal justice. We needed to interrogate the languages of representation employed within the academy and society by those involved in these 'new ways of doing things' — especially how they represented their activities and objectives to the public.

Further we had to recognize and evaluate the level of sectional and individual dissatisfaction with the law. Only when we had begun to unpack and examine all these issues could we return to take part in an examination of those questions, posed in academic circles, which centred on the idea of the end of law or which suggested a deep crisis in legal legitimacy (Cotterrell, 1984). These debates often employ the same quasi-Weberian characterizations of formal justice (law) and informal justice (concerned either with a shift in disciplining regulation or a move away from regulation through law). The possibility of finding configurations of similarity which might suggest general patterns of change required far more specificity in the exploration of sites in which such activity seemed to be developing. Conversely, it was important that we did maintain a perspective which allowed us to traverse different sites in order to analyse potential similarities. For example, looking at what has happened in family law raises some interesting questions in terms of the potential developments in criminal justice.

We can begin by exploring the genesis of the very use of the term 'informal justice' by looking at what it might be taken to represent as well as the actualities of its application. It suggests a set of base characteristics which can be held to identify similarity fundamentally by defining what they are not. By the very use of the term a model of formal justice is presumed against which other patterns can be set. Our starting-point must be that while this term importantly originates in the academy it must be presumed adequately to represent a series of initiatives which might add up to a fundamental shift in ordering. We will return to the actual models used later but first it is useful to consider the setting against which we might begin to test the models employed. Although the academic argument about shifts within the form of ordering, and in particular the use of juridical ordering, has been with us for some time, it is interesting that within the public domain the challenge to 'law' is relatively recent in its specificity of positing 'alternatives' to the formal legal process. Initiatives taken within government agencies, for example the development of certain tribunals, do not seem to have been named and recognized as such fundamental challenges to the hegemony of formal legal ordering as more recent initiatives.[2] This may reflect the ability of those immediately affected to influence such developments. It might also reflect the fact that such shifts were seen as not challenging law as such but rather challenging the efficacy of law in certain areas of work. One important question then is why recent initiatives seem set in a language of difference and celebrated as distinct from the form of legality.

In Britain in particular it cannot be emphasized enough that the practices involved as 'alternatives' to law were diverse, ad hoc and operationalized by activists in particular areas of work — at first most noticeably in the area of family law. These developments were not in their early stages highly theorized or seen as part of an overall pattern of change by the participants. It was only as some activists visited the United States that some saw the need to theorize their work for professional and political purposes. As other possible areas of work became visible to them they began, tentatively, to consider themselves as part of a broader movement within which they could progress. By seeing each development as part of a larger whole they were able to lend strength to its parts particularly those which were under attack.

Thus those involved in mediation on divorce, in part because of the qualified success they enjoyed in this sphere, began to consider other areas of work which mediation could be related to.[3] Given that much of the concentration in divorce has been on the need to sustain continuing relationships the most obvious area of work was inter-neighbour disputes. The first Neighbourhood Mediation Projects got under way and in the same period FIRM (the Forum for Initiatives in Reparation and Mediation, established in 1985) was set up as an umbrella body and potential political lobby group. The most impor-tant elements in FIRM were an amalgam of mediators, probation officers involved in both civil and criminal work (especially repara-tion and victim support schemes) and activists from such religious groups as the Society of Friends. Added to this the support and interest of a number of academics and civil servants in the Home Office, and a 'movement' could not only be talked about but theo-rized. However given the breadth of concerns and interests the key question was how similarity was to be found and melded together into like objectives and practice. The most obvious consensus could be found in distinguishing their initiatives from the adversarial legal model. In this sense it was easier to find coherence in opposition. This representation of their schemes in oppositional terms focused on three themes.

First, that adversarial processes emphasized conflict and inter-party disputes in which individuals were pitted against each other: in the criminal justice system the accused was pitted against the pro-secution and the question for determination was the guilt or inno-cence of the former. In the very starkness of the outcomes of the criminal trial it was said that much violence was done to social reality and the complexity of human behaviour and motivation. Worse, the criminal law itself imposed a somewhat artificial notion of intent in its allocation of criminal responsibility which did not always correspond to popular ideas regarding culpability.

Secondly, insofar as the legal system seemed to offer solutions this was rarely the case even within the terms of its own logic. Thus in the areas of divorce and criminal justice client dissatisfaction and the failure to deliver either 'good parents' or 'reformed offenders' could be turned against the defenders of formal law.

Thirdly, and in the alternative, it could be argued that the objec-tives of formal law were wrong, it was addressing the wrong issues. The task should not be one of deciding who was right and who was wrong with the socially divisive consequences of such an allocation: repair and reintegration rather than revenge and exclusion were to be the proper objectives. Anyway it was not simply that the law was aiming at the wrong target: there was the issue of how law in its operation exacerbated points of conflict and friction. One could not make better parents or citizens through such a process. One could not protect the victims of crime or children when their interests and needs were denied by the law and when they themselves were marginal to the processes of law, if not actually silenced. Thus was found a shared language — in a concern to emphasize processes of consensual agreement and community solidarity[4] against the alienation of law, lawyers and the legal process. This identity found in opposition, with allusions to the symbolic value of consensus and community, served to divert attention from the very real differences both in operational techniques deployed and in the professional knowledges and interests feeding into the sites of activity.

The actual concerns and expertise of each represented group and professional practice are of course specific and in some ways the alliance is quite fragile. The experience of those involved in the early family law mediation schemes serves as a good example.[5]

Schemes such as that which developed in Bristol in 1979 were specifically designed to be a pre-lawyers and pre-court process: though some had hoped that it would be an alternative to both. The majority of those involved, if they had prior professional training at all, were from social work backgrounds. In those cases where a formal change of legal status was sought by the parties their concern was to establish agreement between the parents as to arrangements for parenting which could then be presented to the courts. The scheme at Bristol was only achieved in the face of a great deal of financial constraint which meant that publicity was sought to establish the need for and legitimacy (in terms of success) of such a scheme. It was this which set the tone of much of the debate within Britain. Much of the early published work was of a proselytizing nature which emphasized the fresh approach involved in an area which was characterized as having radically failed to achieve the stability and harmony necessary for the welfare of children. This was followed later by attempts at a more theorized rationale and explanation, or description, of their practice. As this became more established it became clear that other concerns were directly informing their work, most noticeably the concern with the continuation of joint parenting as the norm to be sought for in agreements. In this sense specific theories of adequate parenting were involved and mediation seen as the most suitable way to achieve such an outcome. A second development paralleled this. In the divorce courts the probation officers, acting as court welfare officers, were beginning to take their initiatives. This was initially centred around their function in preparing reports for the courts on children and parents to enable the courts to make decisions in contested custody cases. As Francis

(1981) wrote in a revealing article: '. . . The request for a report is viewed as the entree by means of which the probation officer . . . can become involved in a conciliation role enabling (the parties) to understand what is happening, the effect of their interaction on each other and, most important, the effect on their children.'

Arguing that proper parenting is vital in the fight against producing clients for probation officers in the juvenile courts Francis makes clear his attitude to his client group: 'The parties are not permitted to use the request for a welfare report as an opportunity to relinquish their parental responsibilities . . .' (1981: 72). The formal establishment of a process of conciliation by court officers, and the later involvement of court registrars, employed a similar language, process and set of concerns to that established in what became known as 'out-of-court' schemes. However in one important sense there was a radical difference. The probation officers' schemes evolved in an institutional setting which was much more overtly concerned with third party persuasion towards the correct agreement. The role of the probation services in filing welfare reports in contested cases, as well as the physical and symbolic closeness of the court, could be used to persuade 'difficult' parties of the likelihood that certain agreements would not be validated by the courts, or the very lack of agreement becoming part of the assessment of parental responsibility. The initial criticism of these schemes from other mediators centred on the argument that this form of intervention came too late, the parties were already caught in confrontation and had already encountered the legal profession with all its detrimental baggage.

However this later became subsumed into a more specific critique of the schemes as not really mediation at all but rather a form of persuasion by an individual who wielded too much power in a context in which the parties would be overawed by the institutional setting. This concern became intensified when in a series of related reports the Lord Chancellor's Department decided to encourage 'in-court' schemes and left the 'out-of-court' schemes to fend for themselves. Inevitably the latter began to argue that they were the true upholders of the theory and practice of mediation whereas the in-court schemes became subject to the usual pressures of expediency — particularly in an area of law so overstretched and underfunded. Not only did the differences in practice and setting begin to tell but so did potential client differences, especially in terms of class:

> It is surely important that no particular sector of the population should be denied the opportunity of access to a conciliation scheme . . . It might also be argued that the application of which Sir John Arnold referred to as 'benevolent persuasiveness' (address to the Annual General Meeting of the Central Council of Probation Committees in May 1983) in the context

of an in-court scheme might help to achieve agreement where earlier attempts have failed. Although this has yet to be demonstrated, the probation service, for example, is not entirely unused to working in such a context. (James and Wilson, 1984: 106)

Mediators in family law had won a Pyrrhic victory. In a sense their success had been to offer a legitimating language and a model of practice which became most successfully used in the development of a court-based process which had more to do with the need to save costs and court time than finding alternatives to law. It became fashioned in terms of the practices and concerns of another professional group, probation officers, rather than social workers, and who were still primarily trained in terms of their functions within the criminal justice system. Indeed the establishment of in-court schemes can, and should, be read in terms of the previous practice of probation officers in offering informal advice and assistance (Murch, 1980). Their work prefigured that which was to become institutionalized under the rubric of conciliation. This is not to say that the base line was not changed, or indeed that it is not important to recognize the shift in terms of the representation of that work, but it is to emphasize that presenting developments in oppositional models may hide the patterns of continuity. The particular configurations which employed a language of newness or difference, whether to do with a need for recognition or for a new source of legitimacy, need to be unpacked. Thus the characterization of mediation as an alternative to the adversarial process in family law is seen to be flawed from the beginning. Two points in particular need to be made clear.

The first is that even within the court setting to characterize the process in purely adversarial terms is misleading. Family law, unlike certain other areas, is not a construction of common lawyers but rather a modern amalgam of traditions derived from the ecclesiastical courts, the courts of equity and statute law which has continued to emphasize discretion in court judgment and the importance of the court's responsibility for enquiry. The court as an enquiring court exercising considerable discretion does not rest easily alongside the imagery of adversarial proceedings. Further the courts exercising a jurisdiction in family matters do so in an overlapping, patchwork manner and operate in a context where procedural changes (quite often far-reaching in their effect) have been determined by cost considerations.[6] The reality of family law in the courts is a hotchpotch of procedures and objectives built up over years. It is no wonder that many of those involved find their role frustrating and that there is a high level of consumer dissatisfaction and confusion, but to identify the core of the problem as adversarial proceedings, the epitome of formal law, is to be attacking the wrong target. Why this was the characterization put forward will be considered later.

Secondly, the courts are only a small part of the process. In a sense the mediators recognized this when they included lawyers in their attack. Contested cases in court are usually avoided as a result of bilateral bargaining by lawyers. Ironically the consequence of the establishment of mediation in a court setting is more likely to be an increase in court control over the parties and their lawyers than giving increased party control either through mediation or bilateral bargaining.[7] However this is more likely to affect those sections of society which are least accustomed to making use of professional services, those who are used to feeling the effects of different agencies rather than using them. The overall pattern which seems to be developing is that the out-of-court schemes offer a welcome service for middle-class couples. The success of the model has fed into an interest in developing mediation in other areas of work. We have not seen the rapid growth of professional mediators as in the United States but rather a network of very committed and enthusiastic volunteers. In the setting of such groups as FIRM they ironically meet probation officers who are also extending their sphere of influence, especially in criminal justice.

Before leaving family law we would point out that among lawyers both at local level and in the Law Society there has been a great deal of support for mediation, including the out-of-court schemes. This can be analysed both as a willing vacation of an area which has never been that dear to a lawyer's heart, especially since the changes in legal aid, and as a decision that it is better to work with the emerging initiatives and find a role within them. The picture is complex and in seeking to understand the attitudes of the profession it is important to distinguish between sectional interests within the profession. What we simply want to record here, as has been noted in the American material, is that for a myriad of reasons lawyers are not simply defending their territory under the orthodox rubrics of the need to maintain the principles of formal justice in all areas in which law has been operative. We would however suggest that there are two paradoxical factors at work. One factor is that some lawyers never saw family law as 'true' law at all and are willing to vacate to other professional groups. Conversely other lawyers recognize the plurality involved and are much more sensitive to those elements of their work which are amenable to certain kinds of dispute, finding a role in a type of multi-agency approach, and are able to identify those elements of formal law which they do wish to be able to utilize to the advantage of their client group. Thus, for instance, the forensic elements of due process, the ability to acquire court orders revealing assets, or to challenge certain evidence as unsafe, may be the specific aspects of formal law which they wish to protect rather than the complete package as set up either by the critics or defenders of formality.

Why not criminal law? — conflicts as disputes

One of the most important lessons to be drawn from unpacking the history of developments in family law is the need to distinguish between the different elements which cohabit a site and may share a common language, but may actually be pulling in different directions. The question becomes whether sufficient momentum is built up actually to produce a transformative practice or whether one pre-existing discursive practice or interest becomes dominant. Two issues seem to us to be crucial. The first is the likely difference between initiatives external to an institutional setting, and developments within or under the auspices of an established agency. The second is the distinction between 'new' initiatives and the simple development of one discursive practice into a new site or its increased domination of that site. What may be simply a changing of the boundaries of the sphere of influence, or a recasting of existing practices, or a changed representation of those practices, must be seen as such and not merely read in terms of 'what it is not'. It is not simply that individuals took initiatives against existing orthodoxies, but rather that they constructed models of those orthodoxies and offered alternatives which drew from their own discursive areas. We are not suggesting a picture of subtle conspiracies, rather that it is difficult to understand the depth to which, as individuals, we are imbued with the informing knowledges of our disciplines and professional practices of origin. Part of our task in trying to evaluate these developments must be to decode and interrogate why certain sectional groups have responded to, and built on, specific aspects or themes within the emerging patterns.

We have already referred to the existence of FIRM. Represented within this grouping are four elements involved in the development of 'alternatives' within criminal justice which should be distinguished.

1. The mediators

From the mediators' point of view the starting-point is found in asking two questions of the criminal justice system. The first is concerned with the nature of the 'offence' defined in criminal terms. Why is it that, for instance, an act of theft or violence should be seen as an act to be punished by the state on behalf of the community rather than an act against the individual victim who then has a dispute with the perpetrator of the act? This could be seen as a challenge to definition and objective. It focuses on the individuals concerned, a focus which is re-emphasized when the second question is posed. What is the nature of the pre-existing relationship between the two which has been disrupted or distorted by this event? The model utilized is one of an equilibrium which needs to be re-established.

This process of working outwards from a basis of 'disputes' does not reveal an easily established boundary between criminal and civil law, rather it concentrates on sets of relations and a search for patterns of continuity and reintegration. The obvious difficulties with presuming an equilibrium model and the operational problems of evidence, due process, etc, should not detract from the simple virtue that this at least poses some pertinent questions about both the boundaries and the seeming inflexibility of our model of criminal justice. The reality of attempting such a model in practice displays, however, its limited application.

In practice we know that there are two criminal justice systems operating. The first is that which is initiated by action taken by state agencies, and the second is that initiated by private complaint. Both operate levels of discretion in their decision making. The private individual may choose to see a 'dispute' in those terms, and may therefore choose to attempt to settle the matter privately, either by direct bargaining or through the use of such mechanisms as informal mediation by third parties. Recourse may be had to the civil court system, or at least the threat of it. The fact that the dispute may also involve a possible prosecution and the subsequent focus of penality, but only in reality if the police or prosecution service are willing to act, may be used as one further factor in the process of negotiation and attempted settlement. The threat of legal action, whether civil or criminal, has always been part of a spectrum of bargaining tools. The real point is that the relationship, or lack of relationship, between the parties is the most likely factor to determine recourse to law. The question is then whether a formalized mediation service would be a useful supplement to these processes. This is the point where it is very important to try and distinguish a number of factors.

The first is class. There may be some evidence that when a decision is taken to have recourse to law that, whereas the middle classes might be more likely to visit a solicitor, working-class (at least white working-class) members may be more likely to turn to the police and therefore to criminal law. This results in the complaint that the police are either being misused or overused. It must be obvious that the finding and funding of a solicitor is not the likely response of some sections of the community to a grievance. However what might be less obvious is that on certain occasions the power and symbolism of the criminal law has been judged to be exactly what is needed. Thus women involved in domestic violence may try and 'contain' their grievances and use other mechanisms to try and protect themselves and their children, but might also make the decision that the most effective weapon may be a call to the police and the choice to define the behaviour in criminal terms. Again this may be used more by working-class women, but this should not be used as evidence that they have either chosen an unsuitable route by which to define and deal with their problem, or that it is simply a matter of lack of access to civil remedies.

Understanding the difference between lack of alternatives and choice becomes even more important when outsiders, whether well-meaning volunteers or enthusiastic reformers, choose to confirm the importance of 'relationship' rather than act, and to build systems which presume the importance of reintegration, whether familial or communal. There is too much evidence, particularly from the States, that the offer of alternative forms of dispute resolution too often becomes a system not of choice but of preferred or even compulsory arrangements. It is important to recognize that activists within the areas of family law and criminal law have classically targeted domestic violence as particularly amenable to 'resolution' through mediation. In some situations this has resulted in compulsory diversion from either civil court orders or prosecution. The development of mediation initiatives becomes most dangerous, even in a non-institutionalized setting, when it is imposed on individuals in the misplaced belief that familial and community solidarity will be reinforced by its operation. When such solidarities exist they rarely need this form of intervention. When the image is espoused rather than the reality confirmed, it is too often to the detriment of weaker sections or individuals who are simply not conforming, or attempting not to conform. It is even more worrying when the model of continuing relationships and community solidarity is utilized by institutionalized agencies.

2. Reparation schemes: mark one
It is important to distinguish between the development of reparation schemes derived from a concern with the victim and others (below). Initiatives taken in reparation differ from the outward movement of 'the mediators' in that they arise from within the criminal justice system, as opposed to questioning the definition of the dispute in criminal justice terms. The process of mediating towards an agreed reparation is not only likely to take place in a setting related to the courts, but also as part of the process of criminal proceedings, either

in the form of a diversion scheme or as an 'alternative' to sentencing. Reparation may employ the language of concern with rebuilding relationships, but is more likely to find recourse in a concern with 'victim' satisfaction and therefore, indirectly, a concern with the symbolism of reintegration and community regeneration. Within this context, however, a concern with the victim often becomes confused and conflated with the possibility of using the same process to 're-form' the offender, unsurprisingly given the institutional setting and that the practitioners involved are usually probation officers.

3.   Reparation schemes: mark two
These are the schemes which are also informed by a concern to re-educate the offender by bringing him (or less likely her) into a direct relationship with the victim, in the hope that they might therefore gain a sense of responsibility for the effects of their actions. The fact that these separate initiatives are often conflated can give rise to the kind of consequential thinking that one of us witnessed at a Home Office seminar dealing with Australian initiatives. Outlined during the seminar was the process by which successful mediation might be set up between victim and offender; almost in passing it was mentioned that only one chance at mediation would be offered. Asked to clarify what was meant by this, we were told that if an offender reappeared before the criminal justice system they would not be given a second chance at mediation, although it involved a different offence and a different victim. At this point we return full circle. Having been told that 'formal' law and the adversarial process marginalizes the victim, the balance between a concern to reform the offender and to provide relief for the victim becomes tilted back towards offending offenders. Mediation is to be offered to the deserving; an extension of penalty or an alternative (Roche, 1984)?

4.   Crisis management: efficiency and legitimacy
At this point it is important to distinguish again the different discursive and professional practices operational within the complexity of criminal justice and penality. The specific concerns of, for instance, police, probation officers or the Home Office can, however, at one level, be related on the shared map of operational efficiency and public legitimacy. At a point when it is clear that none of the participating parties can sustain a successful[8] 'war against crime' dependent, primarily, on trial and incarceration (simply the system in its present operational mode will collapse), the need to redraw the terrain is imperative, if only to divert some of the caseload away from the mainstream of courts and prisons. In this light Tony Marshall's carefully argued book *Alternatives to Criminal Courts* (1985) means

exactly that; not alternatives to criminal justice but a diversification within the criminal justice system in the search for greater operational value, or at its broadest the search for more effective forms of containment and control:

> It is opportune to stand back and consider how we employ the law and criminal sanctions. Are there areas where alternative approaches may be more efficient? Is there a tendency to legislate in response to any social problem, without considering whether there may be a more cost-effective means to the same end? (Marshall, 1985: 4)

The development of 'alternatives' may well look to utilizing and incorporating initiatives which might have suggested the possibility of transformative thinking but require some aspect of institutionalized support or funding. At another level support for changes in definition or practice in the face of failure to deliver successful victories against crime, at least in the number of reformed bodies, may look to sharing languages of representation which emphasize community solidarity and the relationship of individuals rather than punishment of the offender. It has been suggested, in relationship to family law, that perhaps the most important symbolic value in the development of mediation is that it has helped to normalize divorce and thus strengthen the institution of marriage (Bottomley, 1985).

Official rhetoric, including that produced by the participating agencies and professional groups, can now partake of an image which emphasizes continuity of familial relationships and therefore of the social fabric, rather than continuing to struggle with an ideology of the threats inherent in divorce. By analogy, the images of exclusion and social destruction utilized in the 'fight against crime' model, may be shifted to target specific offences or groups, while the alternative model of reintegration may be utilized to normalize other areas. Again the question is whether this can provide an environment for true innovation or whether yet again we are caught in the continual movement between repression and reform (Garland, 1985), as actors within the criminal justice system struggle to find better operational techniques and new legitimacies. It is particularly instructive, for instance, to contrast the work of Nils Christie with that of Tony Marshall. For Christie:

> Crime is not a 'thing'. Crime is a concept applicable in certain social situations where it is possible and in the interests of one or several parties to apply it. We can create crime by creating systems that ask for the word. We can extinguish crime by creating the opposite types of systems. (1982: 74)

Christie's model of 'conflict participation' rather than 'conflict management' is both highly idealistic and dependent on therapeutic themes which we find contentious; but the usefulness in turning to such a model is to sharpen the distinction between attempts at 'alternatives' and the system management approach of Tony Marshall (however sophisticated). Christie's critique is also particularly pertinent in considering the espousal of both the imagery of the 'fight against crime' and the concern to find policies within the existing system (rather than attempting to think through and beyond criminal justice and penality) found in much of the work of the 'new' or 'radical' realists in criminology (see Kinsey et al., 1986). This has more in common with the systems management concerns of Marshall, the reproduction of technical knowledge, than the attempts at innovatory thinking and the search for transformative knowledge in the work of Christie. The basic question to ask, in our view, is whether alternatives posed or initiatives offered, or indeed models built in the academy, accept as their basic frame the pre-existing models of a specifity called criminal justice or a mode of disciplining focused on penality. Without interrogating the very idea of crime as a specific social or legal category, we are caught within old languages and models, as effectively as when we are caught within models of formal and informal justice.

To view new initiatives within the context of the continuation of old themes in new languages, is to place such initiatives within the historical backdrop of the interplay between 'justice' and 'welfare', rather than to attempt to portray them as stark choices or truly fresh initiatives (Clarke, 1985). We hope that this is not to seem historically defeatist; we simply wish to recall the historical record to bring a note of realism into a situation which offers the potential of too much enthusiasm for anything which seems to be new (Cohen, 1985). We should recognize the power of representations of 'new' initiatives in our attempts to distinguish between the latest turn in attempts at system management, and the far more difficult struggle of finding possible routes towards emancipatory, transformative thinking and practice.

Of the building of models and representations

We began with our initial dilemma, one which arose from the intersection of trying to name and evaluate shifts within legal and 'alternative' ordering, and attempting to develop the possibility of transformative practices, and therefore necessarily, knowledges. We see it as an intersection because a major aspect of our dilemma was the need to confront and evaluate the languages and models which seemed most readily at hand, in particular the models of formality and informality, of ordering through law and the alternatives.

It is increasingly clear as we begin to examine specific sites more carefully that the simplistic opposition between formal and informal justice is flawed at a number of levels. First, historically the models cannot be sustained as representative of legal practice from which there has been a shift. We mean this in two senses, drawing from the areas of criminal and family law. If formal proceedings are to be identified with a rule-based, court-based adversarial model an examination of the historical record shows that this model has never been sustainable in practice. Both family and criminal law contain strong elements of discretion and inquisitorial styles. This may in part be read within the context of their interesting shared history in the ecclesiastical courts (although this was not the only source of either site) and their constitution as separate areas of law, as defined legal categories, in the nineteenth century. Obviously there are major differences in the development of each site but it is useful to recognize in the genealogy of both the complexity in their development, and in particular the historical confusion in trying to read uniformity or coherence, in terms of structural coherence in either legal form or objective.

As Marshall rightly says: 'The starting point of this analysis will be the assumption that the criminal justice system is not an homogeneous whole, but is an historical accretion of various procedures, intentions and definitions which have grown up pragmatically' (1985: 5). Or as Rose says in relation to family law: 'The first fragmentation must be of "law" itself. The "legal system" is neither totalised nor enclosed, there is no unity to the complex of written codes, judgments, institutions and agents and techniques of judgment which make up "the law"' (1987: 66).

No thinking lawyer needs to be told this. However what is important, and goes beyond simply a model of fragmentation, is that within the complexity of legal discursive practice certain patterns, and representations of those patterns, do coalesce or become dominant. It is this relational configuration which is as important to examine as the, prior, need to fragment. The emergence of specific sites, family or crime, need to be examined in terms of the configurations giving rise to their appearance.

These configurations may well utilize what at one level seem to be distorting patterns of similarity and dissimilarity. This does not make the representations any less important: it is simply to read them for what they are. The interesting aspect of both criminal law and family law is that they both appeared at a time when an emerging parliamentary system utilized legal forms in relation to other emerging modes of discipline and other agencies of knowledge and power. Penality, criminology, etc, created the specific site of criminal law as much as any aspect internal to legal discourse, especially in relation to common law (Garland and Young, 1983). Agencies involved in the construction of particular sites of familial relation created family law as a site as much as the need to reform internal to the legal system. These were always shared sites in which law only played a part. Added to this it was not even 'mainstream' common law, as understood and represented by common lawyers which was the only informing aspect of legal practice. Common lawyers in the nineteenth century were still more comfortable with their traditional areas of work and thinking, the development of doctrine through case argument in the areas of tort, contract and certain aspects of property and commercial relations. It was the combination of these practices with the speaking of political aspirations and legitimacy through languages of law and the rule of law which gave rise to the models of formal justice so beloved of such transmitters of the legal tradition as Dicey.

Of course much more feeds into the picture than this, from the inheritance of a utilization of legal rights arguments against the ancien regime to the attempts to provide political and academic credibility for law and the legal profession in the writings of nineteenth-century jurists. The pragmatic, ad hoc and diverse 'reality' of the legal process became melded into a picture of formal, rational, internally coherent, 'law'. Fed by political languages and professional interests the image became as much part of 'law' as the practice.

Of course we are generalizing from specific sites, sites which have a particular public importance as well as a shared concern with other professional groups and discursive practices. There are areas of law which do more closely conform to the model. What is interesting to us is the paradox that the model of formal justice, espoused and created in a particular historical period, but in practice marginal to the operation of criminal and family law, should be used to critique these very areas of law. The importance of public representations of criminal law in particular, whether emanating from the profession and the historical attempt to mould it in the common law image, or from popular representations, matched with the broader political credibility of law and order, create a complex interaction between images and realities. The second aspect to consider in this relation between image and practice is the fact that the court is anyway marginal to the system: both in the need to operationalize the more formality for the few and the greater need for plea-bargaining for the many, and the number of different agencies operating within the site. For this reason it is important to consider the extension of existing 'informal' practices, mediation in relation to plea-bargaining, etc, rather than simply buying the rhetoric of alternatives to 'formal' justice. We should make clear that we do not rest any case on an argument of disjuncture between image and reality. Our concern is to emphasize the power of both. Shifts in rhetorical practice are as important to track as shifts in other aspects of any discursive system. However in our work this initial unpacking exercise is one that cannot be under-valued.

We began by placing the utilization of a concern with 'alternatives' within their specific setting. We want to end by considering our own specific setting within the academy. In particular we are concerned to recognize the consequence of borrowing models built within sociology and simply adopting them in our own work. The Weberian heritage is marked both in the tendency to build models based on ideal types, which locate categories based on internal coherence and external dissimilarity, and utilization of models of rationality and formality. In work on law this echo of nineteenth-century political aspiration has too often been used as a guide in an attempt to locate and evaluate shifts within law. Much more complexity existed then and exists now. The plurality found in law is not new. Neither is the over-simplistic use of Weberian models. However if we recognize legal discursive practice as incorporating aspirational and evaluative language then we can ask whether there has been a shift at this level, in a sense in the ideology spoken through and about law. How malleable legal discursive practice is to other aspirations being spoken through it, and formulated in different practices, is what is in contention at present. Rather than seeing the models of formality and informality as alternatives, it might be better to recognize their continued presence within different levels of legal discourse. To track the dominance of either the practice or representation, of one over the other in specific sites, is necessarily to recognize complexity within law as well as the effect of different groups and agencies working within 'legal' sites. On the whole we believe that the particular representations of formality and informality are too generalized and too crude. They are presented as models most expressive of the initiatives we have outlined. As working models they require the same level of interrogation as the initiatives themselves. To be caught within them is to be caught in a history rather than to be preparing for a future. We find an analogy with recent developments in criminology. The embrace by some 'realists' of a consumer criminology, which asks people what they think about crime and how it affects them, runs the risk of ignoring its own heritage. To speak of crime qua crime, much as positivist criminology did, is to precisely reproduce the avoidance of a host of awkward, importantly disturbing questions.[9] Condemnation, not of the actors, but of the system or structure of criminal justice in a class society (and one which reproduces racial and gender oppression) has been overtaken by the speaking out of the categories and rhetoric of law and order — a speaking out rendered benevolent by claiming to be giving an effective voice to ordinary people, not the privileged, to the victims of society and crime (see Matthews, 1987; Young, 1987). What is required is a clearer understanding of the languages that are available to ordinary people, and in particular oppressed or marginalized groups, to speak out their fears and aspirations. It is important to read and understand the distortions in these representations because of the limited nature of the political vocabulary available, to distinguish these voices, and the specific sections of society they come from, from either professional interests or academic theories and models. The need to defend specific elements contained within the overdrawn model of formality must not be allowed to detract from the development of transformative practices which is only possible with a fuller understanding of the complexities of legal ordering.

Notes

1. See Abel (1982) and for further discussion on placing this argument within possible shifts around the rule of law see Cotterrell (1984).

2. Indeed 'the law' has recently been brought into the sphere of industrial relations with new targets and new powers (involving the use of both criminal and civil law sanctions) employed. Here the public argument is centred on the inappropriateness of allowing freedom of collective bargaining to decide matters. The language of empowerment and participation is obviously not generally applicable. At a general level this raises the question of why some practices are being brought within law and others pushed away.

3. Of course one has to be careful about overdrawing one's case. For the past two decades welfare professionals have been involved in the negotiation of juvenile justice though this has until recently been primarily a filter operation in concert with local police juvenile liaison bureaux.

4. See Cohen (1983) for a critical view of the easy use of the idea of community and the significance of community initiatives.

5. The terms conciliation and mediation are for our purposes interchangeable. What is important is the developing argument among those involved in practice as to the technical differences between conciliation and mediation and what each professional grouping is actually engaged in.

6. For example the introduction of special procedure for divorce and the withdrawal of legal aid for uncontested divorces. See also the possible transfer of wardship proceedings to the County Court provided for by the Matrimonial Family Proceedings Act 1984 s.38(2) (b) in order to control the rising costs of this increasingly used jurisdiction.

7. See the Report of the Matrimonial Causes Procedure Committee (Chairman: Mrs Justice Booth) (1985) London: HMSO. For an increasingly sceptical view of the 'benefits' of conciliation see Davis (1983) and Davis and Bader (1985).

8. This is using the word aware of the paradoxical nature of success in these terms.
9. See T. Pitch (1985) 'Critical Criminology, Rape and the Role of the Women's Movement', *International Journal of the Sociology of Law*, where she poses some of the problems facing a left (predominantly male) criminology. See also on the question of race P. Stubbs (1987 and 1988).

5   Social Work Contracts and Social Control

David Nelken

'I mean, life is about contracts — my job contract is an agreement — and I think getting him just to think in these terms is useful itself.' [Social worker in a Diversion project]

The increasing resort to 'contracts' and 'working agreements' of various kinds in interventions by welfare, educational and medical professionals may be one of those developments which force us to revise the categories we use for understanding social life. The social work contracts and agreements with which I will be concerned here seem at one time to combine and transcend familiar conceptual distinctions between law and welfare, criminal and civil sanctions, contract and regulation, public and private arenas, formal and informal ordering, and possibly even that between the normative and the technical. Much of this serves as an object lesson in the obfuscation of 'liberal legality' and the need to take the work of Foucault and his collaborators on the 'disciplinary society' as a better starting-point in formulating and resolving the policy dilemmas we now face. But even Foucault's (1977a) contrast between 'the disciplinary' and the 'juridical' seems to distinguish the parts of what is rather an organic unity. This chapter, despite its specific empirical focus, thus represents an effort to re-examine and refine the theoretical conceptualizations we need to use to address related strategies of regulation and control in contemporary western societies.

However, although social work contracts can be seen as something unprecedented (the shape of law to come) they also draw, explicitly and implicitly, on the classical bourgeois ideal of the responsible individual from which contract derives its power to obligate even under imposed social conditions. Yet there are strange incongruities in the current ideological force of the contractual ideal. On the one hand, despite the political significance attached to freedom of choice in Britain, negotiating rights are being withdrawn from sections of the civil service and the teaching unions without apparently eroding the legitimacy of government. On the other hand, the courts insist on the obligations deriving from contract even when the most fun- . damental human interests are at stake, as in the recent American decision concerning the surrogate mother who had a change of heart but was held to her promise to give the child away. Again, within the world of business and the market place empirical studies demonstrate that the trust and benefits arising from long-term business rela- tionships totally outweigh the significance to be attached to mere contractual commitments (Macaulay, 1963; Beale and Dugdale, 1975). Some studies of doctrine even announce the 'Death of Con- tract' by which they mean, that promise *as such* has ceased to be the crux of contract doctrine which has re-approached tort in insisting on damage suffered as a result of disappointed expectations or reliance (Gilmore, 1974). Yet, strangely, it is in the world of welfare that contract *as promise* has apparently been reborn as a phoenix. The failure to honour an agreement here serves to legitimate crucial decisions such as whether to take children into care or to give or deny access to a variety of benefits and privileges, both inside and outside welfare institutions. And contract is endowed with the capacity of reducing, re-forming and even actually replacing burdensome emo- tional relationships between social workers and clients.

What sense can be made of these developments? On some inter- pretations there is no more than an apparent contradiction between contracts and control. Social work agreements are seen as imposed conditions and therefore represent a further illustration of the uni- vocal extension of social control (Cohen, 1979, 1985). But this is too rapid a dismissal of the significance of social work contracts. It lays too much stress on their behaviourist origins and belittles the analogy to legal and political contracts with their very different resonances and practical implications. By suppressing the ambiguity of the dis- course surrounding their use such an approach also fails to consider whether and when the use of agreements could in fact reduce the discretionary powers of professionals and experts. In addition, it neglects the specificity of the way contracts mediate social control and the identifying characteristics of this new modality of power. I would argue instead that social work contracts can be understood neither as contract nor as regulation but rather as an aspect of 'contractulation' — which is to say, *regulation by contract* (Rose, 1986). From this starting-point it may be possible to appreciate more specific differences among types of contract. For example, contracts which arise from efforts to conciliate in families may be distinguish- able from those which specify the details of statutory requirements. These in turn may be contrasted with those which lay down the stages which must be followed in order to overcome a problem such as drug addiction.

However, my main purpose in this chapter is to develop some more nuanced lines of thought about the relationship between social work contracts and social control. I shall start by saying something in general about the use of contracts as a technique of social work and then move on to consider some research findings derived from interviews conducted in Edinburgh and London with over 100 social workers, lawyers and others about their use of contracts and their attitudes towards them. Of course the notion of social control is a rather vague concept. On one view all of the cases in which contracts are used could be characterized as situations involving 'social control'. But as will be seen, the interesting point is that this question of whether contracts are or are not instruments of social control forms part of the debate among social workers over how they should be used.

The rise of social work contracts

Social work contracts are used in a variety of ways and in a variety of settings (Corden and Preston-Shoot, 1987). They are used increasingly in statutory work with families and children, especially in cases where care proceedings are being considered. The most common examples of contracts are with children on 'at risk' registers of potential or suspected abuse, who are being considered for local authority care or who are being released 'on trial' to their natural families. But contracts are also adopted in supervising delinquents and probationers and in facilitating and co-ordinating community placements. They are found in foster care, in mental hospitals, in work with alcoholics and in self-help organizations. They are utilized inside and outside institutional care both as a technique for earning the right to leave 'care' and a method for avoiding being transferred into residential care.

On the other hand, not all social workers use contracts, nor do those who draw up contracts necessarily do so routinely. Most workers are selective in which cases they make use of them. Even what social workers mean by contracts varies enormously. Contracts range from the most formal, lengthy, signed documents (checked by two sets of lawyers) to oral agreements which hardly do more than try to formalize the underlying relationship or service as a contractual one. It is thus difficult to put forward a satisfactory typology of social work contracts. However, their functions include helping to impose statutory conditions, setting up programmes of behaviour modification, delegating social work tasks to lay or quasi-social workers, and creating a framework for dispute processing within families. One important and possibly overriding contrast is between conditional (or conditioning) contracts and co-ordinating contracts (Sheldon, 1978); but as individual contracts may incorporate both of these functions the contrast is not always as clear-cut as it might seem.

A number of factors are associated with the increasing popularity of contract work since its early development in the 1960s in the United States. I shall discuss six of the most important ones, all of which continue to shape theoretical discussions and practical uses of contracts.

The move to taskwork
The use of contracts is closely associated with the increased stress on *task-oriented* social work, in which intervention is geared to improving specific problems within short, time-limited periods. Contracts provide the ideal tool for constructing a framework of such intervention and for identifying an agenda of agreed tasks which fall on the parties concerned (Reid and Shyne, 1969; Reid and Epstein, 1972). One of the other influences on this development, in addition to the declining faith in the success of extended casework, was the approach of behaviour modification. Those writers who emphasize behaviour modification as a catalyst for change in attitudes and feelings (rather than vice versa) argue that contracts help ensure that social workers do not lose sight of this fact (Sheldon, 1978, 1980). These points are brought out in Table 5.1.

The characterizations of task work and traditional social work which figure in Table 5.1 are, of course, idealizations rather than accurate descriptions of how social work takes place. In addition, any given example of social work intervention will probably incorporate elements which are found in both lists. There are also other qualifications to be noted. This characterization of traditional social work undoubtedly exaggerates the extent to which local authority social workers, under the stress of caseloads and crisis work, ever found it practicable to offer sustained and demanding intervention. It should also be remembered that taskwork was originally put forward as a more effective form of client-centred psychodynamic casework, whereas contract work tends to embrace a wide variety of tasks of which work on relationship problems is only one. For the sake of completeness it should also be added that there are a variety of social work activities such as welfare rights advocacy or community work which do not fit at all easily with either model. There are also some uses of contracts, as in behaviour modification programmes in residential homes, or groupwork with self-help groups of alcoholics, addicts or offenders, which are not so directly tied to the growth of

Table 5.1   *Differences between taskwork and traditional social work*

		Task Work	'Traditional' Social Work
Characteristics of work styles	1	Short-term intervention(s)	Long-term involvement
	2	Written agreement	Oral (mis)understanding
	3	Mutually binding promises	Ongoing commitment
	4	Specific focus	Diffuse unrestricted focus
	5	Assistance	Engagement
Nature of work	6	Problem-centred	Client-centred
	7	Target-setting	Developing a relationship
	8	Help to self-help	Friendship and support
	9	Working on agreed tasks	Building up trust
	10	Working to implement solutions (shared definition of problem is the starting-point)	Working to understand causes of the problem (shared definition of problem is the end-point)
Goal of work	11	Apportioning and Monitoring performance of tasks	Identification of problems and remedies
	12	Problem amelioration	Progress towards goal of mental health, normal functioning, etc
	13	What client wants	What client needs
	14	Stress on presenting problem	Stress on underlying problem
	15	Action by client	Insight by client

taskwork. Nonetheless, it would be hard to overemphasize the importance of taskwork for the rise in the use of contracts, both in its own right and in relation to the other factors to be considered.

The return to responsibility

A second factor which explains the rising use of contracts is a renewed stress on personal responsibility. Probation work with offenders and social work supervision have, of course, long embodied or lent themselves to contract work, but the growth of 'diversion', community service and other schemes have increased the scope for such work. Contract work is particularly reinforced by what has been called the 'decline of the rehabilitative ideal'. Disillusion with the 'treatment philosophy', under which offenders were seen as having needs which required expert diagnosis, has led to calls for a 'justice model' of limited intervention in people's lives. Stress is put on asking social workers and probation officers to separate their caring and controlling roles and ensure that the former is restricted to concrete practical assistance rather than intrusive casework. The search is on for a 'non-treatment paradigm' for probation officers in which specified areas of help replace an open-ended casework relationship (Bottoms and McWilliams, 1979). Much of this remains controversial and sometimes out of touch with practice, yet there is no denying the relevance of these debates to the move towards 'agreements' as the (only) legitimate basis for social work intervention. Clients, other than offenders, are now to be treated as free agents capable of determining, like any other consumer, what they wish to take from social workers and what they will choose to do about their own problems. This is manifest, for example, in Collins's plea for greater use of contracts:

> What goals do we seek, and what are the limits we should set, or must set? The terms of the agreement — essentially a contract — should be spelt out. The basis of the contract between worker and client is not so much the meeting of minds as the concept of bargain, the market place and horse trading, the quid pro quo. The client is a consumer and a participant entering into a transactional relationship. If it is to have a basis of trust then the nature of the transaction should be specified as explicitly as possible, as soon as possible. (Collins, 1977)

This rationale for contract shows the continued political and moral resonance of assuming that respect for individuals requires that they be viewed as possessing rights and freedom of choice (Rojek and Collins, 1987).

Deinstitutionalization
The third factor which appears relevant is the decline in the use of institutional and residential facilities for social work. Largely for financial reasons and partly because of a loss of confidence in residential care as the best preparation for life in the community, there has been a considerable upsurge in schemes to empty institutions of all but the most difficult residents. The impact of 'decarceration' (Scull, 1977) for offenders obviously leads to control in the community (Nelken, 1985). But it also has significance for child care because increased adoption, foster care, day care and community care placements all lend themselves to the use of contracts. Nancy Hazel's pioneering community care project, for example, which served as a model for others, laid great stress on contracts (Hazel, 1981). Care in the 'community' requires careful co-ordination of all those dealing with a case and often requires that foster parents, community carers, day carers, etc, be treated as 'para-social workers' delegated to carry out specified social work tasks and paid accordingly. Contracts provide the requisite method of co-ordinating this process and offering

the right degree of 'job description', without expecting or intending these workers to operate as properly trained social workers.

Private and voluntary social work

A further reason for the rise of contracts in social work practice is the encouragement being given to voluntary effort accompanied by increasing pressure on local authorities to ascertain that this effort does not duplicate statutory services and that it offers good value for the grants-in-aid received. Contract work offers a clear method of demonstrating the nature of the tasks being tackled and the commitment to monitor progress being achieved. Thus a threat to its funding helped to explain a shift to contract work in one Family Service Unit (Smith and Corden, 1981). Organizations like the NSPCC and Barnardo's were quick to adopt contracts. The more that local authorities and statutory social workers are made to depend on inputs of social work by voluntary agencies and by volunteers, the more contracts are likely to be used to formalize these arrangements.

Measurable achievements

Pressure to demonstrate results is not restricted to private and voluntary agencies. Social work in general has come under severe, if often ill-informed, criticism and it must be tempting to move towards a form of social work which appears to promise measurable achievements and even a possible yardstick of cost-benefit 'productivity'. However, despite the attractions to management or politicians of requiring a style of work which could so easily be monitored, there is as yet little evidence of erosion of social worker autonomy in choosing how to work.

Accountability

Last, but not least, contracts are seen as providing something of a solution to the problem of making social workers 'accountable' for the exercise of their discretion (Bankowski and Nelken, 1981). Contracts specify the conditions under which a child will be returned home to its natural parents, a probation order will be breached, parental rights will be sought, etc. This is important both for the people affected and those in courts and local authorities who have to take decisions on the basis of social work recommendations. For social workers themselves, contracts allow them to justify and document their decisions and avoid charges of poor communication and liaison. Responsibilities are clearly defined, not least those of the clients who are being encouraged to exercise self-help and avoid dependence on the social work departments.

Contracts and control

Having sketched the background to the growth of social work contracts I now want to focus on their relevance for students of social
control. Social work contracts are certainly not *just* about social
control. The social work literature, for example, gives a quite different, almost opposite, impression. It talks of the value of contracts as a
means of changing the nature and goals of social work involvement:
co-ordinating complex tasks, helping to motivate clients and provide
a record of achievement and improving accountability of social workers (Corden, 1980; Nelken, 1987). It emphasizes that contracts are
merely a tool, although there is some uncertainty about how much
contracts are a means to more successful interventions or more of a
'process-value' in themselves (by allowing greater participation and
choice). Although we should expect to find some gap between the
practicalities of contract use and the aspirations of the literature, it
would be unduly cynical to turn all these claims on their heads so as to
portray contracts as inherently and inevitably a way of increasing
control. What needs to be appreciated rather is when and why
contracts play such a role. Such an enquiry can draw on the views of
social workers because they are often very uneasy about the power
they wield. But their views must be placed within an analytic
framework designed to clarify the relationship between contracts and
control.

Such a framework would distinguish three levels at which social
work contracts could be said to relate to social control. At the most
basic level, contracts may be *abused* in certain ways to strengthen
social workers' ability to manipulate clients. But beyond this, as will
be seen, contracts may also be considered *intrinsically* controlling (as
Marx argued was true of the free wage-contract). In this sense contracts may facilitate the differential exercise of power, *however* they
are used. Finally contracts might be connected to social control in the
broad sense, insofar as they are used to transmit and reproduce
bourgeois conceptions of the responsible individual. In summary
form the first level of analysis defines the controlling role of contract
as that use of power which infringes the autonomy of clients, the
second focuses on how contract generates power for social workers to
use and the third is concerned with the production of autonomy itself
(cf. Lukes, 1973).

Examination of the data derived from my interviews with social
workers reveals that they devote most of their attention to first-level
problems of the acceptable way of using contracts and the dangers of
their abuse. However, at least some social workers, in their dialectical solutions to the dangers they perceive at this level, are then led to

see further difficulties about the operation of contract even where the most blatant misuses are outlawed. I shall therefore discuss in turn the views and disagreements among social workers with regard to each of the three ways of relating contracts and social control.

Contracts and the abuse of power
Many social workers are strong advocates of the use of contracts. Those social workers most in favour of contracts argue that they *curb* power by limiting what would otherwise be relatively unlimited professional discretion. But they do not shirk the fact that power is an inescapable part of their job, especially where their work has a statutory basis. In their view, the use of contracts assists social workers themselves to acknowledge the reality of their powers. In the words of one local authority worker: 'I think most social workers, er, I think the Beckford case highlighted it very clearly, are uncomfortable with their statutory duties. People tend to come into the profession to be things other than policemen but of course a lot of social work involves very heavy policing.'

Contracts are therefore seen to have the legitimate functions of helping to manage encounters with clients and of providing something palpable to remind clients of their commitments. They also serve as a protective device for use at court and a useful means of record keeping. Despite this there is nonetheless considerable disagreement among social workers about *when* it is appropriate to use contracts. For example, some think that contracts take on their main role with difficult clients where they can use them to mobilize threats of various kinds as an incentive to compliance. As one worker put it: 'I suppose I see them as mainly to do with working with resistant people because I feel if people are not resistant you don't need a written agreement'. Or in the words of another, contracts were to be used 'when all the cajoling and nice approach has no effect'. From this it is but a short step to contracts as a weapon to protect social workers in cases where conflict is anticipated. Contracts, explained one social worker, are appropriate 'when we're the last resort for them but we haven't really got anything to offer'. Candidly, she admitted 'it's almost a way of rationalizing and denying the service to people . . . the feeling that this isn't working but we need proof, we need evidence'.

This approach to contracts, which critics would perhaps view as a strategy for 'blaming the victim' reaches its culmination in the design of 'contracts to fail'. Here contracts are drawn up with the expectation that success is unlikely. Yet the social work department cannot lose. If the parents or whoever is involved pass the test, then all is well. If, on the other hand, they fail, as expected, then the social worker has demonstrated to the client and, more importantly perhaps, can prove at court, that the client was unable to reach the required standards of behaviour when the opportunity was presented to him/her.

Such 'contracts to fail' (to use a deliberately exaggerated expression) are particularly common in child care cases, probably because for the social worker it is the child rather than the parent who is their real client. As one NSPCC officer agreed: '. . . Yes, there are times, in most cases, where you ask for more than you can expect'. He went on to describe a particular case as follows: 'They as parents have a responsibility to the child, to act responsibly, and in this case clearly we realized it was going to be extraordinarily hard for them to fulfil these conditions. Actually it would have required a major change in the way they conduct their lives simply to go along with the most basic of these conditions.'

For such workers, making contracts to fail is still not seen as an abuse of contract. This is because they are the first to recommend the client to show the contract to their solicitors. If it contained 'unreasonable terms', then 'their barrister will make mincemeat of it'. In this way legalistic criteria of 'nullity' or 'abuse' (for example, lack of 'consideration' or 'abuse of fiduciary position') are adopted as a correct and sufficient measure of the acceptability of social work contracts. When such contracts fail, social workers may comment, without apparent irony, 'This agreement worked, they ended up breaking it completely'. At other times they may resort to traditional social work interpretations of behaviour (never totally abandoned) so as to 'read' the client's conduct in a way which justifies the outcome of the intervention: 'parental non-co-operation is a clear statement of not wanting their children back'.

On the other hand, other social workers take a diametrically opposed line on contracts. Rather than using them 'when things are getting out of control' or with young children, or backward or resistant clients, they reserve them for the most mature and capable people they deal with and develop them in ways which do not involve obvious coercion. They strongly resist what they see as the 'prostitution' of contracts as techniques of control. As one worker on an Intermediate Treatment project explained: 'We've found that social services children's homes are very keen to actually use it as an extension of their control system, to put things in the contract like, if he misbehaves in the children's home he will be punished by us here by not being allowed as much free time or something. We've just refused to do that . . .'

To avoid such abuse of contracts they object to their use within institutions, and question all routinized versions of contracts. For them there is no place for 'contracts to fail'. On the contrary, too rigid use of contracts is actually self-defeating, in social work terms, by inducing the behaviour you wish to see ended: '. . . their contracts are very tight, there are things like "if I re-offend, I will be expelled from the project". Well that's asking for it really, isn't it — to see whether you will expel them.'

Contracts and the production of power
These efforts to prevent the abuse of contracts as an instrument of manipulation lead some social workers to engage with contracts in terms of the second level of control. Here the concern is with the way contract produces and legitimates social workers' powers by defining and limiting them in a quasi-legal form.

The problems at this level are manifold. Even under ideal conditions (where, for example, there is a strict avoidance of 'contracts to fail') it is hard to accept that social work contracts involve genuinely reciprocal obligations. It seems that, on the one hand, social workers are merely promising to do their job, whereas clients are asked to accept significant and consequential undertakings. Moreover social work 'expertise' gives them the right to interpret the meaning of these requirements in case of doubt or dispute. More than this, from a legal point of view, social work contracts are not comparable to privately bargained contracts. This is because, in case of dispute, whereas the courts are likely to take a dim view of clients who have failed to comply with their volunteered agreements, the same may not be the case for the social work department. Its decision to resile from earlier promises, for example to return a child when set conditions are satisfied, may be applauded rather than criticized. For there is a general public law principle that administrators should not 'fetter their discretion' as to the appropriate action to take in the light of unforeseen circumstances.

Many unquestionable legal contracts, such as the 'standard form' contracts used by government utilities, hire purchase or insurance companies, are also characterized by structured inequality of bargaining powers. But social workers are reluctant to point to these as analogies. Instead they insist on the elements of reciprocity in their contracts which may too easily be overlooked. It can be said that social workers are only agreeing to do what is already their legal obligation, namely to carry out their statutory responsibilities. But many social workers do see themselves as offering something in addition. They bind themselves to devoting time to their cases, keeping appointments and working on their clients' behalf with other agencies. Although these may seem small concessions, social workers are in no doubt that in the actual practice of harassed social service departments they are quite meaningful — and especially in non-statutory cases where workers retain more discretion as to how much effort they will expend. Conversely, clients, in statutory cases at least, are often only agreeing to what is already their legal obligation and therefore are arguably not being asked for anything extra.

A further issue arises from the fact that contracts are used in a context which is biased against clients. Indeed, some social workers insist that contracts are unlikely to succeed unless used in a situation where there is what they call 'leverage': 'It's easier to make contracts with families where we do have some control. They are wanting something. It's difficult to make contracts with families who either reject what you're trying to do or just don't see it in the same terms as you see it.'

Those who reject the use of contracts as an instrument of control recognize that the notion of 'contract' may be intrinsically *disempowering*. They try to tackle this as a problem of both form and substance. 'I don't really like calling them contracts. I prefer agreements. They aren't legally binding. If we start calling them contracts and start using them as evidence in courts that doesn't do anything to reduce the power between worker and client. It actually lowers the client's power.'

There is also the vexed question of consent. Social workers who favour the use of contracts readily concede that the consent obtained from clients, especially in statutory work, is not completely voluntary. But NSPCC inspectors, in particular, insist that this is just the way of the world and that the consent exacted still counts for something: 'They *can* choose. It's a brutal choice and the choice may be work with us or lose your child. Our view is that it's a real choice. They can fight us in court.'

On the other hand, those social workers who worry about the power intrinsic in the practical context in which contracts are used have various recommendations for dealing with it. They argue that contracts should only be set up at the instigation of clients and that they, not the social workers, should identify the problems to be worked on (thus eliminating the power represented in 'fixing the agenda' of what needs to be tackled). In cases of dispute there should be an outside neutral arbitrator available to adjudicate. In general, they argue contracts should only be made for short periods, for days rather than weeks, and clients should be entitled to withdraw at will. Surprisingly, it is those who operate with a behaviourist model of contract who are more likely to seek to tackle the second level of power embedded in contracts. But this is done in the name of *effectiveness* as much if not more than in the cause of *autonomy* (though the two aspirations appear to point in the same direction). They attack the whole notion that contract is about penalizing people into compliance because they argue that this approach only generates resistance. As a child psychiatrist explained: 'It's no more difficult to produce positive contracts than negative contracts. It just requires approaching the whole thing from a more equal point of view'. He went on to illustrate the point: 'All we've done there is to turn the negotiation on its head and now instead of the youngster failing and the teacher responding punitively, the youngster is set up to succeed and the teacher is putting in rewards. It's kind of the opposite of response-cost which would be a punitive setting up and withdrawal of an enforcement. This is setting up of a positive reinforcement.'

The behaviourist approach to contract is distinguished from the legal model because although it also seeks to meet the client's requests it does not do so as a result of bargaining and negotiation. By contrast, the 'legal' approach is explicitly geared to the possibility of conflict and so inevitably involves trading and trade-offs. This results in 'plea-bargaining' when the question of adequate compliance with the contract comes to be assessed — as many social workers admitted. But this is not considered appropriate if a behaviourist contract has been designed successfully.

Contracts and the enforcement of autonomy
However, there is a still more deep-lying problem. This resolution of the power bias inherent in the use of contracts may actually reinforce the most basic sense in which contracts serve as social control. In the words of one proponent: 'Behavioural contracting is to do with setting up agreements to control yourself'. As he went on to say: 'The more individuals persuade themselves to their choices the more they are likely to stick to an agreement'. So a new question now arises. If we get rid of open manipulation of contracts, and even if we avoid contexts in which contracts substantively serve to reduce clients' power, what have we accomplished? Have we prevented contracts from functioning as social control or in fact enabled them to operate as the most insidious form of social control of all?

The argument runs as follows. A contractual approach to welfare problems (like law itself) has a tendency to individualize, to make 'private troubles' out of 'public issues'. The assertion of 'agency' over 'structure' obscures the possibility that the agent's 'choices' are in fact a product of the structural influences which shape and interpellate her 'agency' and desires. It may be claimed that the 'autonomous self', capable of self-monitoring and reflection, which contract work seeks to support, is precisely the bourgeois subject exercising delegated social control. As Nietzsche foresaw, the subject 'must have become not only calculating but himself calculate, regular even to his own perception, if he is to stand a pledge for his own future as a guarantor does' (Nietzsche, 1956).

On this view the gift of contractual freedom is essential because 'autonomy' is an intrinsic feature of this form of social control. A social worker explained the weaknesses of their original use of contracts as follows: 'You have to be careful though ... People who neglected their kids used to be kept very strictly to a routine. "Get up at 7 o'clock. Do this at 7.30." Everything had become so structured that it gave no leeway for error. As soon as one thing goes wrong the whole day is a mess. You had only taught them to be totally structured.'

The ability to choose is therefore at the heart of the contract strategy. Yet, as in the world of the consumer, *what* is chosen is less significant than the habit of choosing. 'If they feel they've a choice between black shoes and black shoes they probably won't want them. If you give them a choice of colours of shoes to buy then it's more likely they'll prefer what it is they buy ... the more choice you give the greater the sense of commitment' (Senior Social Worker).

The question which still needs to be explored is whether the choosing individual encouraged by contracts thereby preserves or acquires the ability to make other choices than the ones set out by the agencies of 'normalization'. It is possible, as Fitzpatrick so persuasively argues, that this modality of social control gives birth simultaneously also to the counter-power of resistance (see Fitzpatrick in this volume). But, as he also stresses, this freedom to choose 'wrongly' does in the end both vindicate and reproduce the conception of the responsible subject. To put the problem in Foucault's language; is the effort devoted to creating a genuinely choosing subject no more than the ultimate form of our subjection by 'the disciplines'? Few of the social workers in my interview sample would accept this viewpoint. But there are indications that this may be an apt characterization at least of some of the uses of contracts in 'normalizing' the behaviour expected of welfare clients.

Conclusion

Although I have concentrated on the practicalities of contract use, the emergence of a new modality of power may also be seen as an index of wider changes in modes of social control. The use of contractual techniques by social workers may be suggestive of changing forms of bourgeois hegemony inasmuch as they operate a peculiar combination of behaviourist and politico-legal strategies which can be seen to represent a way of disciplining even the potential resistance inherent in the 'self-calculating' subject. On the one hand, the politico-legal strand openly acknowledges the possibility of conflict between state and the individual as parties to the social contract, rather than seeking to totally identify their interests. Here legitimation ultimately depends on negotiated consent. On the other hand, the behaviourist approach substitutes conditioning for consent. It seeks to set interventions up so as to avoid all possibilities of conflict. Agreement and need are rendered synonymous. As a check on the potentially dangerous consequences of this alliance between law and behaviourism we have the differences and disagreements among social workers themselves, their flexible application of theories in their praxis and their constant self-examination of their powers. And there is also, for good or ill, the continuing intractability of many of their clients.

Note

Earlier versions of this paper were given at Middlesex Polytechnic Sociology Department, at the Critical Legal Conference at Kent, at Brunel Law Department and at the Vaucresson Centre de Recherches Interdisciplinaires and I am grateful for helpful comments received. I owe special thanks to Stewart Hughan, who was the research assistant on the project on which it draws. Peter Fitzpatrick and David Garland made very valuable comments on an earlier draft.

6 Mediation in the Shadow of the Law: The South Yorkshire Experience

David Smith

Harry Blagg

Nick Derricourt

The scheme to be considered in this chapter was the first court-based scheme in Britain, preceding those funded by the Home Office by over a year. It was run as a 'special project' within the South Yorkshire probation service, with an experimental and developmental brief, for three years from November 1983. Some experience in involving victims in discussing offences had been gained in the previous special project (reported in Celnick, 1985, 1986), and the senior officer was keen to develop the idea. The project was modest in scale, with three full-time workers, the senior and two probation officers, one attached to the area team in Wombwell (near Barnsley), the other to a team in Rotherham. It was hoped that one other officer on each team would also undertake some work with victims, but, for reasons to be explored later, this happened only to a very limited extent. The officers in the special project were to take all requests for social enquiry reports from the Barnsley and Rotherham magistrates' courts relating to offenders in four (later five) specified areas: two (later three) estates in Rotherham, an estate in Barnsley and a pit village (Blackthorpe) near Wombwell. Each area was chosen because it was thought to have both a high rate of crime and a clearly defined local identity. In practice a few cases were dealt with from beyond these areas, when they were referred by another officer because they seemed to have some potential for mediation. Apart from this, the project officers explored the feasibility of mediation in all cases routinely passed to the probation service for reports in the designated areas. An acknowledged limitation on the scope of the project was that it could deal only with cases in which the defendant was remanded on bail, as it had to be possible for the victim and the offender to meet. Because, as will appear, the local magistrates were for the first year of the project barely aware of its existence, they cannot have been remanding cases for social enquiry reports specifically with mediation in mind. The project thus dealt with (roughly) the middle range of cases appearing before the local courts: cases which were serious or problematic enough for the magistrates to ask for a report, but not so serious that they felt they had to remand in custody. The typical offences were burglary from dwellings, various forms of theft, and criminal damage, with some assaults. In twelve cases studied, the magistrates had committed the defendant to the Crown Court for sentence, indicating that they viewed the offence seriously.

The project began by stating its aim as reparation. In this it was in line with much of the early thinking in Britain about the aims of mediation in criminal justice. The assumption (shared throughout most of western Europe — see Dunkel, 1985) was that some material reparation or restitution was an essential element of such schemes. Some very elaborate plans were devised, such as Wright's feasibility study for Coventry (Wright, 1983) to make it possible for offenders to compensate their victims financially; Wright envisaged a special employment scheme, so that offenders could repay victims from their earnings. Nothing as elaborate as this was ever thought necessary in South Yorkshire, where reparation was conceived in terms of practical work for victims rather than as the payment of money. Even so, the emphasis within the project was quickly changed to reconciliation as the aim of mediation, and in recognition of this it became known as the 'mediation' rather than the 'reparation' project, emphasizing, perhaps misleadingly, the process rather than the envisaged outcome. The project's senior (Dixon, 1986) came to see material restitution as 'the Interflora approach to mediation', a phrase which conveys well the strong commitment the project developed to a non-material conception of the aim of mediation, and to the importance of authentic communication between victim and offender. The reason for this shift lay in the view of the project workers that the original assumption that victims would want some form of material reparation had proved largely incorrect. How far this view was justified will be considered later.

This research was based mainly on the first year of the project's work which began in September 1984. Through a series of interviews conducted with twenty-four offenders and twenty-one victims the research focused on the thirteen of the offenders who met 'their' victims and the fifteen victims who met 'their' offenders. In addition to these interviews with victims and offenders, the research also involved a range of methods — interviews, attendance at meetings, participation in the project's own evaluation seminars — intended to establish the views held of the project by the probation officers involved in it, by other officers, and by local magistrates and other criminal justice personnel.

The research is therefore directed towards those cases where 'successful' meetings took place. It would be wrong, however, to regard cases in which no meeting took place as necessarily 'failures'. True, the project consistently emphasized its belief in the importance of a meeting as the context in which authentic reconciliation could be achieved; but it also consistently emphasized the principle of voluntarism, and it is possible that some of those who did not meet regarded the issue as having been adequately settled, so that a meeting was unnecessary. A meeting may be irrelevant in cases where the 'victim' is a large commercial enterprise, such as a chain store or a television rental company, and no one has actually felt personally victimized. Some limits to the feasibility of arranging a meeting also arise from the court-based context. It may be impossible to arrange a meeting in the relatively short time available (usually three weeks) when a case is remanded for a report. It may prove impossible to contact the victim in time; there may be several victims and several co-defendants, so that it is impractical to link each offender with the appropriate victim; and, as mentioned above, the project could only work effectively when the offender was remanded on bail. These are relevant considerations for the feasibility of mediation in this court-based context, and they raise questions of justice and equity — of which the project workers were well aware, and which are discussed later in this chapter.

Victims who did not meet 'their' offenders

Why might victims decide against a meeting? Eleven victims were identified in the study period who could have met 'their' offenders but chose not to do so; that is, the offender was willing and able to meet them. Six of these were interviewed, and for the remainder it was possible to gather information about their reasons for declining the offer of a meeting from the probation officer's records. Four, who had had some previous relationship with the offender, gave as their main reason the fact that they felt so 'let down' by the offender that they did not wish to see him again. (This might not be easy to achieve, especially in Blackthorpe.) Two, seeing the purpose of the proposed meeting in primarily correctional terms, felt that it would achieve nothing because the offenders were 'too old' — that is, they were adults; the idea was all right in principle, but it would 'only work with kids'; by the time they got to the stage where they were being seen by a probation officer, it was already too late for them to change their ways. Two others said that an apology would have been meaningless, because the offence had clearly been premeditated. As one victim of a burglary (motor-cycles had been taken from his garden shed) put it: 'I saw them nosing about the week before. So how could they be sorry?' A further two victims did not wish a meeting, but were prepared to accept an apology conveyed by the probation officer; for them, something like the 'Interflora' approach was, if not what they wanted, all they were ready to accept. Only two victims specifically mentioned that their main interest was in getting financial compensation; they were glad when this was ordered by the court, though inclined to see the slow drip of instalment payments as 'not much, but better than nothing'. One interesting reason given for not wishing a meeting, which was mentioned specifically by two victims and implied by others, was the fear of being thought foolish; they did not want to be seen as the 'silly sod' who accepted an apology from someone who subsequently went around laughing his head off about it. This fear might be expected to operate particularly within a tightly-knit society like Blackthorpe's, where an additional factor could be the fact that the offender was a known 'villain', or at any rate someone with the 'wrong attitude'. This might be revealed in a failure to apologize spontaneously when the chance arose; if so, whatever the offender said in an artificially contrived meeting would be worthless; the 'right' attitude would not suddenly appear. In these ways, previous knowledge of the offender might reduce the perceived value of a meeting, and increase its perceived risks, particularly if there seemed any possibility of publicity — something about which the probation officer could give no guarantees.

Offenders who did not meet 'their' victims

Similar considerations could influence offenders against a meeting. Seven cases were identified in which the offender either definitely decided not to meet, or simply failed to turn up. In one case, the offender thought seriously about it, and was inclined to agree to a meeting, when (as he claimed) he discovered that the victim had been talking in the neighbourhood about the forthcoming meeting; the 'silly sod' factor then worked in the other direction, and the offender decided that it would be 'humiliating' to go through with it; everyone would know, and anyway it seemed unfair; others were 'nicking' too, so why should he alone submit to this extra discomfort? In another case, the offender, who had stolen money from a club in which he had held a position of trust, felt that the victims' interest in a meeting was to humiliate him; he would have had to appear 'before the whole committee', and the news would be 'all round Duffield' (the estate in Rotherham where he lived). He had hoped that the matter might be dealt with without involving the police; when the police were informed, he thought, 'Why be punished twice?' He also said that he feared assault. In another case, it was the victim who was discredited, in much the same way as offenders might be seen as people from whom an apology would be worthless: the father of the (juvenile) offender decided that the victim was inflating the extent of his loss for insurance purposes — a dishonesty which, he said, was typical of this person.

Two other offenders said that they could not face the prospect of a meeting because they were afraid of what might happen. In one case (like that mentioned above) this was expressed as a real fear of violence. The other was the only woman offender interviewed, and her account gives a vivid picture of the tensions and anxieties which offenders may experience. She herself attributed these feelings to her gender ('I think a man's got more guts than a woman'), but, as will appear, this does not seem plausible as a complete explanation. Two appointments were actually made for her to see the victim (the manager of a video rental shop); she meant to keep the second appointment, but after some consideration did not turn up because she was unable to overcome her fears and uncertainties.

Were these victims and offenders in a position to make an authentic and informed choice, as required by the principle of voluntarism? From the interviews, it appeared that they understood what was being asked of them, and on the whole they felt that the probation officer did not put any pressure on them to agree. (They were clear, among other things, that they were being asked to consider mediation, not reparation; there is evidence from this study to support the view of Walklate (1986) that victims at least are not likely to regard the latter with much enthusiasm.) The slight qualification about their perceptions of the probation officer's stance is made because the woman quoted above, whose case arose very early in the life of the scheme, said that 'the first time I thought he was putting a bit of pressure on, because he was just saying, I think it's best that you should go': but, interestingly, in this case the effect of feeling pressure was to promote resistance to the idea. It is noteworthy that offenders who decided against a meeting could be seen as acting against their own interests, since, while the probation officers were careful to avoid any suggestion that agreement to a meeting would necessarily count as mitigation in court, it is hard to see how this possibility can have failed to occur to the offenders, and indeed it was often mentioned in the interviews. The sheer variety and complexity of the ways in which attitudes and feelings arising from these people's social experience in a particular neighbourhood could affect their decisions is striking; would-be mediators should not underestimate the difficulties of their task. These feelings might concern the other party directly, as when he or she was seen as dishonest, or likely to use the meeting as a source of malicious anecdote later; or they might concern the locality as a whole, with its networks of gossip, rumour and intrigue, in which loss of face or honour could be a worse punishment than anything which a court could impose, and more injurious than a crime.

Victims who met 'their' offenders

Fifteen victims were interviewed who had met 'their' offenders as a result of the probation officers' intervention. The questions raised with them were: what had been the effect of the offence on them? How was the initial contact made by the probation officer? Were they given enough information to make a decision on whether to meet, and did they have enough time to think about it? Why had they decided to meet the offender? What happened at the meeting? And what did they feel it had achieved? What did they now think, as people in a position to give an informed opinion, of the idea of mediation? The aim was to elicit an account from the victim's perspective of the process of mediation — in particular, the extent to which they felt that they had been fully voluntary and informed participants — and of its outcomes. Given the shift in emphasis of the project from reparation to reconciliation as the aim of these meetings, it seemed important to ascertain whether the latter could be achieved without the former (which has been doubted by some commentators within the mediation 'movement'). Victims themselves seem evidently the most relevant people to ask.

In summary, nine of these victims gave accounts of their experience of mediation that were almost exclusively positive; four gave accounts which could be taken as reflecting indifference — it had not really been important to them; or cynicism — they doubted if it had made any difference (to the offender); one, the victim of a joint assault by two brothers, felt positively about the process in relation to one of the offenders, and negatively for the other; and one regretted having agreed to the meeting, and felt that the outcome had been damaging. But without exception, they felt that they had been given a chance to make up their own minds on the basis of what seemed to them to be adequate information. Understandably, they were often puzzled by the probation officer's first approach, since, insofar as they had any clear notion of what probation officers did, they thought that they were exclusively concerned with offenders. So the first task for the probation officer could be to get past the initial suspicion of an angry victim that a plea on the offender's behalf was the purpose of the contact: as one man put it, 'I were going to shut the door in her face'. But he did not, and the probation officer was able to explain that this was an experimental project which was not meant to be concerned just with offenders', but also with victims', interests. This was the normal first explanation, given by telephone where possible. At this stage victims were often unclear about what was being proposed; they felt they understood only after the follow-up visit. But of course they had first to agree to this, and their reasons for doing so are of interest.

Some gave curiosity as their initial motive; for example, a farmer who had had some eggs stolen said: 'I felt as though at least I'd have some contact with what had happened on my own property'. Reflecting on the meeting with the offender the victim made the point that: 'Well, I thought there was nothing to lose at all, and I didn't know exactly who the person was at the time . . . You feel so badly about not knowing who's been on your property'. This victim described the feelings left by the offence as 'hurt and bitterness', as well as the sense of failure. For him, actually meeting the offender was essential in coming to terms with the experience of victimization. The meeting was to take place in the probation office, but 'when I went down there, down to Wombwell, I didn't think M. would come'. He described the meeting: 'I could see the guilt and that it did show me that he was in the wrong; he shouldn't have come even though I could have kept him out, if my facilities had been better protected, so he knew he was in the wrong and at least he demonstrated it and it made me feel a bit better, and apologized . . . The probation officer . . . she prompted him from the start and then he eventually spoke quite freely and actually I was amazed at the lad's character and his ability, and I still am . . . He listened all the time, which I was grateful for, and it made me feel a lot better, and I don't feel bitter now because I can see circumstances in their life can be that bad . . . I hoped that he would succeed in life which he was capable of doing, I would say . . . I'd given him a right roasting during the time that these crimes had been committed. He'd been in our yard and he knew he shouldn't have been there and he sort of slunk off . . . he was a different person. This is the point I would like to make — he was a different person that we saw in the yard and who was in that room, so it told a very long story really about people and the situations they get into, shall we say.'

He felt that the meeting had 'worked out so good I can scarcely believe it'. And he said that his views on offenders had changed; he found he was 'more cautious now about making my mind up about people being all wrong and being committed to a life of penal servitude'. He had been impressed by the intelligence and sincerity of his (twenty-year-old) offender, and felt he understood him better when he heard at first hand of the difficult circumstances of his life. Some of the complexity of the emotions involved emerges from the fact that the victim could speak of his gratitude to the offender for acknowledging his guilt; this meant that the worry the victim had that he was somehow to blame was alleviated. But it is interesting too that within this very positive account there emerges an argument against practical reparation, which at the time was still being envisaged by the probation officer. During the meeting M. suggested that he might give some help on the farm: 'I said that that was impossible because I would look a right fool bringing him back onto the farm when all the lads that do help knew the situation, and he said he understood that, and I said there is something you can do to help me, and he said, "What's that?" and I said, "Go straight" — that's one of the things I said and he said that if he got a job he thought that he could.'

Reparation by the poor may more feasibly and justly take a practical than a financial form, but this may in some circumstances at least make it unacceptable to victims. In this case, it seems that both parties understood how and why it would not have been feasible. They shared, in a general sense, a particular social environment — one in which it was very hard to keep some kinds of information private. On the other hand, it was possible to share this environment, to meet in the street or the farmyard, to know by sight and by name, without participating imaginatively in the experience of the other. So while the farmer-victim could relate some gossip about the offender — for instance, he had heard that M.'s uncle was receiving and selling stolen eggs — he had not realized, until the meeting in the probation office, what forces and stresses in the life-experience of this young man might lead him towards crime. And while M. was in one sense familiar enough with the farm, he did not, until the meeting, have any real sense of what the theft of eggs would mean to the victim. M.'s account, referred to later, helps to substantiate the claim made here that this case illustrates, among other things, that reconciliation can be real without reparation — indeed, that a preoccupation with reparation as the desired end would have got in the way of reconciliation.

Some other issues that arose from the interview with victims are illustrated in the following accounts. Mr and Mrs R. were both teachers, and as such were more differentiated in educational background and status from their offender than were most of the Blackthorpe victims. Their lawn-mower was stolen from their garage, and, as with the farmer, they considered that they had contributed to the offence, in this case by leaving the side door unlocked. They agreed to the suggested meeting on grounds which had an educational aspect: 'We felt that if nobody takes part in this new idea, nobody will know whether it works or not. It's got to be tried first'. Their main feeling on learning who the offender was and then meeting him was of surprise: they had thought it would be someone much older. They felt much easier on learning that he was 'just a lad'. They felt 'no need to be angry with him or anything like that'. The boy's mother came with him, and 'took over a bit'; but they regarded her presence as a positive sign, that she was concerned about what had happened. Again the possibility of practical reparation was raised, 'but we've had no reason to call on him for that'. They thought that the meeting was fairly handled and that it was reasonable that an offender's expression of remorse and contrition should influence the court's decision. For them, the main reasons for thinking the meeting worth-while had been that they felt reassured on realizing how young the offender was, instead of a more sophisticated adult criminal, and that they hoped they had been useful to the offender and to the probation service. Several months having elapsed between the offence and the meeting, they no longer felt any anger, but the meeting had other outcomes which they saw as useful. The lapse of time, incidentally, means that any benefits victims might gain from the project were quite distinct from the kind of immediate help a victim support scheme could provide.

The following account, however, shows that anger could persist for longer. The 'victim' in this case was a large TV and rental company, with other interests — in this case a bingo hall. The people actually affected by the offence, however, were the two women who worked there, the manageress and her assistant. The latter, Mrs B., had arrived for work one evening to find evidence of burglary — 'bandits were all scattered about'. The worst thing was that she thought that whoever had done it must still be in the building: 'That's what frightened me most and I daren't go from door to phone police, 'cos I thought if they're still in this building, I didn't know who they were and I didn't know what they would have done to me if I had come in, so I went back out and waited for somebody else, for P. (the man-ageress, Mrs A.) to come.'

In fact there was nobody in the building, because the intruders had got out through a trapdoor which neither woman knew existed. Despite this, they had remained frightened, and whatever else the meeting with the offender achieved, it could not undo this fear:

Mrs A.: I mean by then it were too late, damage were done, I mean still now I wouldn't go up there on my own. At one time I'd go and fetch money out and everything, but I wouldn't now until someone comes in. It's very unnerving.

Mrs B.: I once came in on my own after it happened and a man come and he were having a look at it, when it used to be pictures, he come to have a look, see how it had changed, and I just happened to look up and see him, and I were shaking for an hour after. Nerves of being on my own.

Neither had worried in this way before the offence; it seems likely that the only thing which could have helped reduce their worry would have been the installation of a better security system, which had not happened. The meeting, however, had served some purpose:

Mrs A.: I think he were worse meeting us [i.e. more nervous than they were about meeting him]. We explained what we thought about it and how we felt . . . I just told him he ought to be in bloody Ireland after what he'd done, I mean he put us through it 'cos M. was first one in and she saw it all.

They told him what they thought of him — 'silly little bugger' — but their anger was not all they felt:

Mrs A.: Well, I don't know because in a way I felt sorry for him because he's not a leader. I think he's been led by the other one . . . he's just got in with the wrong set, but I mean I told him point blank that no way would he be allowed in here to play again. He says: 'Is there anything I could do to make up?' and I says 'No, there's no way are you coming in here again to do anything' . . . I think it were a big thing, him having to come and face us . . . he sat here with his head down . . . At least we were able to put our point of view to him . . .'cos I mean if he'd have been in here that night when we came back in and I'd have got hold of him, I'd have wrung his bloody neck, I'll tell you, 'cos it were maddening . . . I think he realized after what a stupid trick he'd done.

Their reaction to the offence was a mixture of fear and anger; it was this that Mrs A. in particular hoped they had conveyed, and the opportunity to ventilate it had been the most positive thing about the meeting. They felt that they would do it again if asked, and that for victims like themselves, who had lost 'only' a sense of safety and ease about going to work, the principle of victim–offender meetings was a good one. There was a hint, at the end of the interview, that the meeting might have made the resumption of some sort of contact between them and the offender easier, because his co-defendant, whom they had not met through the project, would 'look anywhere' when they saw him on the bus rather than at them, whereas the young man they had met had 'started talking to our Deb. He were ashamed to talk to our Deb at one time, but he's started talking to her'. Mrs A. reported this without any comment that he was not the sort of person who should be talking to Deb.

The next account shows how the process of mediation can be

complicated by a closer existing relationship between the parties. It was also one of only two cases studied where some practical reparation was agreed and carried out. The victim was the offender's sister-in-law, married to his brother. He had taken her wristwatch when she was out of the room; it was clear that he was the only possible culprit, and he was quickly seen by the police. The watch was returned within a fortnight. The decision to tell the police was not easy for Mrs G.: 'When I reported him, I didn't want to, it made me feel awful, but we had to do it and it made me feel terrible . . . I didn't like doing it. I was in two minds whether to go or not with being relatives.'

One effect of the probation officer's visit was to make her feel better about having gone to the police ('She eased my mind'). At this visit, some practical reparation was also suggested. 'I said there was the cellar downstairs which wanted clearing out, so she asked him if he'd do it, he said he would, and he came and did it and that satisfied us.' Mr G. thought that it was a good idea: 'but I don't know what it's going to do for the offender myself because I know our P. and to him it's a bit like an easy way of getting out . . . I wasn't angry at him for doing it, I was more angry at her for letting it happen because we know what he's like . . . If I'd known he was coming I'd have moved it out of the way'.

Mrs G. defended herself against this variant of the 'responsible victim' hypothesis by saying that P. had called unexpectedly. P., told by the probation officer that his relatives were willing for him to tidy their cellar, came round and started the work ('he did a smashing job') before the probation officer arrived. Despite his scepticism about the likely effect on his brother, Mr G. was ambivalent about whether he was somehow being let off. 'No angel' himself, and with 'not a lot of time' for the police, he thought that his brother's eventual sentence to community service was perfectly reasonable for such an offence, and that it was fair that trying to make amends should reduce the severity of the sentence. He approved of the idea in general, and would have agreed to meet an offender who was not a relative: but it seemed crucial to the feelings Mrs G. expressed that the offender was not a stranger, and in the resolution of these feelings the act of reparation, as opposed to the act of meeting, seemed less important: 'It might help them (offenders) and it might help people who have reported them and it might make them feel better. It eases everybody's mind. It took me ages to phone . . . It makes you feel guilty if you do report them.' And her husband added: 'I wasn't too keen on her phoning, but when J. [the probation officer] . . . came round, I wasn't too bothered because he wasn't going to go down.' Some complicated feelings are involved here, including an ambivalence about the police and the criminal justice system which is perhaps not surprising in a mining community, and may have been intensified at the time of these interviews by the fact that the miners' strike (very solid in Blackthorpe) was then in progress. The offender's views of this incident are given later in this chapter.

As noted earlier, not all the victims interviewed had seen the meeting as especially important to them or, in all probability, to their offenders. It was also evidently possible for mediation to achieve the opposite of its intended effects, though only one victim interviewed gave an account of this kind. This was a woman who owned a fish-and-chip shop whose window had been broken. The case was complicated by the view of the police that she had been persuaded, after meeting the offender, to withdraw a claim for compensation; this represented a crisis, early in the project, in its relations with the police. Whatever the truth of this, the victim continued to feel uneasy after the meeting, and when her shop window was twice broken in the following months, she suspected, though probably groundlessly, that it was done by the same offender, as an act of revenge for his feelings of having been humiliated at the meeting, when he apologized to her. She regretted having agreed to the meeting, which had only seemed to make things worse. It seems reasonable to emphasize that this case is not typical, and it would have been surprising had the research revealed no negative experiences at all; clients' views of everyday probation practice are not always positive. But the case does underline the need for the practice of mediation to be careful, sensitive and non-coercive; and it may suggest that in some cases the mediation agency — the probation service in this instance — may have a responsibility to check after the meeting on the victim's state of mind.

Offenders who met 'their' victims

Thirteen offenders were interviewed who had met the relevant victims, in at least four cases without the probation officer being present; it seems unlikely that any of these would have approached their victims if it had not been suggested to them, though they and others might certainly have thought about doing so. In interviews with the offenders a range of issues comparable with those which were the focus of the victim interviews was explored: were they clear about what was being suggested? Did they have a chance to make up their own minds? What was their experience of the process of mediation, including the actual meeting? Did the outcome in court seem reasonably fair? And did they approve the idea in principle, as people in a position to make an informed judgement? Broadly speaking, ten of the interviewed offenders gave a positive account of their experience, and felt that it had been helpful in some way; two gave accounts which were categorized as reflecting indifference or cynicism; and only one gave a predominantly negative account. As a generalization, then, offenders' views were overall close to those of the victims, though perhaps a little more positive; and this overall agreement was reflected in accounts of particular cases: where the meeting had been a positive experience for the victim, it was also generally positive for the offender; and cynicism and indifference tended likewise to be mutual evaluations of the experience.

A feature common to several of these accounts was a reported initial reaction of alarm at the prospect of meeting the victim, and this feeling often persisted into the meeting itself. Offenders spoke of being 'a bit scared', not sure they could 'go through with it', or even of being 'terrified' when they first understood what was being proposed. These feelings arose from shame and embarrassment, or from an understandable concern that the victim might 'turn nasty'. So what led them to decide to agree to a meeting despite these initial reactions? One obviously plausible answer is that they thought it might do them some good in court, and this consideration had certainly been present in the minds of some interviewees, although, from their accounts, this did not necessarily make it the main deciding factor. Whatever message the probation officer had tried to convey, there was no doubt that some of these offenders had picked up that it 'would look good in court' if the report could contain a reference to their willingness to face up to the victim and apologize or offer reparation. The following three excerpts from interviews give an indication of the way in which offenders discussed this issue:

> *Offender*: She said it would be a good thing in court, it would help me.
> *Interviewer*: So she could say in her report he's done something, he's met the victim?
> *Offender*: Yes.

> Well I said 'No' at first, because I didn't do anything to apologize for, so I didn't feel I ought to . . . but then I just said 'Yeah' because it will make my report better, you know, I will go and say sorry.

> I thought it might help in court if I apologized and what not . . . but that wasn't the main reason . . . it helps you face up to things. It's a lot harder to apologize than stand up in court and face your fine, because you've never realized what it's like.

This issue may be thought critical in assessing the feasibility of the project's interest in creating opportunities for genuine apologies, genuine forgiveness and genuine reconciliation. It is clearly possible for an apology to be offered cynically or for the convenience of the person making it; this happens in everyday life, and the 'shadow of the law' (Mnookin and Kornhauser, 1979) might seem to encourage such cynicism. But it is not clear that the mere presence of a self-interested consideration necessarily invalidates an apology or an act of reparation, or that it compromises the principle of voluntarism. There is a difference between the 'Agree or you will be prosecuted' message which may be sometimes conveyed in police-based schemes, and a message like: 'One factor which you, as a rational being, may want to consider in coming to a decision on this is how it may affect the court's view. It is reasonable for you to think like this, but I can give no guarantees that the court will in fact be influenced in the way you would wish.' It appears from the interview that in some cases the probation officers in the project may have put the matter more strongly; but a formula like the above seems to allow for a greater degree of authentic choice than (say) is available to a defendant who is told that a prison sentence is the alternative to agreement to being put on probation (on the issue of choice in such circumstances, see Raynor, 1978). The retention of an authentic element of voluntarism in mediation in the context of writing a court report certainly depends on the possession by the mediator of a high level of skill; but it is not impossible.

In fact, the offenders interviewed placed what may seem surprisingly little emphasis on this kind of self-interest as a motive. They may, of course, have been trying to put a good interpretation on their behaviour; but it also seems that the idea of meeting the victim and apologizing at least, and perhaps offering something more, makes sense to offenders as well as to the broad constituency of respectable supporters mentioned earlier. To say that 'you have to have selfish reasons as well' means that you have other, non-selfish reasons. For instance, Mr S., who had burgled a local social club and was going to the Crown Court for sentence, said:

> We were talking and I tell him [the probation officer] I already been up. I did a burglary in '79. I took it off my own bat to see him and he said it were a good idea ...
> *Interviewer*: Did you have in mind that you might get a lesser sentence ...?
> No, not really ... It were just so I could show them that I were *really* sorry for it.

The idea, the principle, of apologizing to the victim was not new to him; it already made sense and was in line with his views on what was a reasonable way of handling an offence. (A point usefully made by Marshall and Walpole (1985) is that an unknown amount of informal resolution of disputes, with or without mediation, goes on anyway; it is not a new discovery by a professional elite.)

Mr P., who had broken into a shed containing park-keepers' tools, said: 'She asked me if I would mind apologizing, you know sorry like for what I'd done, you know I just said "Yes" . . . I've never had to do it before, you know what I mean, apologize to anyone before . . . It's a good idea really'. And Mr B., who with his brother had assaulted a couple on a bus, said: 'I find it hard to approach people, I even did them, but I just thought I'd do it in any case, I tried my best to approach them . . . I felt a bit uneasy at first, but I just did it with calmness, but inside me I didn't feel so comfortable . . . I'd really no grudge against him at all, you know. I didn't dislike him for any reason. It was a duty really, I didn't have to apologize, but I thought it best if I do . . . I think it's a good thing, sorting things out, in a case like mine, apologize and no hard feelings, know what I mean?' He 'knew' that it would help in court as well, and believed that it had done so; but in this he was unlike the two offenders previously quoted, both of whom thought their sentences excessive. Despite this, they were glad that they had agreed to meet their victims and considered this reasonable and appropriate even if it had no effect on the sentence.

So motives other than the hope of a reduced sentence could and did influence offenders given an explicit chance of meeting the victim, and they could find the meetings valuable even when they did not seem to have affected the sentence. This account by Mr P. illustrates several common themes in accounts of the meetings themselves: 'I were very nervous . . . before I wouldn't have gi'ed it a thought, going to court . . . If you've been in trouble you don't like going and facing anybody. If you go with that attitude — "It'll help me out in court" — you'll do summat else. It's the thought of going to people and saying I've done it . . . I mean there's a lot of hardened criminals . . . if you could see them just after they are really sorry, but nobody believes them . . . Them at park, as far as you're concerned there's just someone from park working, but when you get like to go and see them and help out, same people that you've robbed, you think, well it's not just park, it's people there doing the job, and you look at it in a different light . . . and you think, well, I must have been stupid, it's like you don't think of anybody else when you're pinching, and it makes you look at people in a different way . . . you're not just pinching, you're pinching off people like . . . It's changed my attitude to pinching, before I didn't care who I hurt, but . . . I respect people more now . . . I'll think twice before I ever do owt again.'

He made high claims for the correctional effectiveness of the project which were echoed by other respondents, though they would not have been made by the project staff, and should no doubt be treated sceptically. More important may be his emphasis on the way in which a meeting could bring home the human reality of victimization. It is not implausible, especially if the idea of 'techniques of neutralization' (Sykes and Matza, 1957) has any validity, that there might be a correctional effect from this; it certainly seemed to him to make possible a more authentic apology than could be given to a court.

Mr G., whose victim was his sister-in-law, also said that confrontation with the victim had 'put me off pinching', though he had in fact had a subsequent conviction. His cleaning of the cellar seemed to have helped in court, and had been specifically mentioned by the magistrate, but there was a more private, emotional benefit too, apparently associated in this case with the reparative act: 'It made me feel unwanted, specially with it being my family. I wouldn't want to go through it again. He's my eldest brother. I had to face members of my family knowing that they know what I've done. I can talk about it now but I couldn't then . . . I felt terrible about seeing my brother. The only reason I got talking to my parents was that I'd done the work for him . . . It's brought us closer together, I'm glad I did it . . . It should become part of the probation service.' He had thought that in all fairness, if he became a victim, which 'in a funny way' he hoped he would, 'I'd have to meet the offender . . . it's the best way of handling things' — and he believed this to be true whether or not victim and offender were related.

These accounts, taken together with those of the victims, seem to provide support for the project's basic idea that real communication is possible between victims and offenders, even in the shadow of the law, and that in some cases anyway something like reconciliation is possible without reparation, or with only a symbolic reparative gesture. Indeed, in no case where the outcome was perceived as satisfactory by the parties was reparation anything more (or less) than symbolic. It would be wrong, however, to present a wholly positive picture. The context in which the project was working entails the possibility of cynical and self-serving behaviour by offenders, and the risk of this was greater because no elaborate selection process was used; the only criteria which had to be satisfied were those of geography and practicability. Offenders were not assessed as to the genuineness of their remorse before being offered the chance to meet their victims, so that someone who did not really think he had anything to apologize for, as in one case, could be included.

The only thoroughly negative account obtained from an offender was in the one case where the meeting with the victim had lent added importance to the making of a more than symbolic reparation. This was not the only case in which compensation was ordered by the court, but it was the only one in which the probation officer had taken on the role of debt-enforcer, which the offender saw as niggling and unhelpful. Presumably this seemed important to the officer because it represented the fulfilment of a 'contract' entered into at the meeting; it certainly indicates one possible interpretation of the part the probation service (or another agency) might play in schemes emphasizing financial reparation; but it seems doubtful whether it is a role that a social work agency ought to accept (see Nelken in this volume).

Influence on the local criminal justice system

A major aim of the project from the start was to influence sentencing in the local courts towards a greater emphasis on reparation, which would be expressed in a higher use of compensation and community service, and a lower use of retributive or deterrent sentences, including custody. The senior officer in particular also wished to win general acceptance in the local criminal justice system for the principles underlying the project at the expense of those of deterrence and retribution. The research therefore included an effort to get some measure of the influence the project was having on other personnel in the local criminal justice system, including other probation officers as well as, obviously, magistrates, and other relevant figures such as police officers, clerks and solicitors. The limitation that the research covered only the initial period of the project's work needs to be kept in mind during the following discussion; changes certainly occurred after the first year, and indeed the magistrates' awareness of the project was heightened in the course of the research. Probation officers, too, became better informed about the project than they were at the time of the research, both because of efforts to disseminate information within South Yorkshire and because of the higher profile this and other projects achieved in the subsequent two years. It is less clear, however, that sentencing patterns have changed significantly, and the material presented here seems useful in indicating some of the difficulties of innovation in criminal justice, and may provide some guides to thinking about what can reasonably be expected from the continuing proliferation of mediation and reparation schemes.

It is more problematic to draw inferences about causes of changes in sentencing over a short time period than is often supposed. It is understandable that, for example, practitioners in a project intended to provide an alternative to custody should claim success if they find that the local use of custody has in fact dropped in the year following the start of the project compared with the previous year. But in the absence of supporting evidence it would not be justifiable to draw any such conclusion, since marked year-on-year changes in sentencing by any court can arise from a wide variety of factors, and the change may in any case represent a regression to the mean — in other words, the year used as a basis for comparison may have been statistically abnormal. Much longer time periods, and careful control for other variables, are necessary before changes can be thought of as trends, and before these trends can be confidently attributed to a particular cause. So it is not possible from a piece of short-term research such as this to do more than offer a few suggestions about the project's impact on sentencing, based on available figures and on the views of local criminal justice system personnel, especially magistrates.

After the project had been running for just over a year, the senior officer responsible for it claimed in the local media that a sentencing effect was observable, in that a higher proportion of 'reparative' sentences had been made in project cases in which there was a reference in the social enquiry report to contact with the victim than in those in which no such reference was made. This came as a surprise to some local magistrates, and particularly to the chairman of the probation liaison committee in Barnsley, who by any standards was a well-informed and committed magistrate, with a real interest in the work of the probation service. His reaction was that whatever had caused this discrepancy in sentencing, it could not have been magistrates' awareness of the project, since he believed that they were in fact quite unaware of it. After testing this view by a small survey of relevant magistrates, which revealed very patchy awareness of the project, he wrote a report in which he concluded that it would have been better for the magistrates to have been more fully informed about the project at its start, though this would not in itself have affected sentencing; that if no meeting between victim and offender had taken place, the sentence was unlikely to be affected; and that even when a meeting had taken place, the probation officer usually had 'a more optimistic view of the longer-term effect on the offender' and therefore took 'a more lenient approach to sentencing than the magistrates'.

These comments raise a number of issues. First, the project staff clearly overestimated the extent to which the magistrates were aware of their work and attributed to it an influence which the magistrates denied. This is not a surprising situation, as it is natural for people interested in innovation to hope that they are being influential, and to look for evidence to support their hopes. It does, however, highlight the importance in innovation of disseminating information about what is proposed to relevant parties; and this point seems to have special force for this project, since when it began the idea of mediation in criminal justice was much less widely canvassed than it has been since. Secondly, it seems doubtful that magistrates' sentencing would have been unaffected by their awareness of the project, since one could expect a 'Hawthorne effect' to operate — positively for magistrates who broadly supported the project's aims, negatively for any who did not. Thirdly, the comments suggest that sentencing could be affected by the victim's response to the offer of a meeting, rather than by anything within the control of the offender; mere willingness to meet on the offender's part would not count as mitigation. If this is the case, it raises issues of equity, since it might be thought wrong for the sentence to depend on the contingency of whether or not the victim agrees to a meeting, or indeed is available to be met. Finally, the comments suggest that reports by the project officers could contain recommendations that were out of line with magistrates' perceptions in a familiar way, with the probation officer suggesting a sentence that seemed inadequate to the magistrates on grounds of retribution, deterrence or the protection of the public.

There is evidence that in some cases the work of the project did influence sentences in the first year. The view of some offenders that it had indeed 'done them good in court' was mentioned above; that is, the meeting was counted as evidence of genuine remorse, sufficient to lower the severity of the sentence. This seems to have been particularly true of cases which went to the Crown Court. In this respect the project's effect seems similar to many other probation initiatives: a discernible influence in some cases is compatible with the absence of any overall effect. Indeed, it is theoretically possible that the project might tend in some cases to increase the severity of sentences, a worry which some probation officers expressed: since reports from the project contained much more detailed accounts of the perspective of the victim than is usual, magistrates would tend to be more sensitized to the damage done by the offence, and therefore inclined to sentence more severely. No evidence was found, however, to suggest that this was happening in practice.

The project staff formed a number of hypotheses about the influence they were having on sentencing, none of which was strongly supported by the evidence. For instance, it was hoped on the basis of the first year's figures that reports which gave accounts of successful mediation might lead to a lower proportion of sentences entailing long-term work for the probation service; if this was so, it could encourage a belief in the feasibility of generalizing the project's work, since resources could be transferred from long- to short-term work, rather than needing to be increased overall. But the second year's figures did not support this interpretation, illustrating the point about the risks of drawing hasty inferences. The most reasonable conclusion seems to be that the effects of the project on sentencing, at least in its first two years, were marginal. The lack of any quick effect should not be surprising; as its senior noted (Dixon, 1985), the project was attempting something inherently difficult — the introduction into criminal justice of a new language and a new set of concepts, in many ways at odds with traditional views of the aims of the criminal law. Dixon referred to: 'the problems associated with introducing notions of conflict resolution by means of mediation, compromise and consensus into a system which is expected to impose individual penalties through the exercise of power on behalf of the, state' and this formulation seems usefully to summarize just what is entailed.

Perceptions of the project in the local criminal justice system

The point about the difficulty of gaining understanding of the purposes of an innovative project — and the presumably greater difficulty of gaining support — applies equally to the discussion under this heading. The useful data relate mainly to probation officers, because at the time of the research other relevant parties had little knowledge of the project. Although their knowledge certainly increased later, it is significant of the need project staff continued to feel to make their work more widely known that one of the priorities for the last months of its life was to disseminate information about it within the South Yorkshire probation service. It seems appropriate, however, to start with the magistracy.

Two Barnsley magistrates (the chairman of the bench and the chairman of the liaison committee) were interviewed after the latter had begun discussing the project with his colleagues. The chairman of the bench had just discovered that he had in fact dealt with five project cases. Rather surprisingly, he said that even in retrospect he did not feel that the reports he had read in these cases were very different from the usual run of reports. He said of one report that probation had been recommended 'as usual' — in a case which he thought merited a custodial sentence. Of another, he said that since there had been no meeting there was nothing which could count as reparation, and therefore no reason why the sentence should have been influenced. His view was that the value of the scheme lay in the possibility it created for reparation; a mere apology was easily made, and was unlikely to influence the sentence. He and his colleague were therefore sceptical about the shift in the project's main aim from reparation to reconciliation. He thought that the scope of the project would be quite restricted, perhaps to 'subnormal' offenders who were genuinely unaware, until confronted with clear evidence, of the effect their offence had had on the victim. But he modified this judgement during the course of the interview, apparently in response to his colleague's more positive view of it, and said that it could have real value if it brought help to victims. Both magistrates, however, felt that from their perspective mediation and reparation were likely to remain of marginal importance; they drew a contrast with community service, seen as a major innovation. The chairman of the liaison committee mentioned the resource implications and was worried about whether the project was compatible with the *Statement of National Objectives and Priorities* (Home Office, 1984).

Other interviewees (a Rotherham magistrate among them) felt that they knew so little about the project that they could not sensibly express a view — an interesting research finding in itself, but not one that is amenable to extended discussion. For more informed views it is necessary to turn to the probation service itself. It was noted above that the practice of mediation did not spread beyond the project officers as much as had been hoped: only two other officers had any experience at all of arranging a victim-offender meeting. Interviews with officers in the teams focused on this lack of dissemination. Did it stem, for example, from general scepticism about the project's aims, or did they think, rather as the National Association of Probation Officers (NAPO) was suggesting, that the aims were not appropriate for the probation service? Or were more practical considerations, such as those of time and resources, the inhibiting factors? It emerged that while some officers were worried about some aspects of the scheme, there was no outright opposition locally to its basic principles. The factors which restrained officers from trying it themselves tended to be more practical in character. For instance, an officer who was well-informed about the project and much in sympathy with it said: 'I would like to see if it's feasible for the ordinary probation officer working in the field, rather than for someone that's just got a limited caseload ... You see, I find it a strain doing my work with mediation in the foreground, because it is a lot easier to go and do a normal social enquiry report — you don't get too involved, you're not under threat of getting too involved, so whilst I can see the benefits of it perhaps it is easier to slide back to doing traditional probation work ... It's not the caseloads that get in the way, it's the number of reports that come in. I mean if I had a glut of reports ... I would probably not even think about mediation, but if I was given one report a fortnight, something like that — it would be only by chance, these things happen that way — then I probably would do some mediation with them, and that's a worry because you're then singling people out by chance, just chance.'

She refers here to two common worries: that there is no time to do it properly, and that there are elements of chance involved which raise the possibility of random injustices. Time would only become available if there was a substantial reduction in the number of reports required of officers; even then there would still be a problem about multiple offences, with several co-defendants and probably more victims: '. . . the multi-offences and the multi-offenders — as far as I'm concerned . . . it seems to be too much work to do . . . I can't, I haven't the time to do it . . . We have had one where I think it was about fifteen offenders which . . . made three times as many victims. Well, even if you split the work up here I just don't think it would have been feasible.'

Like other officers, she was aware of a shift in focus from reparation to reconciliation, and regarded this as appropriate, especially for an area like Blackthorpe. She saw this not as a 'watering down as such, you're just making the most of what you're best at'. But the change raised the possibility that the project would not be as influential on sentencing as might be hoped. Officers agreed on the whole that sentencing effects ought to be an element in the evaluation of the project. A Rotherham officer, also sympathetic to the project and with some personal experience of mediation, mentioned his concern that the greater focus on the victim in project reports might lead to more severe sentences, especially in relation to compensation orders. He had clearly thought of the scheme as a means of influencing magistrates away from punitive sentences by offering reparation; he had been 'surprised' by the shift to reconciliation as the aim, and was 'wary' of the value of an apology in the eyes of the court. He found it difficult to see how mediation could be justified as a probation task if it had no impact on sentences, and had therefore come to feel uncertain whether it was an appropriate role for the probation service. He felt that this doubt was shared by colleagues, which was one reason why the project had become 'the property of three people'. He felt that the issues of arbitrariness and lack of equity referred to above were not peculiar to the project, since in any case what the probation service could do was 'dictated by the courts'; his uncertainty was focused on the question of sentencing, and he was not optimistic that even reparation would influence the courts in more than a small minority of cases.

Officers in the Wombwell and Rotherham teams were not always as clear about the project's work as might have been expected. For example, one officer regarded the move from talking about reparation as the aim as a merely verbal change: 'A rose by any other name . . . there's been no change in practice that I'm aware of'. Another officer said that she 'didn't know what to make' of the change in emphasis, but 'supposed it was for practical reasons'; she had in fact worked closely with one of the project officers in one case, and had thought that her colleague had persisted in trying to interest the offender in a meeting long after she herself would have given up: 'In time I might learn the art of being more pushy . . . experience in the project gives the confidence to push it . . . she has developed a very crafty — very different interviewing technique from normal'. Her tone here is perhaps half-critical, half-admiring; she seemed unsure that it was the right way to go about it — to 'push' — but she felt that the outcome had been very successful, and that pushing was an art that you might have to learn.

The project workers themselves had come to mediation by different routes — through experience in the previous special project, through an interest in involving the community, through victim support. The senior officer 'wanted to demonstrate that the idea was feasible at the heavy end, not just in minor dispute settlement. I didn't want two parallel systems, but to make the criminal justice system more reparative, and to make punishment secondary, rather than by-passing it as in community-based mediation . . . I didn't want us just to tinker with the periphery . . . There's a need to define what the conflict is in the first place, and to try to widen the range of significant definers . . . An act of faith is involved — you believe people can forgive and wish to resolve angry feelings; therefore they need to move out of role and meet as people. I think this faith has been borne out to some extent — apology and forgiveness have been made possible, and that is an important part of the healing process . . . Hurt cannot simply be translated into £.s.d. . . . The basic philosophy was about people's rights to be involved in events concerning them, not just as roles to be consulted . . . I wanted to put in a set of points on the tramlines laid down by SNOP [the Statement of National Objectives and Priorities]. The SNOP aims have limits. I want another line, looking at issues in a different way — not just alternatives to custody, but in a restorative frame . . . South Yorkshire is a good example — it's very well resourced . . . but three years ago it was one of five areas with above a 4 percent increase in the proportionate use of custody — despite all this we were bottom of the league . . . Why? Maybe all the eggs were in the wrong basket.'

What is sketched here, and has been elaborated in the project's reports and elsewhere, is a radical vision of how the criminal justice system might start to be transformed. Its radicalism might well alarm conservative defenders of that system (Powell, 1985); and indeed, there were occasions during the research when magistrates were clearly alarmed as they listened to such expositions. But the vision was tempered: 'My hopes haven't yet been realized. I'm frustrated in two respects. One is NAPO's decision to limit probation involvement — it bothers me because it will stop the expansion of schemes which would help people to look at it in a new way. The South Yorkshire scheme is the only scheme working and NAPO policy will restrict the development of the other nineteen schemes that are awaiting Home Office funding. The second frustration is . . . how can you make room for change in probation teams, and attempt to involve a wide range of teams so that the work will outlast the project? Non-project officers have hardly been involved at all not through lack of interest but through constraints on time . . . The problem is finding ways of giving them space. Otherwise the same will happen as to other things in probation that come up — if it's not to do with the main task it gets done at the end of the day. That's why I get steamed up — this is a way of redefining the major job, not a frill on the outside to help us do the main job more effectively. This is my main worry.' Only four schemes in the end received Home Office funding, though it is not clear that NAPO's position had much effect on this decision; and subsequent contact with the project suggested that the problems of finding time identified here had not been resolved by the time it ended.

How was the project experienced and understood by the two officers mainly involved in seeing how the vision might work out in practice? Both officers were thoughtful about their work and committed to it, but they differed in their accounts of how successful they felt they had actually been. The Rotherham-based officer, talking of the extent to which his initial hopes had been realized, said: 'From personal experience I haven't got very far, for two reasons, though there may be others. One, the dominance of commercial offences, meaning less personal involvement, and therefore it's more difficult to reach a meeting of persons. Two, a hang-up, a feeling I've been ham-fisted, and I think in some cases I have, because I've not had the confidence based on experience to be myself, because the experience hasn't been particularly confidence-building. I've been uncertain in my approach to mediation . . . but there are several bright spots — the other day in what appeared to be a dead loser, little sparks were flying, so I still feel hopeful . . . My approach will improve by being open about my experience — learning from others and experimenting myself.'

His Wombwell colleague, by contrast, spoke of her work with a good deal of confidence and conviction. She also commented illuminatingly on the reasons why some victims might not want direct practical reparation: 'I felt that more victims would want direct work or something actually done for them . . . but they don't. People do seem very satisfied by an apology, which at first was surprising to me but now isn't. It's partly because of the timing of my contact . . . it's too late, damage has been repaired. But I think it's partly also for a similar reason that a lot of people, when Scouts come round in Bob-a-Job week — you're suddenly faced with someone there saying, "Can I do something for you?" and you just can't think, even though maybe the week before you have been saying, "If only I had someone around to help sweep up these leaves!" It's that type of situation you're suddenly faced with. I think it's also linked in with the fact that they have someone they don't know around the place and feel they have to supervise it in some way.'

Like her colleagues, she was concerned about the effect on sentencing her reports might have, and thought that 'on one or two occasions' a more severe sentence than might have been expected had resulted; but she had come to think that the process of mediation had an independent value: 'It's an experience in itself and it involves a great deal of courage and strength to actually be able to cope with that. I think the majority of offenders feel that they have achieved something when they've got through the meeting, even apart from in court ... I would like to see it having some effect in court in terms of the mediation being taken into consideration, but I think that would probably be secondary to the views and feelings of the people concerned.'

The accounts obtained from victims and offenders suggest that she was right to emphasize the value of the process of meeting, and giving and receiving an apology. But her advocacy of mediation as being capable of producing outcomes which should be regarded as goods in themselves, even if they do not affect the sentence, raises more problematic issues, which are dealt with in the concluding section.

Conclusions

This section attempts to summarize the issues which have emerged in the discussion of the South Yorkshire project, and to relate them to more general questions raised by the development of interest in mediation and reparation. In South Yorkshire it was thought important that the work of mediation should be undertaken by probation officers; this was because of the project's ambition to begin to replace the traditional aims of criminal justice with its own emphasis on reconciliation and forgiveness. But for some advocates of informal justice the use of probation officers as mediators would count as a major criticism of the project. As Marshall and Walpole (1985) make clear, many other schemes regard it as essential that mediation should be undertaken by volunteers, ideally recruited from the same neighbourhood as the victim and/or offender, or at any rate by people who are not professionals in a state agency like the probation service — the Leeds scheme, for instance, used sessionally paid lay mediators, mostly recruited from the ranks of probation volunteers. This concern with de-professionalization is predictable, given the original inspiration of the movement in the critique of the bureaucratic and abstract nature of criminal justice. It may also be predictable because it would be less costly: Marshall and Walpole (1985) comment on this advantage. As the preceding discussion has shown, there are considerable implications for resources if mediation is to be done by workers who already have a wide range of statutory duties, and it is doubtful, to put it no higher, that it could ever become a normal part of (say) probation service practice without an increase in resources on a scale hard to see as realistic.

On the other hand, the South Yorkshire experience, in line with the experience of reparation in Corby reported by Blagg (1985), strongly suggests that successful mediation depends very heavily on the possession by the mediator of a level of skill, commitment and motivation which may well be rare among professional social workers, and can certainly not be assumed to be widespread among potential lay mediators. The Leeds scheme suggests that there may be a large enough pool of people with the relevant skills, motivation and time to make lay mediation feasible in some areas at least; and marriage guidance councils might provide more evidence that it is possible to find lay people willing and able to take on complex and emotionally demanding work, entailing both help and negotiation, on a scale sufficient to provide a consistent service. But neither in the Leeds scheme nor in marriage guidance do the lay workers come free; and marriage guidance councils have never provided universal coverage.

There is a more general argument against the use of probation officers or comparable professionals as mediators, connected with the problems that arise from 'bargaining in the shadow of the law' (Mnookin and Kornhauser, 1979). This shadow may well be more menacing if the mediator is the same person as the writer of a report which may well have an influence on the sentence of the court. This point has been strenuously argued by Davis (1982, 1985) in the context of matrimonial conciliation; he argues that it is just not possible to combine the roles of mediator and report-writer. The parallel between matrimonial and criminal courts is not exact, however: in matrimonial cases the report-writer's recommendation is highly likely to be accepted by the court, with immediate and drastic consequences, where the custody of children is concerned, for the parties involved. And the evidence from South Yorkshire suggests that while there is certainly a potential conflict, it is not an impossible one, if the mediator/probation officer has the skills and awareness needed to resolve it.

Davis and others would argue, however, that the conflict is broader than this, and relates to the fundamental question of whether the interests of victims and offenders are in fact compatible. The South

Yorkshire project, like many others, aimed to affect sentencing, and specifically to reduce the use of custody, and began with the assumption that successful reparation would need to be demonstrated if courts were to be convinced that a non-custodial sentence was appropriate. As has been shown, the aim shifted early on, so that reconciliation came to be seen as a valid end in itself; it seemed to be closer to what both victims and offenders actually wanted, especially in the closely knit community of Blackthorpe. But this position, however intrinsically appealing, is likely to be difficult for the probation service to sustain, especially in the climate established by the Home Office's prioritization of diversion from custody among the aims of the probation service. And if a mediation project were to show success in reducing the use of custody, it would be open to the charge of exploiting victims in order to benefit offenders (Reeves, 1984), since it is not clear how a victim benefits if an offender is diverted from custody. Even if a more 'therapeutic' view is taken of the aim of mediation, the ambiguity remains: is the meeting for the offender's benefit or the victim's, or can it somehow be for the benefit of both? The victim may be regarded as having been used if the aim is to reform the offender (a tempting and politically attractive view, but one resisted in South Yorkshire). And why should offenders wish for a meeting if they can envisage benefits only for the victim? These are real conceptual problems and ambiguities, but the South Yorkshire experience tends to show that they are not irresolvable — given, once more, the possession by the mediator of a high level of skill and awareness of the complexity of the process s/he is engaged in.

The problems of resources discussed in this paper are large and quite possibly intractable; they may well limit the feasibility of generalizing the experience of the South Yorkshire project to probation services and social work agencies elsewhere. But there is much about that experience that seems heartening and attractive — its radicalism, its risk-taking, the evidence emerging from it that conceptual difficulties, tensions and ambiguities can be largely resolved in practice. It seems right that the project's work should inform future debates on the possibility of developing less formal, bureaucratic and especially less coercive ways of responding to offences — and that these debates will take place, as the criminal justice system, now setting new records for incarceration, and no more amenable to effective participation by victims, continues to fail to meet even its own criteria of success.

7 Informal Justice: The British Experience

Tony F. Marshall

From contemporary literature and the stated objectives of schemes in Britain it is possible to identify twelve frequently cited aims (Marshall and Walpole, 1985; Davis et al., 1987). These can be classified as follows:

Traditional criminal policy aims
1. Rehabilitation of offenders.
2. Prevention of trouble (social control).
3. Economy of resources.

Non-traditional criminal policy aim
4. Diversion (but note dangers of latent net-widening or restricted access to law).

Community-related aims
5. Personal involvement.
6. Community involvement (and community control).

Service to individuals
7. Service to disputants.
8. Service to victims: (a) compensation.
                            (b) psychological benefits.
9. Service to offenders.

Longer-range community-service aims.
10. Promote constructive conflict management.
11. Teach cooperative methods and peacemaking.
12. Further reparative justice.

If we take mediation as the key feature of all the recent innovations — that is, non-judgemental third party intervention to facilitate the process of mutual resolution of differences between two parties — then it must be recognized that the idea is far from new in practice. Mediation is well established, generally in Europe and America, in the context of labour relations (for instance ACAS in Britain). There is general acceptance of the value of keeping industrial relations outside the courtroom, despite some reservations, as summarized in Marshall (1985). More recently, mediation has become prevalent in Britain, America, and many other countries, in the context of divorce proceedings, as a means of promoting consensual agreement on child custody and access (in far fewer instances, financial settlements as well) (see Parkinson, 1986). Neither of these will be discussed further here, as I shall concentrate on the even newer developments that relate, directly or indirectly, to the work of criminal courts.

The latter schemes divide rather clearly, on the whole, between those orientated primarily to disputes and those orientated towards offences. Although the two overlap, the distinction is important in terms of the derivation of cases — offences generally arriving via criminal justice agencies and disputes from outside the legal system. Although exactly the same precipitating behaviour may be involved, a prior classification of an incident as relevant to the forces of law may make a good deal of difference to the later process of mediation.

Almost all the dispute-oriented schemes in Britain are community mediation schemes. All of them take cases from a variety of referral sources — community agencies like Citizens' Advice Bureaux, social work departments, solicitors, police, and self-referral all being prominent. Involvement of either party is entirely voluntary. While one party will normally have sought the assistance of the scheme actively, typically the scheme will need to negotiate with the second party to obtain their involvement, and lack of co-operation on their part is a frequent source of case loss. Even where both parties are willing to talk to the scheme's volunteers, they may be less happy about the idea of talking directly to one another in a mediation encounter. The principle of direct negotiation involved in mediation is not one which people who have been in conflict for some time can readily contemplate. Once emotions have been aroused resort will usually be had to advocacy (by a lawyer or a community agency, such as CAB or a consumer department) and a one-sided adversarial battle.

The neutral mediator role is one, then, that needs to be sold, and it is noticeable that this has been achieved more readily in early American community mediation schemes (although even there it has been a problem) than in the first British counterparts, which have usually had to resort to go-between mediation instead of bringing the parties together 'round the table'. Although this may have something to do with the confidence of early schemes and the experience of their mediators, it also seems to reflect the ideology of the scheme itself — whether it sees itself as offering primarily a mediation service, or whether it sees itself as less committed to any one method of conflict resolution and more amenable to the predilections of the parties they are working with.

The Newham Conflict and Change Project stresses community education in constructive conflict management and party empowerment (in terms of skills and knowledge) and thus does not try too hard to impose any particular ideology in terms of how a dispute should be resolved. As a result, face-to-face mediation has been very infrequent compared to go-between mediation or working with one party to advise on effective negotiation. The second major community mediation scheme to be set up in Britain (one year later in January 1985), the Sandwell Mediation Scheme, has had a similar experience. More recent projects attempted to apply a stricter direct mediation approach, either on the American model (such as the Southwark and the Reading Mediation Centres, the first modelled on the American IMCR — Institute for Mediation and Conflict Resolution, and the second particularly fostered by local Quakers, conscious of Quaker schemes in the United States (Beer, 1986) from whom they received initial training), or on the model of divorce conciliation (such as the Bromley Dispute Settlement Centre, which takes referrals entirely from CAB). None of them, however, have yet been able to demonstrate any greater success in getting antagonists together round a table.

All the community schemes use volunteers from the local community to act as mediators, and to carry out the preliminary negotiations (which usually constitute the mediation itself in any case), after a period of training and practice using role-play. Both Newham and Reading projects employ this training as a wider educational device, whether for other schemes yet to begin operation or as a resource for organizations in their area. The Newham project, for instance, has set up courses in conflict management with local police, schools, and so on. One group, the Kingston Friends' Workshop Group, has also set up conflict management training for schools, with the co-operation of the local education authority, and is interested eventually in starting a school-based mediation scheme (Marshall, 1987a).

The management of community schemes is variable. Newham is the only project which is run by a committee of local residents (who are also the volunteer mediators). Although they employ a paid co-ordinator who takes a strong leadership role he is answerable to the committee and cannot act without their agreement. This reflects the origins of the Newham project in grassroots initiatives, rather than of a particular agency or group of agencies, which characterizes the other British schemes. The Southwark scheme developed from inter-agency liaison, with strong leadership from several local churches, and it is based on premises belonging to the local Methodist church. An active group of local volunteers has been recruited, but they do not dominate its management to the same extent as at Newham. The Reading Centre is run by a group of committed local people, among whom the Quakers have taken a leading role. The work of the Kingston Friends referred to above is carried out wholly by Quakers who are not professional mediators, but who have received some training through their American connections and have developed their own training manual for schools. Although they thus act in a semi-professional manner, their emphasis on training others (in a very simple way, accessible even to primary school children) makes the techniques generally available and they are thus not in any way exclusive.

Other schemes have their origins slightly more removed from the community. The Bromley scheme mentioned above has its origins in an initiative of Citizens' Advice Bureaux and uses specifically trained existing CAB volunteers. It takes referrals at present only from CAB. The Sandwell scheme was a probation service initiative, although the service does not actively interfere in day-to-day management, which is left to the paid co-ordinator in liaison with referring agencies and community groups. Apart from such liaison, however, community involvement is limited to the recruitment of volunteer mediators. A project recently started in Northern Ireland was the initiative of EXTERN, a voluntary organization with close ties to probation and the criminal justice system, and operates under the management of an inter-agency committee.

It is difficult to draw firm conclusions when most of these schemes have only recently begun to take cases, but the difference in origins seems to make the biggest difference to whether a scheme is concerned with community development over and above the mediation of specific cases, and much less to its method of operation, given that both Newham and Sandwell schemes in practice operate in similar ways (go-between mediation rather than direct), while Newham is distinct in its long-term orientation to cases and lack of emphasis on achieving a 'final' settlement.

The only other scheme in Britain which was explicitly oriented to disputes was the Juvenile Mediation Project of the Metropolitan Police, the only one which bore any real resemblance to the American Neighborhood Justice Centers. The idea came, indeed, from two researchers, Coline Covington and Sylvia Casale, who had had experience of this kind of scheme in the United States. They acted as consultants and researchers to the project, which was run by the police through inter-agency committees in two districts of London on a trial basis. Cases were to be taken from the criminal process, after a decision to prosecute had been made. If the offender (always a juvenile) and the victim already knew one another, and other circumstances were suitable, the two parties were given the option of proceeding to court or being diverted to mediation, when prosecution would be abandoned. Cases would only proceed to mediation if both parties agreed to this. Mediation was carried out by a pair of mediators, one a police officer not in uniform, the other a local volunteer, both trained specifically for the task.

The project had twin justifications: that offences involving acquainted parties are better dealt with by mediation than by adjudication, and that as many juveniles should be diverted from the criminal process as possible. The first rationale was held in common with the other type of dispute settlement scheme, community mediation, but the other was quite distinct. The Sandwell Mediation Scheme also takes a few offence cases on referral from police inter-agency juvenile panels (see below), but these are regarded as quite distinct from the project's normal community mediation work, and most of the volunteers recruited for the latter are not interested in carrying out victim/offender mediation.

The Juvenile Mediation Project (JMP), then, was a hybrid between the community mediation and criminal justice projects in much the same way as the Neighborhood Justice Centers. This made an important difference to the form that mediation took, which in the case of the JMP was distinctly more formal. Some preliminary negotiation was needed to explain the scheme to the parties and to obtain their agreement to it, but once this was done the emphasis was on setting a date for direct mediation and on settlement at this meeting of the relationship difficulties revealed by the offence. If such direct mediation was not acceptable to the parties the scheme would not be involved further in any way, and the case would proceed to court. This is distinct from community mediation where the mediator may negotiate between the parties or even work with one party alone to assist direct negotiation by themselves. Although the desire to settle disputes is shared, the JMP was also oriented towards settling offences and would not be involved in the former unless the latter could also be achieved. It was therefore primarily a mechanism for removing disputes from the criminal justice arena, rather than a mechanism for resolving disputes generally. Its prime aim may have been valid and useful, but selection of cases was thereby made in terms of criminal justice criteria and priorities, not those of disputants or the wider community. As offences, such cases may be important enough to warrant intervention, but, as disputes, they may be minor or unsuitable in some other way. Mediation was carried out not at the request of the parties initially — who may not have perceived such a problem — but out of the desire of the justice system to divert certain kinds of offence.

The distinction may affect not only the selection of cases, but also other characteristics of the project. Questions of fairness arise, for instance. An offender may agree to mediation largely as the only way to avoid going to court and gaining a criminal record. The fear of consequences may force him/her, especially as a juvenile faced, usually, with an adult victim and two adult mediators, into agreeing with reparative measures that exceed the burden a court may have imposed. This problem is obviated to some extent by allowing the child's parents to be present and to take part in the agreement, but this will only provide a safeguard if they take their child's part rather than that of the others involved, and one cannot rely on that. One can argue that such an extra burden is reasonable if the other party also assumes obligations to improve the state of relations between them, but it is an empirical matter to discover whether the original classification of such cases as offences — with victims and offenders — can be overcome so far as to be able to treat the case as a mutual issue. This would be crucial to the demonstration of the success of such a scheme in other than criminal justice terms.

There is an opposite danger, too, that offenders enter into mediation cynically to avoid prosecution and then refuse to come to any agreement with the other party, which leaves the victim with no recourse, having signed away any rights to a criminal prosecution. The victim may still have the option of a private prosecution or civil litigation, but neither is likely to appeal or to be a practical alternative. The police did retain the option to recommence proceedings if new information came to light bearing on the offence that made it too serious to ignore, but they did agree not to have recourse to such measures unless imperative, and not simply because mediation was unsuccessful.

In practice the scheme encountered problems from the start, because the basis of police decision making with respect to the prosecution of juveniles was altered radically at the same time, so that many more are now cautioned instead of going to court. Although this was formally coincidental, the willingness of the police to co-operate with both measures presumably had a common basis in attitudes at this specific time. This has restricted the number of possible cases for mediation to a very low level (four cases in twelve months). In effect, the diversion aim of the JMP was no longer so necessary, and the project was discontinued.

If it were desired to continue, one option would be to expand the scheme to adults, who are rarely cautioned at present; another would be to consider taking cases that are cautioned as well. If the latter is done, the rationale for committing resources to such intervention in terms of diversion would vanish, and there would need to be some prioritization of cases in terms of the salience of their dispute element. As parties will, without threatened prosecution, be under no pressure to accept mediation, the cases received may be only those where the parties themselves perceive a relationship problem with which they would appreciate help. In this eventuality the scheme could be fairer than when it was run according to its previous design, even though that design derived from a desire to ensure that resources were used solely for diversion and not for net-widening. This illustrates the problem that arises from trying to serve different ends that are not parallel. Net-widening is only a problem if one's aim is solely diversion — or non-intervention — but is irrelevant if the aim is to provide a service that parties willingly desire to use.

All other British mediation schemes are strictly offence, not dispute, oriented. Two types, however, although infrequent, are less intimately tied to the criminal justice system than the others. Both apply after sentence and therefore cannot impinge on adjudication. In one type the process is not tied to a particular offence at all. Mediation takes place between a group of offenders and a group of victims who have suffered from the kinds of crime for which the offenders were responsible, although not specifically at their hands. The intention is simply that offenders should learn to see their victims as real people who suffer and should face up to how they feel about the experience and the damage it has done them; and that victims are provided the chance of expressing their feelings and discovering what offenders are like, what motivates them, etc. Offenders should in theory be chastened by the experience and victims experience some catharsis, while they mutually come to some understanding and acceptance as people that enables both to readjust to normal community life. The first such scheme was set up at Rochester Youth Custody Centre, in liaison with the police and victims' support scheme, for young burglars sentenced there and groups of burglary victims that wanted to avail themselves of the opportunity (see Launay, 1985, for a fuller description).

Without the tie to particular offences, or to criminal justice, parties are free to enter or not into such a process entirely as they please and as they believe it will be advantageous to themselves. It thus has no overtones of hidden pressures or extension of punishment. It is also applicable to any offender who wishes to participate, whether or not his or her particular victim wants to, and to any victim, even if his or her offender was not apprehended. The disadvantage compared to the usual victim/offender mediation is that it is less personalized and probably less powerful in its effects, and does not allow participants to work out their own relationship, which may be important if they are likely to encounter one another again or already know one another. Other custodial institutions have also set up similar groups recently, while the Avon Probation Service has started them for offenders placed on probation. As anyone may be a victim at some time or another, such schemes, if much more prevalent, could provide a valuable learning experience for the public generally. In a way it could be claimed that such schemes, as well as not being dispute-oriented, are not even offence-oriented either, but problem-oriented, treating, say, burglary as a problematic issue and employing those with experience, as offenders and as victims, as well as the police representative who also attends the group sessions at Rochester, to co-operate in trying to understand the nature of the problem and how it might be prevented.

The other type of post-sentence scheme deals with particular offences, bringing the victim and the offender together, rather like the American Victim/Offender Reconciliation Projects, to tie up, as it were, the loose ends of the case after the criminal process has been concluded. Offenders get a chance to apologise and make reparation for what has happened, and victims get a chance to relieve their feelings and achieve equilibrium once again. Again, if there is any relationship between the two, including residence in the same area, there may be more practical achievements in preventing revenge or tackling some underlying relationship issues. As the meeting occurs after state agencies have made their decisions, there is no pressure on anyone to participate, and mediation should only occur when both parties see a real need for it and benefit to be gained. Nevertheless, it may occur a considerable time after the original offence and may for that reason be attenuated in its effects. Only one such scheme operates at the present, in the Rochdale and Bury area of the Greater Manchester Probation Service. It deals with only a small number of cases, as one might imagine given the lack of pressures to take part and the limited benefits for most parties. Even if a reasonable proportion of offenders may see benefit, and an equally large number of victims, the number of cases where both apply could be very small (for example, if one-fifth of either group might see value in it, only 4 percent of cases might involve both a willing victim and a willing offender). This problem of having to obtain the participation of two separate parties, compared to counselling and social work treatments that are carried forth with one alone, bedevils all mediation work and makes it difficult to obtain the number of cases that one might expect.

The bulk of mediation schemes in Britain are more closely tied to criminal justice than the above. One of the major types of these are the court-based projects very similar to the VORPs. While the R in

VORP in North America stands for Reconciliation, with its attendant community notions, the R in British schemes is almost always taken for Reparation, a narrower, more material notion that ties them in more closely with sentencing and traditional criminal justice concerns. While the American VORPs have found it necessary to remove themselves from the justice system somewhat by operating as voluntary organizations taking cases on referral, all but one of the British court-based projects is run by the probation service. Early experience in America led them to reject this model, but the different character of the probation services in the two countries, with the British service having more of the character of social work and less of the character of punitive supervision than its American counterpart, may mean that a probation base is more viable in this country. The process, centrally, is much like the American schemes, or the Rochdale/Bury project, in bringing victims into a face-to-face encounter with their own offenders, with a mediator to facilitate a reasonable exchange, and it has very similar intentions. The difference from the Rochdale/Bury case is that mediation occurs usually between conviction and sentence, during a period of remand for the offender. (In some cases it may not be possible to arrange mediation during the remand period and the scheme will report to the court that both parties are willing to take part, so that it may sentence, if it wishes, in such a way as to enable the mediation to occur.)

The one scheme run outside probation is managed by a voluntary organization, the Crypt Association in Wolverhampton. Mediation has been performed by the paid co-ordinator and by local volunteers he has trained. Referrals can only be obtained, of course, with the co-operation of criminal justice agencies — the courts, probation officers, lawyers, etc — and these have only been gained in the first year as the result of considerable effort at liaison. The evidence is that most probation-run schemes have readier access to referrals — although some of these, especially those with a lower profile, have had a similar problem of a low rate of referral.

The extent to which probation-run schemes involve the local community and attempt a degree of independence from the traditional system varies. The Coventry Reparation Scheme is run by an inter-agency committee, including community organizations. Containing representatives from all the important agencies, such as magistrates, justices' clerks, police, solicitors, it is a useful means of gaining access and co-operation, but it does mean that criminal justice concerns could still dominate the scheme. There is considerable doubt, even with this scheme, whether the most suitable cases are being selected, rather than those where the defence solicitor sees a chance of getting the offender a lighter sentence, or where the court feels the offence is not too serious, etc. The dependence on such agencies for selection, even if guided by the scheme whenever it gets the opportunity — although on very limited information, of course — does mean that the process is subject to the vagaries of personal opinion and imperfect understanding of the potential for mediation.

Mediation at Coventry is carried out by employed staff. Some, like Leeds and north-east Essex, use specially trained volunteers. The north-east Essex scheme also has particularly strong links with local victims' support, which enables it to put more emphasis on victims' interests than other projects. Although all the schemes aim to consider the victim and the offender as equal participants, selection at least is inevitably biased towards features of the offender, given that these are generally all that are known before the victim is contacted by the mediator. This is unfortunate but difficult to circumvent, especially without much wider coverage by victims' support groups. (It is very rare that a victim contacted by one of the reparation schemes has been visited by a victims' support scheme, even if there is one in the area; given the large number of offences they could potentially be dealing with (see Maguire and Corbett, 1987) it is unlikely that victims' support will be able to extend its services to a substantially greater number in the near future. It may be, of course, that the cases selected for reparation tend to involve victims who have suffered little and do not need victims' support. If this is so, then this would reinforce the suspicion that selection of cases for mediation is not working well at present, for it is failing to pick up those where there is particular victim need for such a service.)

The extent to which a scheme involves the community, especially in terms of volunteer mediators, does not appear to have a great deal of impact on its method of working. One of the most aware of its duty to the local community was the recently completed three-year pilot in South Yorkshire which used probation officers as mediators (see Smith, Blagg and Derricourt in this volume). As most of the victims they visited had not been assisted in any other way, they often found themselves providing information about various services for victims and also direct support, if only a sympathetic ear. It could happen, of course, that this effort created a positive image of the scheme which was more likely to persuade victims to take part in mediation, out of sympathy with the mediators rather than for any more substantial reason. Alternatively, it could induce victims to agree to mediation as a way of getting more attention and help from the scheme. The blurring of boundaries between different 'professions' — victims' support and probation — conflicts with the firm policy of the victims' support movement in this country in favour of independence from criminal justice agencies and the use solely of volunteers as visitors.

The director of the National Assocation for Victims' Support Schemes (NAVSS), Helen Reeves (1984), has already referred to the danger of victims being 'used' for other ends (the offender's or those of criminal justice agencies) which such obfuscation of boundaries could produce.

On the other hand, in the present situation of limited coverage by victims' support schemes, any help may be better than none, as long as the development of the voluntary service is not thereby hindered. (By highlighting the absence of support for the majority of victims it should, in fact, encourage such development.) In any case, the discovery of victims' unmet needs may be a valuable lesson for those working with offenders, and especially for those engaged in mediation between victims and offenders. It should increase their awareness of the victim's point of view and reduce their professional orientation towards the offender. In the case of the South Yorkshire project, this increased understanding has led them to a major change of emphasis away from reparation to mediation as the focus of the scheme, for in practice they found that victims were less interested in material compensation than in the sense of involvement they obtained, and other emotional benefits. Too great a stress on working out a financial settlement, or some equivalent in terms of work for the victim, may even interfere with these other, often more important, gains. In many ways a material settlement may also be the easier option for an offender to 'buy himself out', when a more general exchange may be a more powerful challenge to his/her attitudes and irresponsible behaviour. (For an example of the emotional impact on the offender, see the case study in Smith, 1986.) The adjustment in emphasis by the scheme has led them away from the traditional aims of criminal justice and forced them to abandon, at least as a major aim, the original hope that they would influence court sentencing in a reparative direction, for it is hard to get over to magistrates the salience of 'mere' discussion and apology compared to material commitments more akin to court sanctions of a fine or compensation order or community service. The South Yorkshire scheme has not been alone in this development away from traditional criminal justice ends; the experience has been duplicated to a greater or lesser extent by most of the other court-based schemes.

This even applies, perhaps, to the scheme which has tended to be taken as the 'hard end' of reparation in Britain, the Leeds project. This project was deliberately focused on more serious offences (and hence mostly works with Crown Courts rather than Magistrates' Courts). The rationale for this was contained in the emphasis on diversion from custody, a declared aim of the scheme from the beginning. The offenders should therefore be in danger of receiving custodial disposals, so that the reparation obligations voluntarily assumed could provide a direct alternative. The major bias this seemed to give in favour of the offender's interests occasioned considerable criticism from the victims' support movement. The pressure on victims to participate when a crucial decision on a person's future was at stake might be considerable. Paradoxically, however, the emphasis on more serious offences does lead to a greater likelihood of contacting victims with more substantial grievances and need for assistance than in other schemes which deal, by and large, with quite minor events and many victims who are not significantly upset. Moreover, the percentage of cases where direct reparative work for, or compensation to, the victim has resulted seems no higher than in other schemes. The fact that no higher a percentage of victims agrees to participate also indicates that the pressures to take part are not felt to be any greater in practice.

A scheme like Leeds could suffer the dilemma of being unable to divert from custody more than a small proportion of cases because victims concentrate on other purposes than material reparation in most cases (despite the fact that offenders would probably have been rather keen to agree to a material settlement as a more powerful influence on the court). Other schemes have also begun to move, where possible, to higher 'tariff' cases, for the concentration on minor cases, just as much as on serious cases, is biased towards traditional legalistic views and is irrelevant to the growing emphasis on victims' needs, which may occur at any level of offence seriousness and in relation to any type of offender, whether in danger of custody or not.

Other schemes that employ mediation in relation to prosecuted offenders are based on Intermediate Treatment (IT). Such schemes exist primarily in order to divert juvenile offenders from custody by providing intensive 'social work' which may take many different forms, depending on individual needs and the bent of the particular scheme. As part of their total battery of techniques many such schemes employ a reparative approach. They are limited to cases of re-offending by children already in their charge (who they might seek to prevent being brought back to court and sentenced to custody as 'failures' of the IT approach), or to other children brought up for sentence for whom the offer of intensive work, including reparation, may be sufficiently persuasive to the court to give them such an opportunity. IT schemes work with very small numbers of cases and their overwhelming orientation towards helping the offender moulds the concept of mediation in a particular way. A package of measures will often be agreed between the project and the victim beforehand, consciously aimed at the offender's reform, so that the mediation is less natural than it may be in other settings. Even though this may be seen as 'using' the victim, the fact that the offenders are juveniles may often occasion some sympathy and desire to help, the expression of which may be no bad thing and possibly even therapeutic. More information about particular cases would be needed to be clearer about the impact of such schemes (or indeed of any of the other types).

There are many similarities between reparation based on IT schemes, and that based on police juvenile panels, even though the latter are concerned with the decision whether or not to caution, and reparation is employed as an adjunct to caution and not in association with prosecution. Such panels, which have now been instituted by many police forces throughout the country, review all, or virtually all, cases involving juvenile offenders and advise on appropriate dispositions. The panels involve a number of agencies, most centrally the police and social services, but also quite often probation, education, education welfare and youth services. Their intention is explicitly to maximize the diversion of juvenile offenders from court by encouraging more frequent recourse to cautioning. Cautioning is reinforced as a viable option by offering back-up services (acceptance of which is voluntary for the offender) such as social work support. One of the possible back-up measures employed by some of these panels is the offer of arrangements for reparation, which gives victims a chance of satisfaction which they would ordinarily lack if prosecution is foregone. Where concern for the victim is one of the major reasons for contemplating prosecution, the offer of mediation and potential reparation may be crucial to police decisions to discontinue such a course. The Northants Juvenile Liaison Bureaux, situated in Corby, Wellingborough and Northampton, have achieved dramatic falls in the level of juvenile prosecutions (by 80 per cent between 1980 and 1985, see Bowden and Stevens, 1986), even before the recent Home Office circular (1985) recommending sparing use of prosecution for juveniles by all police forces. The Northants panels employ reparation where applicable, as also does the earlier scheme at Exeter (Youth Support Team), although it is only one tool in a whole battery of approaches that may be suggested.

More recent schemes that employ reparation as a major part of what the panel offers (for example, the Cumbria scheme funded experimentally for two years by the Home Office) are more difficult to evaluate for their effects because of substantial changes in 1985/86 in police force cautioning policies as a result of the Home Office circular. This serves to indicate, perhaps, that diversion could be achieved without the use of reparation or any other special measures, and its use in order to achieve diversion may only have been temporary. The Exeter team were concerned about the potential for net-widening, especially in view of the high frequency of first-time offenders in their earlier caseload, offenders who would normally have been cautioned anyway. They have thus decided to concentrate their reparation services on more serious cases, juveniles already known to the police, in order to maintain the centrality of their aim of diversion. The extension of this method of work to adults would provide a much better test of the potential effect of reparation on diversion, as the current rates of cautioning for older people are very low. One such scheme, the Kettering Adult Reparation Bureau, began operation in 1987.

In future, if the cautioning of juveniles becomes more regular, the chief rationale for offering reparation might become concern for the victim, who may be the only loser from the policy of fewer prosecutions. At present, the involvement of victims in the mediation process offered by the juvenile panels or bureaux is much less than it is in relation to, say, the court-based schemes. Direct mediation, for instance, is a relatively rare occurrence, and not one that is regularly sought. Normally a social worker will be assigned to talk with the juvenile and his/her parents and, if they agree to co-operate — as almost always happens — to visit the victim to agree a reparative package. As the offences are typically minor, and the offenders are in any case young and generally impecunious, the settlement will usually involve an apology delivered in person or by letter and little else, although some reparative work or compensation may be included, usually in the form of community work (gardening for an old people's home, say) rather than directly for the victim. As with the IT-based schemes, then, the dominance of the diversion motive concentrates attention on what can be done to influence the offender rather than help the victim, although the latter is a feasible aim in itself, given appropriate attitudes on the part of the schemes. If victims' needs become more prominent, one would expect the rate of direct mediation to increase also.

Achievement of aims by British schemes

In terms of the major aims incorporated into mediation schemes of all kinds, listed at the beginning of this section, current British experience can be summarized as follows.

Rehabilitation of offenders
This aim applies to all the criminal justice-based schemes, but not at all to the community mediation schemes, for whom the victim/offender distinction is not relevant. Insofar as schemes are achieving

more diversion, whether from court or from custody, rehabilitation may be assisted by slowing down the alienation and labelling process, but this is a tenuous argument which only really achieves credibility where the effect is not just on isolated decisions but on many such decisions in relation to the same individual over time. Not only prosecution and sentencing decisions are involved in the process of alienation, but many more informal and possibly more important decisions by ordinary members of the community: neighbours, parents and schoolteachers, for instance. To counteract alienation and work towards the reincorporation of the criminal deviant into the community will call for broad attitude changes that pass beyond anything formal mediation schemes can achieve alone, although they may serve to advertise the basic notions and thus help to bring about such changes in the long term.

More potent than mere diversion, it may be argued, is the experience that meeting the victim and carrying out reparative work affords in taking personal responsibility. It cannot be denied that in many cases the immediate effect on the offender is quite considerable. It is much more personal, direct and emotive than the usual encounters with formal agencies of justice, including even the effect of community service orders, the nearest approach to reparative justice that the courts currently control. Nevertheless, it must be questioned whether even such experiences can survive re-exposure to all the problems and influences that the individual faced beforehand and which helped lead him/her in the direction of crime. It is like a single sail on the horizon in the face of a relentless pounding of waves upon the shore. It will need a much greater frequency of sails to raise hopes significantly for rescue from the desert island of an antisocial career.

In a few cases, especially where work personally for the victim over a period of time is involved, mediation may lead to the creation of an actual relationship between the offender and co-operative community members which bears fruit in a major shift in attitudes and career, but only rarely will the coincidence of circumstances be just right to achieve such alchemy. In general, hopes for rehabilitation must rest on the general change in social attitudes that mediation schemes may ultimately seek to engender rather than on immediate successes with specific offenders.

Prevention of trouble
This aim is applicable to any type of mediation scheme which involves the parties directly in order to calm emotions and promote mutual understanding and some reconciliation. The perfunctory mediation most typical of the juvenile panel and IT-based schemes is unlikely to have any major influence on future relationships. Community media-

tion schemes, however, may well be able to re-orientate a conflict along more productive lines and prevent a deterioration into violence or continual unhappiness. Whether they do this in a superficial way that represses underlying problems or not, however, could be crucial to long-term effects, in that repression could lead to worse conflict in future than would have occurred without intervention. Given our lack of detailed understanding of how conflicts are caused and develop, current community schemes are at the forefront of gaining empirical experience that should ultimately enable realistic policy to be generated concerning the timing and shaping of appropriate intervention. Present approaches are 'rough and ready' and it would be unrealistic to evaluate their effectiveness at such an early stage, before they are reshaped and honed by experience (Marshall, 1987b). At present, the only safeguard against harmful intervention is the sensitivity and awareness of the mediators, which makes selection of volunteers and appropriate training vital. Slow development on a secure basis may be more productive in the long run than a sudden flush of wrong-headed schemes. Repression seems more likely where relationships are asymmetric in power, but current schemes focus predominantly on neighbour relations in which both parties are roughly equivalent, economically and in terms of skills. Where such equivalence is lacking it may be better to create specialist mediation schemes built to cope with the special features involved, as we already have distinct forums for divorce conciliation. Landlord/tenant, employer/employee, business/customer, parent/child, teacher/pupil, etc, are all types of dispute that may need specialist provision. They should not be allowed to dominate the caseloads of community mediation schemes (as, for instance, 'bad cheque' cases brought by business concerns against customers have come to dominate the Columbus, Ohio, Night Prosecutor's Program — 61 percent of all cases according to McGillis and Mullen, 1977; and as debt collection has tended to convert the original aims of small claims courts — Ison, 1972; Nader and Singer, 1976).

Victim/offender mediation can be similar to that occurring in community dispute settlement schemes where a prior relationship between the victim and the offender is the root of the offence, and the subject of the mediation is a dispute rather than the aftermath of crime. The problem of timing intervention, however, is less problematic, as this has already occurred to some extent, and expectations of some sort of short-term resolution created. Even where there has been no past relationship to speak of, the crime, by creating a potential relationship — the parties re-encountering one another in the same neighbourhood, the victim seeking revenge for the crime, the offender seeking revenge for being reported by the victim — can be a source of future trouble that mediation may prevent. Such effects could be more tangible than any long-term influence on the parties as individuals, such as rehabilitation. In the case of victims and offenders, for the most part, there would be no alternative forum for working out their differences. There would be a strong argument for postulating prevention of trouble as the primary aim of mediation in relation to victims and offenders, and attempting to employ it, at any feasible stage in the legal process (which proceeds at its own pace unrelated to extrinsic social developments) whenever there seemed to be some potential for subsequent disorder.

Economy of resources

The longer-term cost-effectiveness of new programmes is always difficult to establish. Mediation schemes could be financially justified in time if enough disputes were prevented from getting to the pitch that necessitated legal intervention. We cannot at the moment estimate such potential, however. In the short term community mediation, as a new service, inevitably involves more resources and increased costs, without any immediate compensatory savings. The only schemes that might be able to claim economies in the shorter term are those that directly divert cases from legal processing, and then only if the input of work costs less than what would otherwise have occurred. The police juvenile panel schemes save the costs of court adjudication for those cases they successfully divert, but given that they mostly involve minor offences, the time and cost savings are probably not large, while the time spent on negotiating reparation agreements is not inconsiderable, even though the latter is far less than in the court-based projects. Economies, even if they occur, therefore, will not be large. Moreover, the same rate of diversion could probably be attained even more cheaply without mediation.

The only schemes, therefore, that might justify themselves on economic grounds alone (in the short term) are those that achieve diversion from custody, which is a very expensive option. Even though considerable time may be spent in negotiations, this could probably be recouped entirely by saving one week's custody. It then becomes a matter of the rate of success in altering sentences to non-custodial ones, which depends on many factors — accuracy in selecting cases at risk of custody, percentage of parties willing to participate, percentage of mediations that produce agreements, and the ability of the agreements obtained to persuade a court to alter its decision.

Diversion

Some diversion from custody seems to be occurring as a result of reparation schemes. Substantial increases in cautioning have occurred, along with reductions in prosecution, for juveniles, but it has been argued above that this may have been achievable without reparation. It will be interesting to witness the success of the new Northants scheme in Kettering that will extend the juvenile panel idea to adult offenders. While there would seem to be more potential here for greater effect, one can expect a lower success rate in achieving either victim participation or police acceptance of alternatives to prosecution. There is little evidence of net-widening — in the areas covered by the Northants schemes the numbers of juveniles dealt with by the police overall have indeed declined (Bowden and Stevens, 1986). Insofar as the cases dealt with would have been cautioned in any case, there has been an increase in the resources devoted to intervention, but this may be justified by other gains — victim satisfaction, perhaps, or a more successful way of dealing with offenders. Altogether, it is doubtful whether victim/offender mediation can be justified solely in terms of diversion, and the latter aim may even interfere with its proper functioning by becoming the dominant concern of a scheme's practitioners.

Community mediation schemes are not, of course, predicated on diversion, although they may achieve this indirectly through early intervention and the prevention of violence. There is, however, a danger of such schemes restricting access to the law. Given police reluctance (traditionally at least, although attitudes may be changing in some areas now) to become involved in domestic violence cases, a community dispute settlement scheme might provide a ready excuse for referral that would maintain the low rate at which wife-battery reaches court. (While the women's movement strongly favours increased rates of prosecution for such offences, and one can see the justification for this in the effect it could have on general attitudes if the legal system dealt more severely with male violence against women, it is by no means sure that prosecution is at all beneficial to most individual victims, for it may well exacerbate the underlying problems. Firm police action and readiness to intervene to defuse critical situations, keeping both options of prosecution and referral to mediation or other assistance, according to victim preference, may be the ideal option. Such an arrangement would not restrict access to the law, but increase the powers of choice of the complainant.) Solicitors may also find referral to community mediation a useful means of avoiding involvement in unprofitable civil litigation of petty squabbles. Even so, the parties retain the freedom not to participate in such an option, and to maintain their right to go to law, while they at least have another option. Voluntariness can, however, be corrupted by the persuasive powers of other interested parties, especially where the latter are seen as knowledgeable or professional, and the actual use made of dispute settlement programmes will need to be scrutinized for such abuse.

Restriction of access to the law (for the victim) is always the obverse of the coin of diversion (for the offender). As the victim, in practice, gets little out of the criminal process, this may not be of great importance at present. Insofar as the victim does gain from prosecution, by obtaining compensation for material loss, reparation schemes at least allow for alternative means of recompense. (These do rely, admittedly, on the co-operation of the offender in carrying out the agreement, while a compensation order of the court is backed by further sanctions, although in practice there has been no major problem of default in reparation schemes, certainly far less than that pertaining to compensation orders, where it is about one-fifth — see Newburn, forthcoming).

Personal involvement
The legal process is a formal system. It deals with the potential for trouble between individuals by keeping them separate, and seeks fairness through uniformity and routinization that leaves little room for personal influence and creativity. There is little doubt, whatever else may be achieved, that mediation offers the parties immediately concerned a chance of personal involvement in a process that they can understand and influence. One of the major findings of Shapland et al. (1985) was that victims of crime missed such involvement in the aftermath of their own victimization. Mediation offers such a chance. The degree to which it does so depends on the role assumed by the mediator, the degree to which the third party manipulates and seeks to control the process and/or the outcome. Where the mediator acts largely as a go-between, he/she maintains considerable power over the process. Certainly personal involvement in the police panel schemes is not very substantial for the victim, although it may still be much better than no contact at all, while it makes few demands on the victim. Direct mediation, on the other hand, at least gives parties the chance to control their own interaction and thereby to gain much more from the experience. Blagg (1985) has raised the problem of the 'impersonal' victim — the corporate concern. In his study of the reparation process in Northants, he found that offenders were usually more affected by meeting a personal victim than the representative of a corporate body who had not personally suffered from the crime. Many schemes, however, have used mediation with corporate bodies to good effect, and the difference appears to rest on how the process

is managed and the commitment of the 'victim', rather than implying a blanket criticism of the involvement of all corporate victims.

In the case of community mediation where, as we have seen, go-between negotiation is often resorted to through lack of any other means, the same problem of third party manipulation may arise. It could also arise that the existence of such a scheme might induce people to seek intervention where they would otherwise have sorted matters out directly, thus reducing personal involvement. It would therefore seem to be a responsibility of community-based schemes to encourage parties seeking their help either to take part in direct mediation or to negotiate with the disputant themselves, after taking advice from the mediation scheme, and to be wary of 'taking over' conflicts from the hands of the parties themselves.

Community involvement
All the community mediation projects would endorse community involvement as a major aim and all employ local volunteers as mediators. The degree to which the local community actually controls operations, however, is variable. The Newham project, as we have seen, has taken the most determined strides to maintain community control. The problem, as with all voluntary organizations, is to maintain enough local interest and investment of time. The San Francisco Community Boards Programs expend a good deal of effort in encouraging a high profile in the local neighbourhoods and in trying to make their activities interesting and exciting for the average resident. There would seem to be no alternative to continued effort of this sort for any community scheme which valued being of and for the community rather than just in it.

A degree of community control is valuable in preventing the corruption of dispute settlement into a repressive mechanism of control by the state (although the opposite danger of local vigilantism has not yet been properly addressed). It is still possible to provide a valued service to local residents, however, without total local commitment and with some professional direction. Indeed, professional ethics and standards can provide the needed safeguards against corruption of a scheme's aims by any one interest group, and can avoid wasteful and debilitating involvement in local politics. In view of the argument above that no modern urban project can hope to be an entirely grassroots initiative involving anything more than a small minority of the local population, and certainly not a typical cross-section, a certain degree of professionalism may be essential. Every project will then be involved in a delicate balance of professional and community interests which cannot be solved by opting entirely for one or the other.

None of the victim/offender mediation schemes seeks community control beyond management by a local inter-agency committee of professionals or quasi-professionals. Some employ volunteer mediators, others professionals (usually social workers). Whether the employment of volunteers amounts to exploitation of a cheap resource or not will be answered in practice by the turnover of volunteers in reaction to the satisfaction inherent in the job. Direct mediation, as distinct from go-between negotiation, is often seen as a challenging and fulfilling experience by volunteers in the longer-running American schemes.

Although professionals introduce a personal service ethic and standards that may preserve a scheme from other interests, they may emphasize certain aims over others. The overwhelming interest of the social workers involved in juvenile panels and IT schemes in helping individual offenders and in achieving diversion certainly colours their activity so far as to place victims' interests somewhat in the shade. Court-based schemes, on the other hand, even though run largely by professionals (mostly probation officers), are able to maintain a more equal consideration of both victim and offender, given that there is usually only a vague goal in terms of affecting the ultimate disposal of the latter. The context of such schemes, however, within the criminal process, leads inevitably to a bias in selection in terms of the characteristics of the offender, which only very close active liaison with a vigorous victims' support scheme might overcome. At present, the development of victims' support has not reached such a stage that this is really possible.

Service to disputants

Only the community mediation schemes in Britain, plus the erstwhile MPD Juvenile Mediation Project, are primarily oriented to dispute settlement. The demand for such a service has yet to be measured. Inevitably growth has been slow at the beginning. The problem is not the lack of conflicts, but the difficulty in persuading people to adopt an unaccustomed non-adversarial approach to their disputes and thus to take responsibility for negotiating some kind of settlement. This appears to be particularly a problem in British culture, compared to American or Australian experience, but is not unique to this country.

Although it is not a primary concern, many of the cases referred to victim/offender mediation do involve related parties and the potential for dispute settlement, although this circumstance has only been sporadically capitalized on, given the dominant emphasis on agreeing reparation in order to make an impression on criminal justice decision makers. If, as seem likely, the emphasis on material reparation and on altering sentence declines, there will then be more scope to emphasize the underlying dispute and relationship problems, which may well provide a more relevant service to the parties, even if less directly relevant to the courts. The scope for diverting disputes from the criminal process has not yet been explored in Britain, in contrast to the United States. Strangely, there are indications that victims who already know the offender are less keen to engage in mediation than those who are strangers (O'Brien, 1986), such reluctance possibly stemming from the fact that some of them are not entirely guilt-free themselves, so that they may lose some advantage in shifting from victim to disputant status, from 'whiter than white' to somewhat 'muddy'.

Service to victims

There are two ways in which victims may be helped, materially and psychologically. The first is catered for to some extent within the present justice system, at least as far as offenders are identified and brought to trial. Mediation schemes are similarly limited to those victims whose offenders are caught and admit responsibility, although they can extend material compensation to cautioned cases. Even so, victims themselves often stress the emotional benefits over the material ones. In this latter respect the meeting with the offender is a unique experience which is apparently found very valuable to some victims. Exactly which victims benefit most, and in what circumstances, are issues with which the experimental schemes are only just beginning to grapple, however. Too great an emphasis on the offender has prevented many schemes from paying more attention to victims' benefits.

Service to offenders

Offenders may benefit by less rigorous treatment at the hands of the law, or by an experience which changes the pattern of their lives. Such benefits have been covered above — if, indeed, they are benefits from the point of view of the offender, rather than from that of others on his/her behalf. Diversion alone might be a mixed blessing; of short-term benefit but making no difference in the long run. The addition of the mediation experience to diversion, ensuring that, even if punishment is to some extent escaped, responsibility is not, may make the whole process much more meaningful, a learning process rather than just a sigh of relief. The greatest benefit that mediation may represent is as part of a process of reincorporation into the community to counteract the process of alienation that the offender has already begun to experience. As such it will probably only be really successful in conjunction with wider changes in how delinquency is approached.

Constructive conflict management
Mediation and reparation are technical words referring, respectively,
to a method of approach to intervention and an outcome of it. Both
are unnecessarily restrictive. In the United States, where there is
much more activity related loosely in some way to 'dispute resolution', a more general theoretical orientation is beginning to emerge
which is at present only glimpsed in a rudimentary way in Britain. It
would, moreover, be contrary to the flexibility and creativity of this
orientation to regard either mediation or reparation as defining what
one was trying to achieve. Both too easily come to be taken as
ultimate aims, when they are really only means to further ends or
possible options among many others. Mediation is only of benefit if it
provides something to the parties involved — the ability to perceive
the conflict for what it is and to be able to work with others, even
apparent opponents, for common ends. Reparation is of no value in
itself, but only achieves value in the context of an exchange which
affects the victim, and also the offender, beneficially.

Most schemes in Britain have found that they have moved outside
the restraints they imposed on themselves at the outset when they
have encountered, almost incidentally, cases which could benefit
from the approach they represented, even though outside the formal
criteria for acceptance. Thus the Leeds Reparation Scheme accepted
one manslaughter case for which the offender was already placed in
custody (that is without any prospect of diversion) because of the
potential for revenge and the unsatisfied emotions that were still
prevalent in the local community where the involved families lived.
The co-ordinator of the Wolverhampton project has attempted to
involve fuel supply boards, as frequent victims, not only in specific
cases but generally in a dialogue about possibilities for alternative
approaches for preventing or coping with the problems they face
continually. This more creative approach, passing beyond the mediation of a particular case, is one answer to the problems of meaningfully
involving corporate victims raised by Blagg (see above). As schemes
develop, it already seems inapposite to refer to most of them as
reparation schemes, in that reparation — of a material kind at least —
is typically involved in only a minority of cases, and even mediation
comes to occupy centre stage less often. The more general concept of
problem solving in collaboration with the involved parties may better
represent the orientation of the more mature projects.

Education in peacemaking skills
There are several ways in which current projects may contribute to
such general educational aims. Those that train volunteer mediators,
given the natural turnover among them, are gradually educating

more and more members of the general public in negotiation skills and in awareness of the potential (positive and negative) of conflicts. Others who take part as disputants or victims and offenders are also made aware of the potential for collaborative problem solving. Growing awareness of such schemes, especially in mass media reports, may also convey a general message that adversariality is not an inevitable result of differences. Nevertheless, the general impact of such schemes must remain extremely limited for the foreseeable future. Those who would take this particular aim most seriously will need to employ more direct educative approaches, especially using conflict resolution training in schools (see Marshall, 1987a), as the Newham project and the Kingston group are beginning to do.

Further reparative justice
The impact of most schemes on criminal justice agencies has so far been minimal. Although the juvenile panel schemes have fostered diversion from the court, reparation has only been a small element in the total effort. The influence of the court-based schemes on sentencing practice has yet to be established. In any case, as long as schemes connected to criminal justice remain committed to traditional justice aims — rehabilitation, diversion, etc — they will fail to challenge the underlying philosophy of the law. It is only as they gain experience and begin more positively to stress what they offer as something quite aside from the perennial concerns of formal justice that they may have an impact. As they demonstrate the need for victim involvement, the potential of positive orientations to crime and conflict, the importance of 'community' in its more general sense, and the power that comes from maintaining personal responsibility, not destroying it, then they may begin to define a new approach to justice.

Conclusion

What we witness in Britain at present in the name of mediation or reparation is diverse, fragmentary and tentative. There is little in the way of an integrated philosophy or a central core of concerted action. The only existing organization of practitioners and other interested parties that attempts to cross institutional boundaries is the Forum for Initiatives in Reparation and Mediation (FIRM), which is still small and building up its identity, and which until very recently, was run entirely by voluntary effort on the part of members. Although it has played an important role in keeping practitioners in touch with one another and in circulating information, it did not begin to assume any particular position — beyond advocacy of mediation — which might influence future development and give some thrust to the movement in Britain until it had been granted sufficient funds to set up a permanent office with paid staff in March 1988.

Its future success will depend on whether it can overcome its present condition as a pragmatic network of those who share an interest in a particular technique but who may not have any more general aspirations or aims in common. The situation in this country contrasts with that in the United States and Canada, where the 'alternative dispute resolution' — ADR — movement has a strong identity across all institutional boundaries, especially as represented in the National Conference on Peacemaking and Conflict Resolution, whose membership has grown exponentially since its first conference in 1983. While the British FIRM was, until this year, largely limited to people involved in community mediation or criminal justice reparation schemes, NCPCR has always been much more generalist, covering people mediating in organizations, international conflict, divorce settlements, labour relations, education, environmental and public policy debates, and so on.

The lack of any integrated philosophy in Britain has several drawbacks. It means, in the first place, that individual efforts tend to be unfocused, with eclectic adoption of any aims that offer themselves — so that it would not be unusual for a particular scheme to see itself as serving more or less equally all, or virtually all, the objectives discussed in the last section. Secondly, it makes it easier for schemes to be subverted to ends other than those with which they started, especially in reaction to the grassroots problems of obtaining funding and public acceptability. These latter forces tend to be 'conservative', in that it is easier to gain acceptance for something that offers a service for traditional objectives that everyone already understands and with which they can be readily sympathetic. It is thus easier to 'sell' a new scheme for, say, diversion from criminal justice, rather than, say, reparative justice or people's rights in their own conflicts. Callers at community dispute resolution schemes are more likely to be seeking advocates for their side of a conflict than a neutral party who will not take sides at all, as well as someone who will take the unpleasant business out of their hands rather than someone who will reinforce the need for their personal involvement and responsibility. Thirdly, the lack of any core theory makes it difficult to proselytize beyond existing boundaries, to seek out new arenas in which mediation could be as, or even more, important.

One can see the effects of this in Britain in the dominance of new schemes that relate to criminal justice and in the way they are in turn dominated by traditional criminal justice ends — in everyday practice, if not in theory — that is by the primacy of the need to divert offenders from the courts or by the desire to alter sentencing practice to reduce the punitiveness of disposals. It is this primacy of criminal justice ends that led to the demise of the Juvenile Mediation Project in London, not because it failed in its central aims of mediating relationships, but for quite extraneous reasons that it was no longer necessary to achieve diversion. Most of the diversion schemes, indeed, were instituted by those who were already criminal justice practitioners — social workers, probation officers, police officers — whose main motivation lay in their belief in the efficacy or propriety of diversion, rather than in the wider notions of conflict resolution or reparative justice. The lesser clarity and certainty of affecting the ongoing criminal process that applies to the court-based schemes has perhaps helped some of them shift from this emphasis to other concerns more freely — for instance to serving victims or promoting general social responsibility for crime. The schemes that seemed originally to be less of an 'alternative' because they did not divert from the courts, now appear to be more of an alternative because of their reduced ability to serve traditional ends and the necessity to emphasize different aims.

A fourth consequence of the fragmentation of mediation in Britain is the failure to realize the full potential for reform that the new ideas could represent. The terms themselves — mediation, reparation — have become too formalized, too reified, as if they were the ultimate ends themselves, rather than just means to something much more challenging. More important than terms such as these, if one is to see the emergence of 'liberating social control' or of 'new justice principles', is awareness of the more general value of 'co-operative problem solving' that injects meaning into these technical terms, by keeping to the forefront the central issues of participation, prevention rather than punishment, and flexibility (or creativity).

It is, of course, more difficult to evaluate performance in terms of aims such as these, which relate the worth of any particular outcome to the exigencies of specific cases, than in terms of more easily generalized measures such as numbers of offenders removed from prosecution. It would involve an analysis of individual cases rather than the usual statistical approach, for it is only in what actually transpires 'on the ground' that one can distinguish those features that make for more or less repressive or more or less liberating control, for democratic justice or otherwise. Despite the drawbacks of the present situation in Britain, the fragmentation that presently exists at least leads to a multiplicity of project designs and activities, and substantial freedom of choice in how they operate for members of the projects, whether professionals or volunteers, that at least contributes to healthy experimentation and a wealth of experience. The mere involvement of a greater number of people, whether of non-legal specialists or of laypeople, creates the opportunities for genuine reform, even if these are not always achieved and whatever the intentions of those who instituted the experimental schemes in the first place, as Cohen (1985) observes:

> The sheer statistical chance that community projects might be able to function in this way are increased ... by their very looseness and vagueness, by the fact that most of them do not actually have the slightest idea what they are doing. By being — however ambiguously — 'in' the community rather than behind closed walls, it is sometimes easier to assemble a package deal of useful services.

Without greater coherence, however, there is a distinct possibility of such experience being dissipated without the real lessons being learned. Mediation runs the risk of becoming yet another failed technique to be thrown in the dustbin of history, if its actual potential, that passes beyond mere technique, fails to be realized. To do that, practitioners will have to define their aims in their own terms, and not those of traditional processes based on a distinct philosophy and set of assumptions. Such independence from the established system is the only way in which practitioners can guard against the dangers of net-widening and increasing state intrusion (with their associated economic and social costs) that so many commentators have warned against, and also the only way that sufficient flexibility of approach can be assured that will allow adaptation to different cultural contexts and individual predilections of parties. As Blagg (1986) asserts in his review of Abel and Marsh's book *Punishment and Restitution: a Restitutionary Approach to Crime and the Criminal*:

> The present system would surely manage to assimilate material restitution within an unreformed punishment paradigm ... Victim offender mediation schemes have been running for some years and I was surprised that the authors did not make even passing reference to them. It is clear from victim surveys in this country and from evaluation of reparation schemes that a large percentage of victims do not want material recompense from the offender, but wish instead to have their anxieties about the offence resolved; something that can be best achieved by mediation. Similarly, offenders may be educated by this process more effectively than by any judicial and penal system, be it punitive or restitutory.

Independence of aims, however, does not have to entail the absence of material ties to formal justice. It is important not only to establish alternative systems but also to civilize existing ones, and this can only be done in interaction with them. In the case of mediation schemes, or any other projects involving co-operative problem solving, the essential independence comes from allowing all parties an equal share in, and commitment to, the process and its outcomes, which is the key principle in guarding against the substitution of one professional ideology for another (as social work treatment for legal retribution) that has dragged down so many other well-intentioned efforts at reform. While the Home Office Discussion Document relating to reparation (1986) mostly took a narrow view of its functions as yet another sentencing alternative, the response to that document indicated public interest in a wider perspective, which is reflected in any case in the range of experimental schemes funded by the Home Office and the research monitoring they are receiving. Until the findings of this research (see Marshall and Merry, 1988) and other independent evaluations, are available — and perhaps beyond then — the appropriate relationship between the new 'mediation' ideas and criminal justice will remain problematic. Although there is little sign at present that existing schemes are likely to offend principles of fairness and justice, or to extend state control, there is also little sign of dramatic achievements of a more positive kind, and much grassroots developmental work remains to be done to make the new ideas for dealing with crime and disputes operational and to match results to the degree of effort involved.

8 The Rise and Rise of Informalism

Peter Fitzpatrick

The Caliph Haroun el-Raschid was sitting in disguise one evening in a company of dervishes.
One of those present said:
'Rules can only function well with people for whom they were explicitly prepared.'
Haroun, who was dresssed as a visiting merchant, objected:
'But surely this is a dangerous doctrine, for it would mean, if believed, that people could deny that laws applied to them.'
A Sufi ancient who was present said:
'Such a lack of understanding is, in reality, rare. If, on one of his secret nightly visits to various parts of this city, the Caliph heard of the belief in the limitation of laws, he might indeed be shallow enough to summon us to answer the following morning at his Court. Otherwise, it is not harmful.' (Shah, 1974: 113)

There is a strangely persistent concern with the informal in the legal scholarship of the left. Again and again the informal has been dismissed as a mask or mere agent for such as state power or social control. Yet these very dismissals often accompany a vague and uneasy acclaim for some untouched core of informalism vibrant with unalienated humanity or integral community. Not only that, but explorations of the informal constantly and tantalizingly suggest that they could have something else, something fundamental to say about law: they throw out 'clues to the underlying fabric of contradictions and conflicts upon which the entire symbolic and operational edifice of the law rests' (Spitzer, 1982: 170). In this chapter, I want to unite a certain persistence of informalism with that 'something else', and to show that law and the informal are indeed fundamentally related.

At the outset, I position the argument in a first rise and reduction of the informal. Modes of dispute settlement alternative to formal law or, taking another example, the community as a site of penal practice were attributed by their advocates with a self-contained particularity and an inherent worth. Such assertions were soon met with devastating studies which reduced the informal to a simulacrum essentially contained or incorporated in encompassing systems of control, the state being the leading examplar. This divide between a self-contained particularity attributed to the informal and its reduction in terms of some other entity also characterizes a more recent use of the informal, which I call the new informalism. But the divide and these elevations of the informal do point towards a new perspective building on ideas of power. More particularly, they point towards two distinct but inseparable dimensions of power in modern western societies. One is a dimension of connection between powers in which they are combined as particular and distinct. The other is a dimension of coherence which unifies and condenses powers in hegemonic dominations. What I attempt here is not a dismissal but a drawing on previous work about the informal and the effecting, with Foucault's considerable help, of some axial shift in that work.

It is such an axial shift through focusing on simultaneous dimensions of power that brings a basic constitutive connection between law and the informal into alignment. This connection is elaborated in dual strands. With one, the informal is seen as created in law and in a liberal social ordering made by law. The other strand has the informal returning the favour, as it were, by maintaining the identity of law as liberal legality in the face of social relations otherwise destructive of that identity. I end with a practical analysis of what this relation to the informal says about a politics of law, about 'taking law seriously'. As for a politics of state law, I conclude with a barely qualified pessimism. But I do locate and explore intimations of optimism in a politics outside the state, a politics of alternative law.

Rise and reduction of the informal

The initial rise of informalism need not be observed minutely. It is well documented in acute critical studies and extensive bibliographies (Harrington, 1982, 1985; Marshall and Walpole, 1985: 67–89). In this manifestation, informalism covered, and continues to cover, many things. It extended to mediation and other types of dispute settlement alternative to traditional courts, varieties of delegalization and various, so-called community adaptations of penal and psychiatric regulation. These were seen as essentially alternative and resistant to formal systems and, usually, as operating in diminution of them. More positive bases for informalism were found in populist, even millenarian visions of community, humanity and tradition.

This idyll could, in academic terms, scarcely survive the ensuing onslaught upon it, notably in many of the penetrating analyses and revealing case studies in the volumes edited by Abel (1982a). These lines of argument see the informal as neither alternative nor resistant to formal systems of control but as contained or incorporated within state power or as providing a subordinated vehicle for its expansion. The experience of 'community policing' in Britain, for example, reveals not only the shallowness of community but the subjection of its remnants or pretensions to a more pervasive policing (Nelken, 1985). Other lines of attack see informalism as reinforcing oppression in sites of power besides the state. Mediation and conciliation in matrimonial disputes reassert and reinforce patriarchal and 'middle-class' values (Bottomley, 1984: Cain, 1985b: 336–40, and in this collection). What has to be appreciated here, and Cohen (1985: 83–5) makes the point forcefully, is that the family is not a site of power distinct from the state but a mode through which state power operates. Some accounts would deny the informal any distinct identity at all, seeing it not just as instrumental in the cause of an extensive formal power but as constituted by and within such power (Fitzpatrick, 1984).

The new informalism

Formidable as this critical array has been, its own ranks have harboured a persistent if uneasy dissent. Thus Abel leaves his devastatingly critical collection on informal justice on the line, 'the struggle for informal justice never ends' (1982d: 13). Critical legal scholars in the United States have condemned and advocated informalist solutions to present difficulties (Delgado, 1987: 312–15). Cain detects the occasional 'attenuated left-wing squeak of hope that by some dialectical feat a "genuinely" human and popular form of justice may emerge in spite of all' (Cain, 1985b: 335, and in this collection). But if we search beyond the critics of informal justice, we encounter not so much a squeak but a hydra-like roar. There is now a profusion of academic perspectives bearing on the informal — varieties of post-structuralism and post-modernism, of feminism and anti-racism, of hermeneutics and cultural critique. By and large, these would oppose surpassing reductions of the informal and would espouse difference and diversity. There is also sympathetic work not explicitly situated within these intellectual developments. The revival of the scholarship of legal pluralism, for example, has much in common with the pervasive post-modern temper even if the links between them have not actually been made. I will draw indicatively on these various sources to illustrate a new informalism. This will be in large part a factitious exercise because I want to show that, apart from its innovations, the 'new' informalism manifests much the same tension as that involved in the initial rise and reduction of the informal.

Legal pluralism has recently moved beyond the constant rediscovery of legal orders outside of the state towards delineating the interaction between legal orders, including state law, and towards locating elements of the informal embedded in formal state law (Allott and Woodman, 1985; Arthurs, 1985). These perspectives have been much refined in luminous recent work in the anthropology and sociology of law (Cain, 1986; Dezalay, 1985; O'Malley, 1987; Yngvesson, 1985). One significant strand of this work and of the revived legal pluralism questions the primacy and encompassing nature of the state and of imperatives of social control. This questioning is pushed productively in the direction of Foucault's ideas of power in Rose's work (Rose, 1986b, 1987). Particular sites of power such as psychiatry and the family have to be 'taken seriously' in their relation to law and otherwise. They are to be accorded a specific existence and not reduced in terms of a general social control. But they do not stand alone. They join with numerous other sites of power through 'links, relays and alliances' (Rose, 1986: 58). In this way they take on a general efficacy. For Rose, the dynamics of linkage move from within, and stay grounded within, the particular sites of power.

Other strands of the new informalism have sought to maintain a holistic position that is not inexorably reductionist but responsive to particular sites. Dialectical contradiction is a leading contender here. O'Malley (1987) looks at efforts relying on it and considers them, with justification in my view, to be mechanistic; in the result, they come closer to the reductionist response. Henry seeks to establish a more palpable mode of connection in the 'integrated theorizing' derived from his accounts of 'private justice' in the workplace (Henry, 1983, 1985). His 'central argument is that formal law and private justice are integrally related. Each is mutually interdependent upon the other'; but each retains also a 'semi-autonomous' nature (Henry, 1983: vii–viii). He establishes abundantly that state law 'penetrates' deeply into the rules, values, forms and procedures of private justice. However his guiding focus on private justice in the workplace does not enable him to complete the picture of interdependence, to make out that half of it is concerned with the penetration of state law by private justice. The surpassing position of the state thus tends to be confirmed. In Teubner's finely concentrated vision, law itself, as a possibly emerging 'reflexive law', is to provide an overall coherence of what he calls semi-autonomous sub-systems, or sub-units (Teubner, 1983, 1986). Contrary to its historic mission, law would 'restrain' itself and recognize that it could not control these systems or units. Thenceforth it would be confined to the co-ordination of action between and within them. With this scenario, the encompassing coherence provided by law would exist along with a heightened distinctness and autonomy of law and of these systems or units. This seeming paradox is reflected in my later argument. Santos has recently extended an invitation to an even more panoramic adventure (Santos, 1985). He seeks 'modes of production of social power and law' by exploring certain relations between four sites chosen because of a unique 'structural autonomy' he attributes to each. Although Santos does indicate some constitutive connections between these sites, and although the abrupt choosing and privileging of them does imply some wider structure, the picture is as yet radically incomplete. The sites remain essentially distinct within an attributed particularity.

In a more unrestrained mode Cohen has incorporated elements of the new informalism into his gargantuan restatement of the critical reductionist thesis of social control — a social control linking the particular sites in an encompassing unity (Cohen, 1985). A path-breaking variant has been created by Cain (in this volume). She approaches and definitively evaluates informal justice in a way that is 'standpoint-specific', the standpoint being seen as that of the working class. This, in terms of her title, is to move 'beyond informal justice'. Whether or not informal justice is then left behind may be beside her point. But operatively, the specificity of the informal is denied.

In short, the new informalism sustains a divide broadly similar to that which characterized the initial rise and reduction of the informal. On one side of the divide, the informal and sites of the informal are attributed a distinct, even autonomous, identity. On the other side, the informal and its sites are denied such an identity and reduced essentially in terms of some other surpassing identity. I now want to explore this divide, not to dismiss or dissolve it, much less to provide the resolution that it may seem to call for, but rather to see it and to see the work done around it as illuminating a key dynamic in modern modes of power. I will now start to do this by extracting two strands from Foucault's work on power, strands which are evocative of the divide.

Foucault and power

Foucault's ideas of power in modern, western societies derive from specific instances of its operation. Although often presented in terms of abstract generality, I take these as ideas, even descriptions, of the historically specific. They are set against the notion of power as merely or characteristically prohibition or coercion, that which is subjected to power being otherwise 'free'. Foucault seeks to counter the prevalent notion that 'power is essentially that which represses. Power represses nature, the instincts, a class, individuals' (Foucault, 1980a: 89–90). Such a repressive power is typified in the figure of the centralized 'Law-and-Sovereign' which occasionally and discontinuously intervenes in society (Foucault, 1981: 88–9, 97). This mode of power does retain significance in the form of law (Foucault, 1980: 144). But Foucault sees the more typical mode of modern power as positive and productive, as disciplinary and continuously regulative, and as pervasively and constitutively inhabiting social relations. One could instance a large range of overlapping powers dealing with crime and the prison, health, education, urban space, the control of mobility, recreation, morality, the workplace, the asylum, race and sexuality. Perhaps the most spectacular contrast Foucault provides is that between the conventional view of the negative repression, 'the refusal of recognition', of sexuality in systems of power in the west in the nineteenth century and the view in the first volume of his 'history of sexuality' which reveals the burgeoning of sexuality in this period in, and as a site of, 'public' controls and 'private' self-regulation (Foucault, 1981: 69).

In terms of its dynamics, 'power must be understood in the first instance as the multiplicity of force relations immanent in the sphere in which they operate and which constitute their own organization' (Foucault, 1981: 92). 'Force relations' would seem to be the basic encapsulation of the dynamics of power. These force relations find 'support ... in one another, thus forming a chain or a system' (Foucault, 1981: 92). They operate through 'strategies ... whose general design or institutional crystallization is embodied in the state apparatus, in the formulation of the law, in the various social hegemonies' (Foucault, 1981: 92–3). Such strategies incorporate and generalize, yet integrally depend on, local exercises of power (*e.g.* Foucault, 1981: 99–100). Although I will put some emphasis on generalizing and cohering elements, this should not obscure Foucault's prime concern with the 'manifold' nature of force relations nor be seen as a counter to his denial of 'the primary existence of a central point', or to his denial of the containing locus of a 'unique Law-and-Sovereign' as the source of power (Foucault, 1981: 91, 93). Rather, '[p]ower comes from below; ... the manifold relationships of force that take shape and come into play in the machinery of production, in families, limited groups, and institutions, are the basis for wide-ranging effects of cleavage that run through the social body as a whole' (Foucault, 1981: 94). Power is domination but it is not solely binary, to be exercised by one who has power over the other who has not. Rather, power is relational and in this subject to constant modifications and continual shifts. It inheres as 'relations of power' in all other social relations. Such relations of power 'are the immediate effects of the divisions, inequalities, and disequilibriums' occurring in social relations, 'and conversely they are the internal conditions of these differentiations'; relations of power have not 'merely a role of prohibition or accompaniment; they have a directly productive role' (Foucault, 1980: 94).

This emphasis on particular relations and local sites of power is not to deny general 'major dominations' sustained by them nor, apparently, does it run counter to the characteristic concern of modern forms of power with the ordering of whole 'populations' or 'societies' (Donzelot, 1980; Foucault, 1979b). Rather, the linkages between general dimensions and particular dimensions of power are integral and inseparable. Thus the general type of modern disciplinary power is constituted by and constitutes a host of particular relations which, for example, generate detailed regulations of 'personal' health and of sexuality. Through a 'micro-physics' of power, discipline pervasively and intimately informs social relations, even those of the most 'private' and 'personal' kind.

Power's ineluctable reach appears to leave little, if any, scope for resistance. Indeed, it is a common view that for Foucault power is not only pervasively and amorphously inescapable but ultimately irresistable (Dews, 1979; Poulantzas, 1978: 149–51). Yet Foucault's ideas on power and of the efficacy of resistances were not always consistent. I would like to suggest that they contain a productive contradiction, one that can be explored in building on Foucault's 'theoretically unelaborated' (Dews, 1984: 90) notion of resistance.

For Foucault '[w]here there is power there is resistance, and yet, or rather consequently, this resistance is never in a position of exteriority in relation to power' (Foucault, 1981: 95). The very existence of 'power relationships . . . depends on a multiplicity of points of resistance: these play the role of adversary, target, support or handle in power relations' (Foucault, 1981: 95). Although contained within power, resistances are 'inscribed' in relations of power 'as an irreducible opposite' (Foucault, 1981: 96). So, although it is 'in' power, resistance cannot be reduced to it. As with power, there is no comprehensively dominating centre but rather 'there is a plurality of resistances' (Foucault, 1981: 96).

But Foucault also seems to conceive of resistances as 'in a position of exteriority in relation to power'. In the same account of resistance as plural and as internal to power, he says that there can be a 'strategic codification of these points of resistance that makes a revolution possible' (Foucault, 1981: 96). The point at least suggests that resistance is not ultimately contained within power relations but can in ways be 'exterior' to them, and be autonomous and outflanking of power. There is also an unresolved naturalism in Foucault's work, one strand of which would posit a pure, seemingly innate type of resistance to power, the resistance of the body and the resistance of the 'pleb', a type that ceases to count as resistance as soon as it engages with or is in complicity with power (Foucault, 1980: 138). Less spectacularly, and less clearly, there are miscellaneous mentions of resistances which seem to be in essential ways external to power. Foucault saw his genealogies, his particular histories of the conditions of emergence of sites of power such as the penitentiary and the asylum, as 'bringing into play . . . subjugated knowledges', the knowledges of historically and institutionally suppressed people, and these knowledges fuelled 'criticism' of and 'struggles' against power (Foucault, 1980: 82–5). In a related vein, he advocated more general 'antiauthority struggles' such as 'opposition to the power of men over women, . . . psychiatry over the mentally ill . . . of medicine over the population' (Foucault, 1982: 211). He also looked 'towards the possibility of a new form of right' with which to resist disciplinary power (Foucault, 1980: 108).

Counter-power and syncretic power

I will develop two dimensions of power suggested by this account: one a dimension of connection between distinct powers, the other a dimension of coherence serving to unify them. For that dimension of connection, I will continue with Foucault's intriguing location of resistance in and outside power and the related notions of resistance as compromised by and yet opposed to power. For Foucault there is not a settled structure or hierarchy of power pointing it in the one direction. Power is made up of 'the disjunctions and contradictions which isolate . . . [force relations] from one another' (Foucault, 1981: 92). Power relations are not 'univocal'; 'they define innumerable points of confrontation, focuses of instability, each of which has its own risks of conflict, of struggles, and of at least temporary inversion of the power relations' (Foucault, 1979a: 27). Power, it would seem, resists power. Discarding the dubious possibility of some naturalistic nihilism, I would argue that an act of resistance entails, even if sometimes implicitly, some positive project of power which engages with and seeks, at least in part, to reverse or modify the power it opposes. That engagement will, in turn, act back on and shape resistance. So, resistance is in power not just negatively 'as an irreducible opposite' (Foucault, 1981: 96). It is also in power positively and supportively as counter-power, and as counter-power, as another power, it will also be outside power. As Foucault has it, powers find 'support ... in one another, thus forming a chain or a system' or they are isolated from one another by 'disjunctions and contradictions' (Foucault, 1981: 92). What I am arguing is that they can be in both situations at once. That is, a power exists in conterminous relations of opposition and support with other powers.

In its relations with a counter-power, I would argue that power operates, usually simultaneously, in two broad modes and relations of domination: that of inclusion and that of exclusion. Power includes counter-power by disaggregating and appropriating elements of it, transforming them in its terms of power. In the mode of exclusion, power seeks to deny counter-effects, or significance or even existence to counter-power remaining external to it. Counter-power, for example, is often denied by being presented as inert nature: on the constitution of 'the feminine character', Adorno notes that '[w]hatever is in the context of bourgeois delusion called nature, is merely the scar of social mutilation' (Adorno, 1978: 95). Or counter-power is contained in so-called small-scale sites such as the modern family. Or a counter-power is isolated from, even set in opposition to, companionable counter-powers, especially where these could all take on a challenging unity in their resistance to power: divisions along ethnic or racial lines provide an example that is both commonplace and monumental.

It follows that the existence or significance of counter-power is not to be measured in empirical presences. Whether or not a counter-power has or is denied a certain operative form, whether or not it operates in isolation from other counter-powers are not issues simply 'internal' to the counter-power. Form, scale and position are themselves effects, and usually connected effects, of power, of the relations between counter-power and power. The more telling a counter-power, the more fundamental its challenge, then the more it has to be denied significance or even existence. Measures taken within power to constitute counter-powers as small-scale or to deny them operative form, or to divert their cumulative impact will, in turn, shape power itself. Take the often-asserted weakness or inchoate nature of capitalist class formation, especially of the proletariat, in many nations of the so-called Third World. Some would thus assert that such class division is of minor significance and that ethnic division is more central. But ethnic division is central in large part because it is a response to challenges, and potential challenges of class (Fitzpatrick, 1980: 18). This defence has, in turn, profoundly shaped the nature and operation of the power of imperialism. As well, such power derives contents from counter-power. Ethnic division, in this example, is not just the creation of this power but also something appropriated from 'outside' it. The constitutive history of a power and of its containing forms is constrained and complex:

> Thus the whole history of a thing, an organ, a custom, becomes a continuous *chain* of reinterpretations and rearrangements ... [This history] is a sequence of more or less profound, more or less independent processes of appropriation, including the resistances used in each instance, the attempted transformations for purposes of defence or reaction, as well as the results of successful counterattacks. (Nietzsche, 1956: Second Essay, XII, his emphasis)

Let us look at two hard cases to illustrate the argument, cases of the extreme denial of operative form or even of existence to counter-power. E.P. Thompson's studies of 'the moral economy of the English crowd in the eighteenth century' find a coherence, effectivity and moral restraint in forms of popular protest labelled as mobs and riots, as 'loose and disorderly', by rulers, and as spasmodic, instinctive and even degenerate by historians less inspired than he (Thompson, 1971, 1978). There was, he finds, a reciprocity between a dominant and a popular power basic to that social formation. Domination certainly was domination but it was bound in terms of its ties to popular power. If these terms were transgressed, the crowd sought to enforce them. Dominant elements who tried to profit from breaking these terms, as they increasingly did, were met with assertions of popular justice, assertions of a general view of society, of social morality and responsibility, supported by extensive organization and extensive strategic knowledges. Although indigenous, these resources creatively and conveniently absorbed elements of dominant culture: thus we have 'the consciousness of the "free-born Englishman", who took to himself some of the constitutionalist rhetoric of his rulers, and defended stubbornly his rights at law and his rights to protest ...' (Thompson, 1978: 158). Yet this definitional relation contained also an essential opposition, for 'the plebeian culture' was in part constituted by 'antagonisms to the definitions of the polite culture' (Thompson, 1978: 161).

The second case of a provocatively extreme 'informality' comes from the colonial situation, a situation in which the very ability of the colonized to act in a formal, systematic framework is denied. Colonial constructs such as law, a foundational mode of the civilizing mission, can operate only *on* the inert, diffused mass of the colonized. In a study of transformations in forms of law and of labour in Papua New Guinea, I have presented a dramatically different picture (Fitzpatrick, 1987). The very exercise of colonial power provoked counter-powers which were extensively and effectively organized. These powers, in turn, drew on vital traditions pre-dating colonization. Although for the colonists these counter-powers were aberrant, insignificant or non-existent, it was the same counter-powers that entered constitutively into colonial power providing a prime impetus for what humanity, fairness and universality law had in that situation. It was the barbarians who provided these elements of civilization which the colonists claimed as their own essence and prerogative. But the transformation of law through counter-power operated back, as it were, on counter-power. It was now accorded some legal recognition, as regulated trade unions, and thereby partly assimilated and neutralized within colonial power.

A power, then, takes identity in modes and relations of inclusion and exclusion, of fusion yet separation. For convenience, and for short, I will use the term syncretic power for this dimension of integral connection between power and counter-power. The term is meant to bring out the key element of connection and of combination of things *as* different and distinct. For that other dimension of power, a dimension of coherence which seeks to unify component powers into a singular power and which I will now explore, the term synoptic power will be used. As with the syncretic dimension, an element of combination is imported but one which here makes for some condensed generality drawn from different powers: such powers are invested with a certain definitive unity. Like 'the synoptic gospels', they can be seen as arranged from the same point of view.

Synoptic power

Powers do not support each other in singular, meandering connections, nor do they stand in random opposition. 'Domination is in fact a general structure of power' (Foucault, 1982: 226). And powers do, in Foucault's scheme, configure in 'hegemonic' dominations (Foucault, 1981: 94). I will develop the point in terms of the idea of synoptic power. A synoptic configuration of power in this hegemonic sense can be seen, 'in the sphere' in which it operates (Foucault, 1981: 92), as occupying the field, more or less successfully, and organizing the action of subjects or the subject, more or less comprehensively. This picture of synoptic power must not be 'overstructured'. Such power can be a loose, labile configuration despite, and even because of, its claims to comprehensiveness. It does not exclusively contain or exclusively give definition to its constituent powers. Nor is it a settled resultant but, rather, it and its configuring powers are constantly resisted. Contrary to its frequent claims, such as those of the nation-state, it is not a supreme organizing authority. Nor do the different spheres of synoptic powers relate in a hierarchical way. The sphere of the nation-state, for example, overlaps with but cannot contain all the powers brought to bear in the sphere of the capitalist economy and neither of them can completely encompass the sphere of the family or the individual.

The essence of synoptic power lies not only in its generalizing, encompassing dynamics. It is also a synopsis, an operative representation of its component powers or sites of power. The key to this ability can be found in Foucault's revelatory emphasis on a certain materiality of power (Foucault, 1982: 217, 219: see also Giddens, 1981; Mann, 1986). When explicitly addressing 'power', Foucault is constantly concerned with its 'mechanisms', 'procedures' and 'techniques' (e.g. Foucault, 1980: 92–108). It is in the modes of modern power most compendiously described as disciplinary, modes of surveillance and normalization for example, that an adequate synopsis can be constituted. That is, such modes enable the generalizing synoptic dimension of power to draw on yet sustain the particularities of its syncretic dimension. The modern individual provides a telling example. Disciplinary power provides techniques which render everyone notable in their individuality but which also produce the individual as integral, as a normal, sound character (Foucault, 1979a: 191–3). 'The individual ... is not the *vis-a-vis* of power; it is, I believe, one of its prime effects' (Foucault, 1980:98). These techniques operate in the most general dimensions yet they are also oriented towards the creation of a 'voluntary' self-responsibility on the part of the subject — self-identity and self-control being inculcated, for example, in extensive social campaigns ostensibly aimed at securing probity in sexual relations (Foucault, 1967: ch. 9; 1981). In the creation of the self-responsible subject, these techniques can operate in most intimate, tentacular and pervasive ways that rely on and invest even the closest social relations. The new modern individual was free but it was 'a culpable freedom', one attended with 'the stifling anguish of responsibility' (Foucault, 1967: 182, 247): '[m]en were thought of as "free" so that they could become *guilty*' (Nietzsche, 1968: 53, his emphasis). In short, subjectification was integral to and a condition of subjection (Foucault, 1981: 60).

This line of argument is pivotal and I will borrow another example to take it further. The modern family can be seen, with Donzelot, as having been constituted 'as a positive form of solution to the problems posed by a liberal definition of the state' (Donzelot, 1980: 53). In operating through the family, the state couples its effects with relations internal to and distinctive of the family, relations with a necessary autonomy in their connection with the state: 'It could even be said that this familial mechanism is effective only to the extent that the family does not reproduce the established order, to the extent that its juridical rigidity or the imposition of state norms do not freeze the aspirations it entertains ...' (Donzelot, 1980: 94).

Combining the two dimensions of power, a synoptic configuration of power can be seen in its particularity as itself a power entering into syncretic relations with other powers. It includes elements of other powers, of counter-powers, shaping them and according them some counter-identity or, to borrow a phrase, a relative autonomy — an autonomy relative to the terms of that sphere of synoptic power. This is not simply a matter of powers being reduced to the encompassing content of a sphere of synoptic power. The modes of modern disciplinary power create integrating homologies between different sites of power, yet in this very process enable them to remain differentiated. Further, the inclusion of counter-powers does not exhaust the syncretic dimension of power. An appropriating power also excludes elements of counter-power which remain 'counter, original, spare, strange'. I will now extend this analysis to an exploration of the mutual constitution of law and the informal.

Law and the creation of the informal

Law provides the form of that synoptic power configuring in the 'liberal' state. 'According to the rule of law, in the liberal-bourgeois state the law must do everything and therefore it can do anything' (van den Bergh, 1984: 35). Law becomes 'an immanent principle that unites the parts into a whole, that makes this whole the object of a general knowledge and will whose sanctions are merely derivative of a judgement and an application directed at the rebellious parts' (Deleuze and Guattari, 1983: 212). In this, law relies integrally on disciplinary power to constitute a massive, non-rebellious normality. To dramatize the point in a contrary case from Kafka's 'The Great Wall of China', there can be 'no contemporary law' where '[l]ong-dead emperors are set on the throne in our villages, and one that only lives in song recently had a proclamation of his read out by the priest before the altar' (Kafka, 1961: 78, 80). The pervasive, normalizing effects of disciplinary power are the necessary 'dark side' of law (Foucault, 1979a: 194, 222). Liberal legality would prove too delicate for a society founded on coercive authority, were not this authority embedded indistinguishably through discipline in the domain of the normal, of the unremarkable. The actions of individuals need only be forcibly constrained, and can only legitimately be so constrained, through forms of the 'rule of law'. Law marks out an area of action in which the subject is 'free' to accept the dictates of disciplinary power. It is thus constitutive of the free-acting individual, the individual 'as posited by nature', as the 'starting-point of history' (Marx, 1973: 346). This is the individual who is 'the *vis-a-vis* of power' and who is essentially apart from it. In terms of an alternative formulation, power as the rule of law is of the 'public' domain. It occasionally intervenes as coercion in an autonomous 'private' domain in which the subject is otherwise free. Such interventions can only be through law and, in this, law is constitutive of the domains of the public and the private and provides the line and the ties between them. Power is, in short, presented through law as a negative constraint leaving intact an otherwise unbounded freedom, and so the coercive operation of a positive creative disciplinary power is masked and rendered acceptable (Foucault, 1980: 104; 1981: 86, 144). The form of power, the source of its homogeneity, its guiding metaphor and its 'truth' are found in 'Law-and-Sovereign' (Foucault, 1981: 88–9, 97).

In this way, law creates both the general space of the informal and forms of the informal. The informal exists in a clear domain of non-power, a domain of freedom. It is founded on the self-realizing individual who is located outside power and unbounded by form. It is the free individual who voluntarily agrees to and constitutes such informal modes as mediation and conciliation, 'private justice', the consensual community, and behaviour modification 'contracts' with welfare agencies (as to the last, cf. Nelken in this volume). Such an individual cannot be a disordered maverick. The subject must assume a complex self-responsibility, an assessing, ordered and ordering self-conception: the subject 'must have become not only calculating but himself calculable, regular even to his own perception, if he is to stand a pledge for his own future as a guarantor does' (Nietzsche, 1956: Second Essay, I). But what of the usage of 'informal' in relation to processes and standards operating integrally within frameworks of legal coercion? Administrative tribunals may, for example, be absolved from following formal rules of evidence and be allowed to follow more informal procedures, or administrative regulation may contain a large measure of informal negotiation (Harrington, 1987). To take another example, broad standards, as we will see later, about what is 'reasonable' and such allow power to enter as informal into law. All these adventures in the informal posit and seek the same thing: a realm where people are or could be truly, or even normally, themselves, a realm apart from the artifices of form, a realm of a natural and undifferentiated reality. Only here can we find, for instance, 'what a dispute is all about' or 'actual substantive relationships in ongoing communities' (Lempert and Sanders, 1986: 478).

But far from being outside power, it is in the very arrogation of such an un-formed, such a limitless realm that disciplinary powers can be brought to bear yet denied — and denied, in particular, as constitutive conditions of law. The informal itself thus serves to deny the integrity of that community, that realm of the private (and so on) of which it is supposed to be an essence. Critics of informalism have indeed recognized the informal as mask or mere agent for some site or type of power. But where, as in the reductionist invocations of social control or the state, such power is itself accorded a limitless and intractable dimension, the underlying terms of informalism are confirmed. This is not to deny significance to the reductionist vision. The family as 'private' and 'informal', for example, does operate as a conduit for state power (Cohen, 1985: 83–5). In the syncretic dimension of power the state does include the family. But what enables the state to do this is not simply a power distinct to itself. Rather, the state draws on and gives effect to precise modes of power, of legal power and disciplinary power, which are neither wholly contained within the state nor themselves limitless. The state can, drawing on disciplinary power, operate through the family *as* different and distinct. This is not an ultimate appropriation by the state of the family's identity. In the syncretic dimension, the state excludes elements of the family, elements which sustain the sphere of the family in opposition to the state, and such opposition has indeed been effective in countering the state's efforts to incorporate and utilize the family.

The informal and the integrity of law

The informal can also be seen as created through law and as sustaining the integrity of law by buffering the oppositions between law as synoptic power and law as sycretic power. As synoptic power law assumes a universal, encompassing aspect and the ability, potentially, to 'do anything'. In its syncretic dimension, law is a power constituted by the limits drawn in its relations with other powers. The informal, in its flexibility and intangibility and in its evocation of the natural, provides modes accommodating the oppositions between these dimensions of law. This line of argument has, in effect, just been illustrated with the informal 'coming between' law and disciplinary power, maintaining the integrity of law as synoptic power in the face of its syncretic-type dependence on disciplinary powers.

Such modes of accommodation are of two broad, overlapping kinds, both operating in the dynamics of syncretic power. One could be called a mode of reduction and disaggregation, the other a mode of mediation. I will take certain constitutive connections between bourgeois law and the wage-labour relation as instancing the first mode. The exchange of commodities, including labour power, is a basis of law, as liberal legality, from which it derives elements of the freedom and equality of the legal subject (Pashukanis, 1978). But in the capitalist mode of production, exchange is integral to production and within the labour relation production is based on a hierarchic subordination of the worker. If, in seeking to 'do anything', law enters the labour relation directly it courts two dangers. One is the legal compulsion of workers which would undermine their 'free' status and thus undermine a basis of law. The other danger is the importing into the labour relation of the elements of the freedom and equality of legal subjects within law, thus undermining the domination resident in immediate relations of production. The opposition here is reduced and, in class terms, disaggregated through the individual as the ultimate site of the informal. As an embodiment of the limitless range of the informal, the individual can 'freely' join the community of the workplace and agree to the subordination characteristic of the labour relation. A more precise and localized instance of accommodating the opposition between law and the labour relation can be found in Henry's penetrating case studies of the use of law in 'workplace discipline' in Britain (Henry, 1982). When law was used to regulate the labour relation internally, it did so not in direct but in oblique and truncated ways which skirted the opposition just outlined. In this, it drew on elements of informal ordering, of 'private justice', existing or incipient in the workplace. There resulted, Henry found, some 'tension' between the involvement of workers in such informal ordering and the potentiality that that had to 'undermine management's ability to control' (Henry, 1982: 374). But such challenges were reduced and disaggregated by using the intangibility of the informal to restrict workers' involvement to procedural matters, thus avoiding any substantive engagement with the terms of immediate relations of production (Henry, 1982: 375–7). In this account, the element of counter-power in the labour relation was made effective in the assertion of workers through 'informal' processes in the workplace. These processes were disaggregated and reduced, thus enabling elements of them to be incorporated supportively into law. 'Substantive' elements which would challenge domination within immediate relations of production were excluded.

In the mode of mediation, elements of power which would challenge law's synoptic integrity are rendered informal. To stay with the same opposition for examples, the power of employers in the labour relation is taken sympathetically into law in processes of conciliation or through lay members of tribunals being appointed from within 'industry'; or the rationalities of domination are absorbed in broad adjudicative standards, in what is 'reasonable', 'justifiable' or 'fair' (Fitzpatrick, 1987). These infinitely responsive processes and open, yet irreducible, discretions serve to avoid any definitive testing of law's power in its connection with the labour relation. They effect the obfuscating entry into law of what the power of the capitalist 'is all about'.

I would like finally to explore what this analysis has to say about the politics of law. I will have to argue for pessimistic cautions about the prospects for 'struggles' in or around state law or about the promise of 'taking law seriously'. Various optimisms are, however, then located in a politics of alternative law.

Informalism and the politics of state law

Powers constitutive of law are integrally linked to 'external' counter-powers and this relation could provide an entry and support for effecting change in or through law. Identifying the impact of such a counter-power could well reveal areas that are unsettled and provide focal points for implementing change. To return to Henry's case study for an example, that 'private justice' in the workplace reliant on the participation of workers if pushed by them beyond procedural matters could more significantly confront and change the legal–economic domination of capitalism.

Even that tentative optimism must be inhibited in its application to informalism. Informal modes of accommodation operate not by recognizing opposition and seeking to resolve it. To do that would be to recognize limits on law's necessary integrity as synoptic power. Such modes of accommodation operate by denying the existence or significance of the opposition. The dynamic of denial here comes from law itself. One could then hardly expect law to recognise counter-power adequately, much less give full effect to it. Indeed it could be argued that the greater the challenge from counter-powers, the more will there be a resort to obfuscating modes of accommodation. Hence, with the advance of disciplinary power, Cohen notes the increasing 'blurring' of boundaries between formal and informal modes of control (Cohen, 1985: 57, 69, 83–5). There are also other modes of obscuring the opposition besides, if often related to, the informal. There is, for example, the identification of judges with the power of a dominant class and the permeation of that power through the manifold and irreducible discretions of the legal process (Fitzpatrick, 1987). And ultimately, should challenges become established in law, law does not cede their ultimate origins outside its own self-regulation, and it makes their existence contingent on change or abolition through legislation or some other purposive 'sovereign' process.[1] In all, law in its necessarily synoptic dimension is radically inadmissible to any assured appropriation in its syncretic relations.

But there is a perversely positive 'moral' to the story. In one way the point is obvious, even tautologous. The effectiveness of a counter-power that becomes engaged with law cannot be assured in law. It can only be assured if the terms of the engagement are adequately set and supported outside law. To work through law there must be a basis in counter-powers against law. In this light, Cain's advocacy and analysis of a 'standpoint-specific' approach to informal justice can be applied to formal law as well (Cain in this volume). Santos provides an exciting account of this line of argument in action with his study of how squatters in Recife, Brazil, defended eviction proceedings against them (Santos, 1984). The squatters who were successful first set and then sustained the political terms of their engagement with law and constantly sought to subordinate law and its powers to those terms.

Informalism and alternative law

The work of Cain and Santos points towards a positive politics of informalism, one which is projective in its sustained appropriation of power. It contrasts sharply with the informal as an absence of power or as a mere conduit for its operation. Such a politics would, I suggest, nullify the informal as an essentialist notion and reveal it as an effect of relations of power. This would also lead to the identification of counter-powers otherwise denied or obscured in the domain of the informal. Might not law inhabit and give effect to such counter-powers? It is the finding and the viability of such alternative law that will concern me here.

There are problems about appropriating the idea of law. To accept much that is usually taken to typify law would be to cede the terrain at the outset to the self-presentation of liberal society. Alternative legal orders could either be constrained in attributed characteristics of bourgeois law or they could be found deficient in lacking such characteristics, thus confirming those claims of superiority or exclusiveness intrinsic to bourgeois law. The challenge of alternative legal orders to the arrogation of power in bourgeois law would thus be blunted or denied. What may be required is an idea of law adequate to that challenge. 'Law' need not continue to reside definitively with the state. Such a location is not a matter of eternal definition but is itself a political appropriation. Law, or elements of it, can be added to such instances as 'individual conscience, norms of sexuality, the security of a population' as 'constantly being "turned around"' between power and counter-power (Gordon, 1980: 256). Indeed, if we set aside those sociological and jurisprudential arrogations of law as simply emblematic of 'society', law is revealed as an object of unresolved contestation between different sites of power and not as located definitively with the state. The negation of form or the attribution of the informal are ways of denying law, or law of a comparable power, to the opposition. Arthurs's study of the battle over law between professional lawyers and reforming administrators in nineteenth-century Britain graphically makes the point (Arthurs, 1985). But it may be that the idea of law as integral is not redeemable, in which case we could try to locate social-legal practices of, for example, legislating, causidical reasoning and hearing disputes. As an expedient, I will adopt that course here. But this does not end the difficulty. Law's definitive association with the nation-state involves a reduction and rejection of counter-powers, including their legal elements. The consolidation of bourgeois law entailed 'a strange mixture of historicism and juridical positivism which is reduced to negating every law except the official law' (Pashukanis, 1978: 69). An adequate search for alternative law must follow the plangent absurdity of trying to find what is not and to find out why it is not. In this chapter I do not take the search much beyond intimations of what is not. But the search does clearly link up with political dimensions of that 'new informalism' outlined earlier.

We may look for encouraging indications in places where the vitality of alternative traditions and the relative absence of disciplinary power have restricted the ability of state law to present an adequate synopsis of power and society. 'Alternative courts' comprehensively challenging state law now abound in India. They often operate not only to settle disputes but as a focus for a general alternative ordering (Baxi, 1985). Santos has provided a case study of how an urban community in Brazil constructed its own legality counter to, yet drawing on, state law (Santos, 1977). Christie finds intimations of counter-power denied in the popular vitality of a court hearing in Tanzania (Christie, 1977). This prompts his vision of the appropriation of conflict by 'professionals' in western societies as denying people their 'property' in conflict, denying them popular legal powers involved in dealing with conflict, and these are the sorts of powers — 'a potential for activity, for participation' (Christie, 1977: 7) — which would widely challenge hegemonic dominations. What could add further point to his argument is that the hearing and settling of disputes is something 'ordinary', non-professional people seem to do well (Garlock, 1982). In western societies it may well be that the pervasiveness of disciplinary power and its constitutive effects on the individual promote popular legal abilities.

Disciplinary imperatives of self-responsibility and self-control import an 'internalization of the juridical instance' (Foucault, 1967: 267), one in which the subject is invested with that autonomy and that capacity for sustained self-evaluation necessary for these attributes. There are a great diversity of conflicting powers and counter-powers that come to bear constitutively on the subject. Those disciplinary powers which Foucault sees as constitutive of the subject are diverse and conflicting enough, but there are other varying powers to be added to these which are constitutive of and call for a 'free' subject. Legal subjectivity itself is a site for the operation of power, the legal subject being constituted historically in terms of subjective responsibility, of facilitative, self-realizing power and of individual autonomy. The subject has then to be enormously skilled and paradoxically powerful in her/his own subjection, in organizing and sustaining some stably operative unity of a multitude of divergent powers and effects of power. The necessarily evaluative, distanced, even critical element of 'the juridical' and this ability of organization could be seen as capable of being 'turned around' and countering other elements of subjection.

What is, I hope, starting to emerge is a picture of the denial of alternative law, not because it has been rendered insignificant in modern society, but because it is so significant. As I argued earlier, and illustrated in the connection between class and ethnic identity in the 'Third World', the more significant a counter-power the more will it be denied significance in its opposing power. That is good reason for not being inhibited about seemingly speculative conjunctions. To return again to Henry's example, the extension of worker involvement in 'private justice' beyond procedural matters could draw on 'substantive' normative regulation of the workplace and challenge the imperatives of domination in immediate relations of production.

Conclusion

Positively then, the informal can point towards power, or counter-power, denied. There are obvious difficulties in proceeding with this search for silences. Even scholars committed to such searches can see their object as something unformed and inferior in its 'pre-political' and unorganized nature (e.g. Hobsbawm, 1959: 2; Scott, 1985: 33). There are triumphant exceptions. E.P. Thompson's studies of the organization subsumed and denied in the 'mob' and the 'crowd' were considered earlier. Increasingly, these silences are becoming eloquent with previously unrecognized significance and form in studies of the extensive organization of popular resistance, of politically coherent cultures and even civilizations of resistance, and of 'hidden histories' and 'subjugated knowledges' (see e.g. Gilroy, 1982; Nandy, 1984; cf. Foucault, 1980: 80–87). The critical and political potentialities of this work are manifold. It locates sites of counter-power denied and extracts their effective forms. Resistance, as counter-power, is shown to have a constitutive hold on and a potential to challenge that power being resisted. The hidden terms of the engagement between such resistance and power are made explicit and subject to contestation. Rather than being contained passively in the intrinsically informal, resistance is freed to join supportively with other counter-powers in incipient hegemonies. All of which may be more in the nature of a prospectus with pockets of progress than an extensive achievement. But enough of this work has been done to justify continued emulation of Rushdie's large-nosed hero in his ability to 'sniff absences through the walls' (Rushdie, 1982: 435).

Notes

Rarely can conviviality and intellectual excitement have been combined so generously as in the Amherst Legal Process Group, for whom much of this paper was first prepared. Thanks also to Christine Harrington, Alan Hunt, Boaventura de Sousa Santos, Fariborz Shafai and David Sugarman for invaluable comments.

1. Laws that are constitutionally entrenched may give some greater security for a politics of law if it is difficult to amend the constitution. I am grateful to Stuart Scheingold for this point.

References

Abel, R. (1980) 'Delegalisation' in E. Blankenburg, E.K. Jansa and H.R. Hleuthner (eds), *Alternative Rechtsformen und Alternative zum Recht*. Westdeutscher Verlag.

Abel, R. (1981) 'Conservative Conflict and the Reproduction of Capitalism: the Role of Informal Justice', *International Journal of the Sociology of Law*, 9: 245–67.

Abel, R. (1982a) *The Politics of Informal Justice*, 2 Vols. New York: Academic Press.

Abel, R. (1982b) 'Introduction', in R. Abel (ed.), *The Politics of Informal Justice*, Vol. 1. New York: Academic Press.

Abel, R. (1982c) 'The Contradictions of Informal Justice', in R. Abel (ed.) *The Politics of Informal Justice*, Vol. 1. New York: Academic Press.

Abel, R. (1982d) 'Introduction' in R. Abel (ed.) *The Politics of Informal Justice*, Vol. 2. New York: Academic Press.

Abel, R. (1986) 'The Transformation of the American Legal Profession', *Law and Society Review*, 20 (1): 1–14.

Abel-Smith, B. and R. Stevens (1967) *Lawyers and the Courts*. London: Heinemann.

Adorno, T. (1978) *Minima Moralia: Reflections from Damaged Life*. London: NLB (Verso).

Allott, A. and G.R. Woodman (eds) (1985) *People's Law and State Law: The Bellagio Papers*. Dordrecht: Foris.

Arthurs, H.W. (1985) *'Without the Law': Administrative Justice and Legal Pluralism in Nineteenth-Century England*. Toronto: University of Toronto Press.

Auerbach, J. (1976) *Unequal Justice: Lawyers and Social Change in Modern America*. New York: Oxford University Press.

Auerbach, J. (1983) *Justice Without Law?* New York: Oxford University Press.

Bankowski, Z. and G. Mungham (1976) *Images of Law*. London: Routledge & Kegan Paul.

Bankowski, Z. and J. McManus (1983) 'Lay Justices in Scotland: a Study of the District Courts', unpublished ms, University of Edinburgh.

Bankowski, Z. and G. Mungham (1981) 'Laypeople and Lawpeople and the Administration of the Lower Courts', *International Journal of the Sociology of Law*, 9: 85–100.

Bankowski, Z. and D. Nelken (1981) 'Discretion as a Social Problem', pp. 247–68 in M. Adler and S. Asquith (eds), *Discretion and Welfare*. London: Hutchinson.

Baxi, U. (1985) 'Popular Justice, Participatory Development and Power Politics: the Lok Adalat in Turmoil', pp. 171–86 in A. Allott and G.R. Woodman (eds), *People's Law and State Law: The Bellagio Papers*. Dordrecht: Foris.

Beale, H. and T. Dugdale (1975) 'Contracts between Businessmen: Planning the Use of Contractural Remedies', *British Journal of Law and Society*, 2: 45–60.

Beer, J. (1986) *Peacemaking in Your Neighborhood: Reflections on an Experiment in Community Mediation*. Philadelphia, PA: New Society.

Bell, K. (1969) *Tribunals in the Social Services*. London: Routledge & Kegan Paul.

Bergh, van den, G.C.J.J. (1984) 'What Law for Whose Development? — Some

Theoretical Reflections on Law and Development', pp. 29–44 in *Unification and Comparative Law in Theory and Practice: Contributions in Honour of Jean Georges Sauveplanne*. Deventer/Netherlands: Kluwer.

Berki, R. (1986) *Security and Society: Reflections on Law, Order and Politics*. London: Dent and Sons.

Blagg, H. (1985) 'Reparation and Justice for Juveniles: the Corby Experience', *British Journal of Criminology*, 25: 267–79.

Blagg, H. (1986) 'Review of *Punishment and Restitution* by C.F. Abel and F.H. Marsh, Greenwood Press', *British Journal of Criminology*, 26: 303–6.

Blankenburg, E. and U. Reifner (1981) 'Conditions of Legal and Political Culture Limiting the Transferability of Access to Law Innovations', pp. 217–43 in M. Cappelletti (ed.), *Access to Justice and the Welfare State*. Florence: Le Monnier.

Blegvad, B.-M. (1983) 'Accessibility and Dispute Treatment: the Case of the Consumer in Denmark', in M. Cain and K. Kulcsar (eds), *Disputes and the Law*. Budapest: Akademiai Kiado.

Boigeol, A. (1984) 'French lawyers', paper prepared for a meeting of the Working Group for Comparative Study of Legal Professions of the ISA Research Committee on Sociology of Law, Bellagio, Italy (first draft).

Bottomley, A. (1984) 'Resolving Family Disputes: A Critical View', pp. 293–303 in M.D.A. Freeman (ed.), *State, Law and the Family, Critical Perspectives*. London: Tavistock.

Bottomley, A. (1985) 'What is Happening to Family Law? A Feminist Critique of Conciliation', in J. Brophy and C. Smart (eds), *Women in Law. Explorations in Law, Family and Sexuality*. London: Routledge & Kegan Paul.

Bottomley, A. and S. Olley (1983) 'Conciliation in the USA', *LAG Bulletin*, January.

Bottoms, A. and W. McWilliams (1979) 'A Non-treatment Paradigm for Probation Practice', *British Journal of Social Work*, 9 (2).

Bowden, J. and M. Stevens (1986) 'Juvenile Justice: a Corporate Strategy in Northampton', *Justice of the Peace*, 150: 326–9 and 345–7.

Brady, J.P. (1981) 'Towards a Popular Justice in the United States: the Dialectics of Community Action', *Contemporary Crises*, 5: 155–92.

Brakel, S. (1978) *American Indian Tribal Courts: the Costs of Separate Justice*. Chicago: American Bar Foundation.

Brooke, R. (1969) 'Civic Rights and Social Services', *Political Quarterly*, 40.

Brooke, R. (1979) *Law, Justice, and Social Policy*. London: Croom Helm.

Brosznat, M. (1981) *The Hitler State*. London: Longman.

Bureau of Justice Statistics (1984) *Victim/Witness Legislation: an Overview*. Washington, DC: US Department of Justice.

Cain, M. (1976) 'Necessarily Out of Touch: Thoughts on the Social Organisation of the Bar', in P. Carlen (ed.), *Sociological Review Monograph 23*. Keele University, Staffordshire.

Cain, M. (1979) 'The General Practice Lawyer and the Client: Towards a Radical Conception', *International Journal of the Sociology of Law*, 7 (4).

Cain, M. (1983) 'Where Are the Disputes? A Study of a First Instance Civil Court in the UK', in M. Cain and K. Kulcsar (eds), *Disputes: the Law*. Budapest: Akademiai Kiado.

Cain, M. (1985a) 'Is Rapprochement between Marxist and Feminist Methodology Possible? (And Does this Matter for Sociology of Law?)', paper presented to ISA Research Committee on Sociology of Law, Aix-en-Provence, August.

Cain, M. (1985b) 'Beyond Informal Justice', *Contemporary Crises*, 9: 335–73.

Cain, M. (1986) 'Who Loses Out on Paradise Island? The Case of Defendant Debtors in County Court', pp. 101–46 in Iain Ramsey (ed.), *Debtors and Creditors*. Abingdon: Professional Books.

Cain, M. and J. Finch (1981) 'Towards a Rehabilitation of Data', in P. Abrams et al. (eds), *Practice and Progress: British Sociology 1950–1980*. London: Allen and Unwin.

Cain, M. and K. Kulcsar (1982) 'Thinking Disputes: an Essay on the Origins of the Dispute Industry', *Law & Society Review*, 16: 375–402.

Cappelletti, M. (ed.) (1981) *Access To Justice and The Welfare State*. Florence: European University Institute.

Carlen, P. (1983) 'On Rights and Powers: Some Notes on Penal Politics', in D. Garland and P. Young (eds), *The Power to Punish*. London: Heinemann.

Carlin, J. (1970) 'Store Front Lawyers in San Francisco', *Trans Action*, April: 64–74.

Carson, W. (1981) *The Other Price of Britain's Oil*. London: Heinemann.

Celnick, A. (1985) 'From Paradigm to Practice in a Special Probation Project', *British Journal of Social Work*, 15: 223–41.

Celnick, A. (1986) 'Negotiating Alternatives to Custody: A Quantitative Study of an Experiment', *British Journal of Social Work*, 16: 353–74.

Christie, N. (1977) 'Conflicts as Property', *British Journal of Criminology*, 17: 1–15.

Christie, N. (1982) *Limits to Pain*. Oxford: Martin Robertson.

Clarke, J. (1985) 'The Politics of Juvenile Justice', *International Journal of the Sociology of Law*, 13 (4): 405–21.

Clarke, M. (1976) 'Community as Dustbin', *New Society*, 29 July, 234–5.

Cloward, R. and M. Elman (1970) 'Advocacy in the Ghetto', pp. 105–21 in A. Blumberg (ed.), *Scales of Justice*. Chicago: Aldine.

Cohen, S. (1979) 'The Punitive City: Notes on the Dispersal of Social Control', *Contemporary Crises*, 3: 339–63.

Cohen, S. (1983) 'Social-Control Talk: Telling Stories about Correctional Change', in D. Garland and P. Young (eds), *The Power to Punish*. London: Heinemann.

Cohen, S. (1984) 'The Deeper Structures of Law; or Beware The Rulers Bearing Justice', *Contemporary Crises*, 8: 83–93.

Cohen, S. (1985) *Visions of Social Control*. Cambridge: Polity Press.

Cohen, S. (1987) 'Taking Decentralisation Seriously: Values, Visions and Policies', in J. Lowman, R. Menzies and T. Palys (eds), *Transcarceration: Essays in the Sociology of Social Control*. Aldershot: Gower.

Collins, H. (1987) 'The Decline of Privacy in Private Law', *Journal of Law and Society*, 14 (1), Spring: 91–105.

Collins, J. (1977) 'A Contractual Approach to Social Work Intervention', *Social Work Today*, 8: 11–19.

Colwill, J. (1984) Paper on the origins of National Insurance Legislation, privately circulated.

Cook, F., J. Roehl and D. Sheppard (1980) *Neighborhood Justice Centers Field Test — Final Evaluation Report*. Washington, DC: American Bar Association.

Corden, J. (1980) 'Contracts in Social Work Practice', *British Journal of Social Work*, 10: 143–62.

Corden, J. and M. Preston-Shoot (1987) *Contracts in Social Work*. Aldershot: Gower.

Coser, L. (1956) *Functions of Social Conflict*. Glencoe: Free Press.

Cotterrell, R. (1984) *The Sociology of Law: An Introduction*. London: Butterworth.

Dahl, T. (1982) 'Towards a Housewives' Law: the Case of National Insurance Provision for Handicapped Children in Norway', *International Journal of the Sociology of Law*, 10 (2): 169–87.

Danzig, R. (1973) 'Towards the Creation of a Complementary, Decentralized System of Criminal Justice', *Stanford Law Review*, 26 (1): 1–54.

Danzig, R. and M. Lowy (1975) 'Everyday Disputes and Mediation in the United States: a Reply to Professor Felstiner', *Law and Society Review*, 9: 659 ff, 675–83.

Davis, G. (1982) 'Conciliation: A Dilemma for the Divorce Court Welfare Service', *Probation Journal*, 29: 123–8.

Davis, G. (1983) 'Conciliation and the Professions', *Family Law*, 13: 6–13.

Davis, G. (1985) 'The Theft of Conciliation', *Probation Journal*, 32: 7–10.

Davis, G. and K. Bader (1985) 'In-court Mediation: the Consumer View', *Family Law*, 15: 42–9, 82.

Davis, G., J. Boucherat and D. Watson (1987) *A Preliminary Study of Victim/ Offender Mediation and Reparation Schemes in England and Wales*. Research and Planning Unit Paper 43. London: Home Office.

Dawson, J. (1960) *A History of Lay Judges*. Cambridge, MA: Harvard University Press.

Deleuze, G. and F. Guattari (1983) *Anti-Oedipus: Capitalism and Schizophrenia*. Minneapolis: University of Minnesota Press.

Delgado, R. (1987) 'The Ethereal Scholar: Does Critical Legal Studies Have What Minorities Want?', *Harvard Civil Rights–Civil Liberties Law Review*, 22: 301–22.

Dews, P. (1979) 'The *Nouvelle Philosophie* and Foucault', *Economy and Society*, 8 (2): 127–71.

Dews, P. (1984) 'Power and Subjectivity in Foucault', *New Left Review*, 144: 72–95.

Dezalay, Y. (1985) 'Des Affaires Disciplinaires au Droit Disciplinaire: La Jurisdictionnalisation des Affaires Disciplinaires Comme Enjeu Social et Professionnel', *Annales de Vaucresson*, 23 (2): 51–71.

Dickens, L. (1983) 'The Role and Influence of Industrial Tribunal Lay Members', *Personnel Management*, November.

Dixon, P.A. (1985) *SYPS Victim–Offender Mediation Project — Interim Report on First Twelve Months*. Sheffield: South Yorkshire Probation Service.

Dixon, P.A. (1986) Speech to FIRM conference, Chelsea College, London.

Donzelot, J. (1980) *The Policing of Families: Welfare versus the State*. London: Hutchinson.

Dunkel, F. (1985) 'Comparative International Research on the Possibilities and Practice of Reparation and Offender–Victim Conciliation', pp. 13–28 in *The Victim, the Offender and the Probation Service*. Hertogenbosch: CEP.

Eaton, M. (1980) 'The Better Business Bureau: the Voice of the People in the Market Place', in L. Nader (ed.), *No Access to Law*. New York: Academic Press.

Edelman, B. (1979) *Ownership of the Image*. London: Routledge & Kegan Paul.

Eisenstein, M. (1979) 'The Swedish Public Complaints Board: its Vital Role in a System of Consumer Protection', in M. Cappelletti and J. Weisner (eds), *Access to Justice Vol II Book II: Promising Institutions*. The Hague: Sijthoff.

Engel, D. (1984) 'The Oven Bird's Song: Insiders and Outsiders and Personal Injuries in an American Community', *Law and Society Review*, 18: 552–82.

Engels, F. (1970) 'Origin of the Family, Private Property, and the State', pp. 191–334 in *Marx and Engels: Selected Works, Vol III*. Moscow: Progress.

Erlanger, H., E. Chambliss and M. Melli (1987) 'Participation and Flexibility in Informal Processes: Cautions from the Divorce Context', *Law and Society Review*, 21 (4): 585–604.

Ewing, S. (1987) 'Formal Justice and the Spirit of Capitalism', *Law and Society Review*, 21 (3): 487–512.

Farmer, J.A. (1974) *Tribunals and Government*. London: Weidenfeld & Nicolson.

Di Federico, B. (1976) 'The Italian Judicial Profession and its Bureaucratic Setting', in D.N. MacCormick (ed.), *Lawyers in their Social Setting*. Edinburgh: W. Green and Son.

Felstiner, W. (1974) 'Influences of Social Organisation on Dispute Processing', *Law and Society Review*, 9 (1): 63–94.

Felstiner, W. and L. Williams (1980) *Community Mediation in Dorchester, Massachusetts*. Washington, DC: US Department of Justice, National Institute of Justice.

Fielding, N. (1986) 'Social Control and the Community', *Howard Journal*, 25: 172–89.

Fisher, E. (1975) 'Community Courts: An Alternative to Conventional Criminal Adjudication', *American University Law Review*, 24, Summer: 1253–69.

Fisher, R. and W. Ury (1981) *Getting to Yes: Negotiating Agreement Without Giving In*. Boston: Houghton Mifflin.

Fitzpatrick, P. (1980) *Law and State in Papua New Guinea*. London and New York: Academic Press.

Fitzpatrick, P. (1984) 'Traditionalism and Traditional Law', *Journal of African Law*, 28 (1 & 2): 20–27.

Fitzpatrick, P. (1987) 'Racism and the Innocence of Law', pp. 119–32 in P. Fitzpatrick and A. Hunt (eds), *Critical Legal Studies*. Oxford: Basil Blackwell.

Fitzpatrick, P. (1987) 'Transformations of Law and Labour in Papua New Guinea', in F. Snyder and D. Hay (eds), *Labour, Law and Crime in Historical Perspective*. London: Tavistock.

Foucault, M. (1967) *Madness and Civilization: A History of Insanity in the Age of Reason*. London: Tavistock.

Foucault, M. (1977) 'Intellectuals and Power', pp. 205–17 in *Language, Counter-Memory, Practice*. Oxford: Basil Blackwell.

Foucault, M. (1977a) *Discipline and Punish: The Birth of the Prison*. Harmondsworth: Penguin.

Foucault, M. (1978) *A History of Sexuality*. Vol. 1. Harmondsworth: Penguin.

Foucault, M. (1979a) *Discipline and Punish: The Birth of the Prison*. Harmondsworth: Penguin.

Foucault, M. (1979b) 'Governmentality', *Ideology and Consciousness*, 6 (Autumn): 5–21.

Foucault, M. (1980a) *Power/Knowledge: Selected Interviews and Other Writings 1972–1977*. Brighton: Harvester Press.

Foucault, M. (1980b) 'On Popular Justice: a Discussion with Maoists', pp. 1–36 in *Power/Knowledge*. Brighton: Harvester.

Foucault, M. (1981) *The History of Sexuality, Volume 1: An Introduction*. Harmondsworth: Penguin.

Foucault, M. (1982) 'Afterword: The Subject and Power', pp. 208–26 in H.L. Dreyfus and P. Rabinow (eds), *Michel Foucault: Beyond Structuralism and Hermeneutics*. Brighton: Harvester Press.

Francis, P. (1981) 'Divorce and the Law and Order Lobby', *Family Law*, 11: 69.

Franks Committee Report (1957) *Administrative Tribunals and Enquiries*. Cmnd. 218. London: HMSO.

Frost, A. and C. Howard (1977) *Representation and Administrative Tribunals*. London: Routledge & Kegan Paul.

Galanter, M. (1980) 'Legality and its Discontents', in Blankenburg et al. *Alternative Rechtsformen und Alternativen Zum Recht*. Westdeutscher Verlag.

Galanter, M. (1985a) 'A Settlement Judge: Not a Trial Judge, Judicial Mediation in the United States', *Journal of Law and Society*, 12 (1), Spring: 1–18.

Galanter, M. (1985b) 'The Legal Malaise, or Justice Observed', *Law and Society Review*, 19 (4): 537–56.

Galanter, M. (1986) 'The Day After the Litigation Explosion', *Maryland Law Review*, 36 (1): 3–39.

Garafolo, J. and K. Connelly (1980) 'Dispute Resolution Centres Part One: Major Features and Processes', *Criminal Justice Abstracts*, Vol. 12, September: 416–39.

Garland, D. (1985) *Punishment and Welfare*. Aldershot: Gower.

Garland, D. and P. Young (1983) *The Power to Punish*. London: Heinemann.

Garlock, J. (1982) 'The Knights of Labor Courts: a Case Study of Popular Justice', pp. 17–33 in R. Abel (ed.) *The Politics of Informal Justice*, Vol. 1. New York: Academic Press.

Garth, B. (1982) 'The Movement towards Procedural Informalism in North America and Western Europe: a Critical Survey', in R. Abel (ed.), *The Politics of Informal Justice*. Vol. 2. New York: Academic Press.

Giddens, A. (1981) *A Contemporary Critique of Historical Materialism: Vol. 1 Power, Property and the State*. London & Basingstoke: Macmillan.

Gilmore, G. (1974) *The Death of Contract*. Ohio University Press.

Gilroy, P. (1982) 'Steppin' out of Babylon — Race, Class and Autonomy', pp. 276–314 in Centre for Contemporary Cultural Studies (ed.), *The Empire Strikes Back: Race and Racism in 70s Britain*. London: Hutchinson.

Ginger, A. (1972) *The Relevant Lawyers*. New York: Simon & Schuster.

Gordon, C. (1980) 'Afterword', pp. 229–59 in M. Foucault (1980), *Power/Knowledge: Selected Interviews and Other Writings 1972–1977*. Brighton: Harvester Press.

Grace, L. and P. Lefevre (1984) 'Lawyers and the Base', paper presented at the European Conference on Critical Legal Studies, Kent, April. Mimeo. Available from Brent Community Law Centre.

Grace, L. and P. Lefevre (1985) 'Draining the Swamp', *Law and Policy Quarterly*, 7 (1): 97–112.

Gramsci, A. (1971) *Selections from the Prison Notebooks*. London: Lawrence & Wishart.

Grossman, J. (1965) *Lawyers and Judges*. New York: Wiley.

Habermas, J. (1975) *Legitimation Crisis*. Boston: Beacon.

Haley, J. (1982) 'The Politics of Informal Justice: the Japanese Experience, 1922–1942', in R. Abel (ed.), *The Politics of Informal Justice Vol. 1*. New York: Academic Press.

Hall, S. (1980) *Drifting into a Law and Order Society*. London: Cobden Trust.

Handler, J., E. Hollingsworth and H. Erlanger (1978). *Lawyers and the Pursuit of Legal Rights*. New York: Academic Press.

Harrington, C.B. (1982) 'Delegalization Reform Movements: A Historical Analysis', pp. 35–71 in R.L. Abel (ed.), *The Politics of Informal Justice: Vol. 1: The American Experience*. New York: Academic Press.

Harrington, C.B. (1985) *Shadow Justice? The Ideology and Institutionalization of Alternatives to Court*. Westport & London: Greenwood Press.

Harrington, C.B. (1987) 'Creating Gaps and Making Markets: Dispute Processing and Regulatory Reform'. Paper presented at the European Conference of Critical Legal Studies, Centre de Recherches Interdisciplinaires de Vaucresson, Paris, 9–11 April.

Hartsock, N. (1983) 'The Feminist Standpoint: Developing the Ground for a Specifically Feminist Historical Materialism', in S. Harding and M. Hintikka (eds), *Discovering Reality*. Boston: D. Reidel.

Hazel, N. (1981) *A Bridge to Independence*. Oxford: Basil Blackwell.

Henry, S. (1982) 'Factory Law: The Changing Disciplinary Technology of Industrial Social Control', *International Journal of the Sociology of Law*, 10 (4): 365–83.

Henry, S. (1983) *Private Justice: Towards Integrated Theorizing in the Sociology of Law*. London: Routledge & Kegan Paul.

Henry, S. (1985) 'Community Justice, Capitalist Society and Human Agency: The Dialectics of Collective Law in the Co-operative', *Law and Society Review*, 19: 303–27.

Hetzler, A. (1982) 'The Role of Lay Councils in Democratic Decision Making', *International Journal of the Sociology of Law*, 10 (4): 395–407.

Hillyard, P. (1985) 'Popular Justice in Northern Ireland: Communities and Change', in S. Spitzer (ed.), *Research in Law, Deviance and Social Control*. Vol. 7. Connecticut: JAI Press.

Hobsbawm, E.J. (1959) *Primitive Rebels: Studies in Archaic Forms of Social Movement in the 19th and 20th Centuries*. Manchester: Manchester University Press.

Hofrichter, R. (1982) 'Neighborhood Justice and the Social Control Problems of American Capitalism: a Perspective', in R. Abel (ed.), *The Politics of Informal Justice*. Vol. 1. New York: Academic Press.

Home Office (1984) *Statement of National Objectives and Priorities*. London: Home Office.

Home Office (1986) *Reparation: a Discussion Document*. London: Home Office.

Honore, A. (1962) 'Social Justice', *McGill Law Journal*, 8: 78.

Hough, M. and P. Mayhew (1985) *Taking Account of Crime: Key Findings from the Second British Crime Survey*. London: HMSO, Home Office Research & Planning Unit, Report 85.

Hunt, A. (1986) 'A Theory of Critical Legal Studies', *Oxford Journal of Legal Studies*, 6 (1): 1–39

Ietswaart, H. (1982) 'The Discourse of Summary Justice and the Discourse of Popular Justice: an Analysis of Legal Rhetoric in Argentina', in R. Abel (ed.), *The Politics of Informal Justice*. Vol. 2. New York: Academic Press.

Ison, T. (1972) 'Small Claims', *Modern Law Review*, 35: 18.

James, M. (1973) *The People's Lawyers*. New York: Holt, Rinehart & Winston.

James, A. and K. Wilson (1984) 'Conciliation — The Way Ahead', *Family Law*, 14: 104–7.

Jessop, R. (1982) *The Capitalist State: Marxist Theories and Methods*. Oxford: Martin Robertson.

Kafka, F. (1961) *Metamorphosis and Other Stories*. Harmondsworth: Penguin.

Karst, K. et al. (1973) *The Evolution of Law in the Barios of Caracas*. Los Angeles: University of California, Latin American Centre.

Kilbrandon Committee (1964) *Report of the Committee on Children and Young Persons*. Cmnd 1306. Scotland: HMSO.

Kinsey, R., J. Lea and J. Young (1986) *Losing the Fight against Crime*. Oxford: Basil Blackwell.

Kirchheimer, O. (1940) 'Criminal Law in National Socialist Germany', *Studies in Philosophy and Social Science*, 8: 444–63.

Kirchheimer, O. (1969) 'The Legal Order of National Socialism' (pp. 88–109) and 'Politics and Justice' (pp. 408–427), in S. Burin and K. Shell (eds), *Politics, Law and Social Change*. New York: Columbia University Press.

Launay, G. (1985) 'Bringing Victims and Offenders Together: a Comparison of Two Models', *Howard Journal*, 24: 200–12.

Lazerson, M. (1982) 'In The Halls of Justice: Only Justice in The Halls', in R. Abel (ed.), *The Politics of Informal Justice*, Vol 1. New York: Academic Press.

Lea, J. (1987) 'Left Realism: A Defense,' *Contemporary Crises*, 11: 1–30.

Lefcourt, C. (1984) 'Women, Mediation and Family Law', *Clearinghouse Review*, 18: 266–9.

Lefcourt, R. (1971) *Law against the People*. New York: Random House.

Lempert, R. and J. Sanders (1986) *An Invitation to Law and Social Science: Desert, Disputes and Distribution*. New York & London: Longman.

Lerman, P. (1975) *Community Treatment and Social Control: a Critical Analysis of Juvenile Correction Policy*. Chicago: Chicago University Press.

Longmire, M. (1981) 'A Popular Justice System: A Radical Alternative to the Criminal Justice System', *Contemporary Crises*, 5: 15–30.

Lukes, S. (1973) *Power : A Radical View*. London: Macmillan.

Macaulay, S. (1963) 'Non-Contractual Relations in Business: A Preliminary Study', *American Sociological Review*, 28: 55–67.

Macauley, S. (1987) 'Images of Law in Everyday Life: The Lessons of School Entertainment and Spectator Sports', *Law and Society Review*, 21 (2): 184–218.

McBarnet, D. (1976) 'Law, the State, and the Construction of Justice', in P. Carlen (ed.), *Sociological Review Monograph 23: The Sociology of Law*. University of Keele, Staffordshire.

McBarnet, D. (1983) *Convictions*. London: Macmillan.

McEwen, C. and R. Maiman (1984) 'Mediation in a Small Claims Court: Achieving Compliance Through Consent', *Law and Society Review*, 18.

McGillis, D. and J. Mullen (1977) *Neighborhood Justice Centers: an Analysis of Potential Models*. Washington, DC: US Department of Justice.

Maguire, M. and C. Corbett (1987) *The Effects of Crime and the Work of Victims' Support Schemes*. Aldershot: Gower.

Mann, M. (1986) *The Sources of Social Power: Volume 1: A History of Power from the Beginning to AD 1760*. Cambridge: Cambridge University Press.

Marshall, T.F. (1985) *Alternatives to Criminal Courts*. Aldershot: Gower.

Marshall, T.F. (1987) 'Mediation: a New Mode of Establishing Order in Schools', *Howard Journal*, 26: 33–46.

Marshall, T.F. and S. Merry (1988) *Crime and Accountability*. Home Office Research Study. London: HMSO.

Marshall, T.F. and M. Walpole (1985) *Bringing People Together: Mediation and Reparation Projects in Great Britain*. London: Home Office Research & Planning Unit, Paper 33.

Marx, K. (1954) *Capital*. Vol. 1, ch. 10, sec. 6. London: Lawrence & Wishart.

Marx, K. (1969) 'The Civil War in France', pp. 195–244 in *Marx and Engels: Selected Works*, Vol. II. Moscow: Progress.

Marx, K. (1973) *Grundrisse: Foundations of the Critique of Political Economy*. Harmondsworth: Penguin.

Matthews, R. (1987) 'Decarceration and Social Control: Fantasies and Realities', in J. Lowman, R. Menzies and T. Palys (eds), *Transcarceration: Essays in The Sociology of Social Control*. Aldershot: Gower.

Matthews, R. (1987) 'Taking Realist Criminology Seriously', *Contemporary Crises*, 11: 371–401.

Mathiesen, T. (1980) 'The Absorbent State', ch. 6 of *Law, Society, and Political Action: Towards a Strategy under Late Capitalism*. London: Academic Press.

Medcalf, L. (1978) *Law and Identity: Lawyers, Native Americans, and Legal Practice*. Beverly Hills: Sage.

Merry, S. (1979) 'Going to Court: Strategies of Dispute Management in an Urban American Neighbourhood', *Law and Society Review*, 13 (4): 891–925.

Merry, S. (1982a) 'The Social Organisation of Mediation in Non-Industrial Societies:

Implications for Informal Community Justice in America', in R. Abel (ed.), *The Politics of Informal Justice*, Vol. 2. Academic Press.

Merry, S. (1982b) 'Defining "Success" in the Neighbourhood Justice Movement', in R. Tomasic (ed.), *Neighbourhood Justice: An Assessment of An Emerging Idea.* London: Longman.

Merry, S. and S. Silbey (1984) 'What Do Plaintiffs Want? Re-examining The Concept of Dispute', *The Justice System Journal*, 9 (2): 150–77.

Miller, D. (1976) *Social Justice.* London: Oxford University Press.

Miller, E.J. (1986) *Conflict and Reconciliation: the Newham Experiment.* London: Tavistock Institute Occasional Paper 9.

Mnookin, R. and L. Kornhauser (1979) 'Bargaining in The Shadow of the Law: The Case of Divorce', *The Yale Law Journal*, 88: 950–97.

Moore, B. and F. Harris (1976) 'Class Action', in L. Nader and M. Greene (eds), *Verdicts on Lawyers.* New York: Thomas Y. Cromwell.

Morris A., H. Giller, E. Szwed and H. Geach (1980) *Justice For Children.* London: Macmillan.

Morris, A. and M. McIsaac (1978) *Juvenile Justice.* London: Heinemann.

Morrison, W. (1975) 'The North West Mounted Police in the Klondike Gold Rush', in G. Mosse (ed.), *Police Forces in History.* London: Sage

Munck, R. (1985) 'Repression, Insurgency and Popular Justice: the Irish Case', *Crime and Social Justice*, 21/22: 81–94.

Murch, M. (1980) *Justice and Welfare in Divorce.* London: Sweet & Maxwell.

Nader, L. (ed.) (1980) *No Access to Law: Alternatives to the American Judicial System.* New York: Academic Press.

Nader, L. and L. Singer (1976) 'Dispute Resolution — What Are The Choices?', *California State Bar Journal*, 51: 281–320.

Nandy, A. (1984) 'Culture, State and the Rediscovery of Indian Politics', *Economic and Political Weekly*, XIX (49): 2078–83.

Napier, R. (1979) 'The French Labour Courts: an Institution in Transition', *Modern Law Review*, 42: 270–84.

Nelken, D. (1982) 'Is There a Crisis in Law and Legal Ideology?', *British Journal of Law and Society*, 9.

Nelken, D. (1985) 'Community Involvement in Crime Control', *Current Legal Problems*, 38: 239–67.

Nelken, D. (1987) 'The Use of "Contracts" as a Social Work Technique', in J. Jowell and R. Rideout (eds), *Current Legal Problems.* London: Sweet & Maxwell.

Neumann, F. (1957) *The Democratic and the Authoritarian State.* New York: The Free Press.

Newburn, T. (forthcoming) *The Use and Enforcement of Compensation Orders in Magistrates' Courts.* Home Office Research Study. London: HMSO.

Nietzsche, F. (1956) 'The Genealogy of Morals', in *The Birth of Tragedy and The Genealogy of Morals.* New York: Doubleday (Anchor).

Nietzsche, F. (1968) 'Twilight of the Idols', in *Twilight of the Idols and The Anti-Christ.* Harmondsworth: Penguin.

O'Brien, E. (1986) *Asking the Victim: a Study of the Attitudes of Some Victims of Crime to Reparation and the Criminal Justice System.* Gloucestershire Probation Service.

O'Malley, P. (1987) 'Regulating Contradictions. The Australian Press Council and the "Dispersal of Social Control"', *Law and Society Review*, 21 (1): 83–108.

Parkinson, L. (1986) *Conciliation in Separation and Divorce.* London: Croom Helm.

Pashukanis, E.B. (1978) *Law and Marxism: A General Theory.* London: Ink Links.

Pashukanis, E. (1980) 'The General Theory of Law and Marxism', and 'Lenin and

Problems of Law', pp. 133–64 in P. Beirne and R. Sharlett (eds), *Pashukanis: Selected Writings on Marxism and Law*. London: Academic Press. Translation by P. Maggs.

Paternoster, R. and T. Bynum (1982) 'The Justice Model As Ideology. A Critical Look at the Impetus of Sentencing Reform', *Contemporary Crises*, 6 (1): 7–25.

Pearson, R. (1980) 'Lay Magistrates and Popular Justice', in Z. Bankowski and G. Mungham (eds), *Essays in Law and Society*. London: Routledge & Kegan Paul.

Phillips, D. (1977) *Crime and Authority in Victorian England*. London: Croom Helm.

Platt, S. (1986) 'Farewell to Arms', *New Society*, 7 November: 8–9.

Poulantzas, N. (1974) *Fascism and Dictatorship*. London: New Left Books.

Poulantzas, N. (1978) *State, Power, Socialism*. London: New Left Books.

Powell, E. (1985) Speech to Cambridge University Conservative Association, 20 October.

Pratt, J. (1986) 'Diversion from the Juvenile Court: a History of Inflation and a Critique of Progress', *British Journal of Criminology*, 26: 212–33.

Rajchman, J. (1983/4) 'The Story of Foucault's History', *Social Text*, Winter: 1–32.

Raynor, P. (1978) 'Compulsory Persuasion: A Problem for Correctional Social Work', *British Journal of Social Work*, 8 (4): 411–21.

Raynor, P. (1985) *Social Work, Justice and Control*. Oxford: Basil Blackwell.

Reeves, Helen (1984) 'The Victim and Reparation', *Probation Journal*, 31: 136–9.

Reich, C. (1964) 'The New Property', *Yale Law Journal*, 73 (5): 733–87.

Reid, W. J. and A. Shyne (1969) *Brief and Extended Casework*. New York: Columbia University Press.

Reid, W.J. and L. Epstein (1972) *Task Centred Casework*. New York: Columbia University Press.

Reifner, U. (1982) 'Individualistic and Collective Legalisation: the Theory and Practice of Legal Advice for Workers in Prefascist Germany', pp. 81–123 in R. Abel (ed.), *The Politics of Informal Justice*, Vol. II. New York: Academic Press.

Roche, J. (1984) 'Why such Enthusiasm for Mediation?', *Legal Action*, December, 12: 12–14.

Rojeck, C. and S. Collins (1987) 'Contract or Con Trick?', *British Journal of Social Work*, 17: 199–211.

Rose, N. (1986a) 'Law, Rights and Psychiatry', in P. Miller and N. Rose (eds), *The Power of Psychiatry*. Cambridge: Polity Press.

Rose, N. (1986b) 'Psychiatry: the Discipline of Mental Health' and 'Law, Rights and Psychiatry', pp. 43–84 and 177–213 in P. Miller and N. Rose (eds), *The Power of Psychiatry*. Cambridge: Polity Press.

Rose, N. (1987) 'Beyond the Public/Private Division: Law, Power and the Family', pp. 61–76 in P. Fitzpatrick and A. Hunt (eds), *Critical Legal Studies*. Oxford: Basil Blackwell.

Rose, N. (1987) 'Beyond the Public/Private Division: Law, Power and the Family', *Journal of Law and Society*, 14 (1): 61.

Rosenbaum, D. (1986) *Community Crime Prevention: Does It Work?* Beverly Hills: Sage Publications.

Royal Commission on Legal Services (1979) *Final Report, Vol. I*, 'Law Centres' (ch. 8), Cmnd 7648. London: HMSO.

Rushdie, S. (1982) *Midnight's Children*. London: Pan Books.

Sachs, A. (1979) 'Mozambique: the Survival of Legal Doctrine in a Revolutionary Society', *International Journal of the Sociology of Law*, 7 (1): 31–6.

Sachs, A. (1985) 'The Two Dimensions of Socialist Legality: Recent Experience in Mozambique', *International Journal of the Sociology of Law*, 13 (2): 133–46.

Sander, F. (1983) 'The Multidoor Courthouse', *National Forum*, 63: 24–5.

Santos, B. de Sousa (1977) 'The Law of the Oppressed: The Construction and Reproduction of Legality in Pasargada', *Law and Society Review*, 12 (1): 5–126.

Santos, B. de Sousa (1979) 'Popular Justice, Dual Power, and Socialist Strategy', in NDC/CSE (eds), *Capitalism and the Rule of Law*. London: Macmillan.

Santos, B. de Sousa (1980) 'Law and Community: the Changing Nature of State Power in Late Capitalism', *International Journal of the Sociology of Law*, 8 (4): 379 ff.

Santos, B. de Sousa (1981) 'Science and Politics: Doing Research in Rio's Squatter Settlements', in R. Luckham (ed.) *Law and Social Enquiry*. Scandinavian Institute of African Studies.

Santos, B. de Sousa (1984) 'Law, State and Urban Struggles in Recife, Brazil', Disputes Processing Research Program Working Paper, University of Wisconsin.

Santos, B. de Sousa (1985) 'Modes of Production of Law and Social Power', *International Journal of the Sociology of Law*, 13 (4): 299–336.

Santos, B. de Sousa (1987) 'Law, a Map of Misreading: Toward a Postmodern Conception of Law', *Journal of Law and Society*, 14 (3): 279–302.

Schwendinger, J. and H. Schwendinger (1978) 'Studying Rape: Integrating Research and Social Change', in C. Smart and B. Smart (eds), *Women, Sexuality and Social Control*. London: Routledge & Kegan Paul.

Scott, J.C. (1985) *Weapons of the Weak, Everyday Forms of Peasant Resistance*. New Haven: Yale University Press.

Scull, A. (1977) *Decarceration*. Englewood Cliffs: Prentice-Hall.

Scull, A. (1982) 'Community Corrections: Panacea, Progress or Pretense?', in R. Abel (ed.), *The Politics of Informal Justice*, Vol. 1. New York: Academic Press.

Shah, I. (1974) *Thinkers of the East*. Harmondsworth: Penguin.

Shapland, J., J. Wilmore and P. Duff (1985) *Victims in the Criminal Justice System*. Aldershot: Gower.

Sheldon, B. (1978) 'Making Contracts to Please', *Community Care*, 24: 24–32.

Sheldon, B. (1980) 'The Use of Contracts in Social Work,' *Practice Note Series*, BASW.

Shonholtz, R. (1984) 'Neighborhood Justice Systems: Work, Structure, and Guiding Principles', *Mediation Quarterly*, 5: 3–30.

Smart, B. (1986) 'The Politics of Truth and The Problem of Hegemony', in D. Hoy (ed.), *Foucault: A Critical Reader*. Oxford: Blackwell.

Smith, A. and J. Corden (1981) 'The Introduction of Contracts in a Family Service Unit', *British Journal of Social Work*, 11: 1–14.

Smith, J. (1986) 'Mediation in Practice: an Example of Victim/Offender Mediation from the South Yorkshire Scheme', *Mediation*, 2 (2): 2–4.

Spence, J. (1982) 'Institutionalizing Neighborhood Courts: Two Chilean Experiences', pp. 215–49 in R. Abel (ed.), *The Politics of Informal Justice*. Vol. II. New York: Academic Press.

Spitzer, S. (1982) 'The Dialectics of Formal and Informal Control', pp. 167–205 in R. Abel (ed.), *The Politics of Informal Justice*. New York: Academic Press.

Stephens, M. (1980) 'The Law Centre Movement', in G. Mungham and Z. Bankowski (eds), *Essays in Law and Society*. London: Routledge & Kegan Paul.

Strathern, M. (1985) 'Discovering "Social Control"', *Journal of Law & Society*, 12: 111–34.

Stubbs, P. (1987) 'Crime, Community and the Multi-Agency Approach', *Critical Social Policy*, 20, 30.

Stubbs, P. (1988) 'Relationships with the Police; Intermediate Treatment and the Multi-Agency Approach', *Youth and Policy*, Spring, 24, 16.

Sykes, G.M. and D. Matza (1957) 'Techniques of Neutralization: A Theory of Delinquency', *American Sociological Review*, 23: 664–70.

Teubner, G. (1983) 'Substantive and Reflexive Elements in Modern Law', *Law and Society Review*, 17 (2): 239–85.

Teubner, G. (1986) 'After Legal Instrumentalism? Strategic Models of Post-Regulatory Law', pp. 299–325 in G. Teubner (ed.), *Dilemmas of Law in the Welfare State*. Berlin and New York: Walter de Gruyter.

Thompson, B. (1983) 'The Planning Appeals Commission of Northern Ireland: an Essay on Lay and Professional Justice', *International Journal of the Sociology of Law*, 11 (4).

Thompson, E.P. (1971) 'The Moral Economy of the English Crowd in the Eighteenth Century', *Past & Present*, 50: 76–136.

Thompson, E.P. (1975) *Whigs and Hunters*. London: Allen Lane.

Thompson, E.P. (1978) 'Eighteenth-century English Society: Class Struggle Without Class?', *Social History*, 3: 133–65.

Tomasic, R. (1980) *Mediation as an Alternative to Adjudication: Rhetoric and Reality in the Neighborhood Justice Movement*. Dispute Processing Research Program, Madison, Wisconsin. Reprinted in R. Tomasic and M. Feeley (1982).

Tomasic, R. and M. Feeley (1982) *Neighborhood Justice: Assessment of an Emerging Idea*. New York: Longman.

Touraine, A. (1985) 'An Introduction to the Study of Social Movements', *Social Research*, 20 (4): 749–87.

Trubek, D. (1984) 'Turning Away From Law?', *Michigan Law Review*, 82: 824–35.

Umbrett, M. (1985) *Crime and Reconciliation: Creative Options for Victims and Offenders*. Nashville: Abingdon Press.

Unger, R. (1975) *Knowledge and Politics*. New York: Free Press.

Unger, R. (1976) *Law in Modern Society: Towards a Criticism of Social Theory*. New York: Free Press.

Vidmar, N. (1984) 'The Small Claims Court: A Reconceptualisation of Disputes and An Empirical Investigation', *Law and Society Review*, 18: 515–39.

Vogler, R. (1984) 'The Development of Summary Jurisdiction in England and Wales in Relation to Civil Disorder'. PhD dissertation. University of Cambridge.

Wahrhaftig, P. (1982) 'An Overview of Community-oriented Citizen Dispute Resolution Programs in the United States', in R. Abel (ed.), *The Politics of Informal Justice*, Vol 1. New York: Academic Press.

Walklate, S. (1986) 'Reparation: A Merseyside View', *British Journal of Criminology*, 26: 287–98.

Weber, M. (1954) *On Law in Economy and Society*. M. Rheinstein (ed.) Cambridge, MA: Harvard University Press.

Wilson, G. and E. Brydolf (1980) 'Grass Roots Solutions', in L. Nader (ed.), *No Access to Law*. New York: Academic Press.

Winkler, J. (n.d.) 'The Changing Role of the State and the Administration of Welfare', mimeo, Cranfield Institute of Technology, UK.

Wraith, R. and P. Hutchesson (1973) *Administrative Tribunals*. London: Allen & Unwin.

Wright, M. (1983) *Victim/Offender Reparation Agreements — Feasibility Study in Coventry*. Unpublished mimeograph.

Yngvesson, B. (1985) 'Legal Ideology and Community Justice in the Clerk's Office', *Legal Studies Forum*, 9: 71–87.

Yngvesson, B. and P. Hennessey (1975) 'Small Claims, Complex Disputes: A Review of The Small Claims Literature', *Law and Society Review*, 9: 269.

Young, J. (1986) 'The Failure of Criminology: The Need for Radical Realism', in R. Matthews and J. Young (eds), *Confronting Crime*. London: Sage Publications.

Young, J. (1987) 'The Tasks Facing Realist Criminology', *Contemporary Crises*, 11.

Zander, M. (1978) *Legal Services for the Community*. London: Temple Smith.

Zehr, H. (1985) *Retributive Justice, Restorative Justice*. Elkhart, Indiana: MCC US Office of Criminal Justice, Occasional Paper 4.

Zemans, F. (ed.) (1979) *Perspectives on Legal Aid: an International Survey*. London: Frances Pinter.

Index